Colborne:
A Singular Talent for War

Colborne:
A Singular Talent for War
The Napoleonic Wars Career of
One of Wellington's Most Highly Valued
Officers in Egypt, Holland, Italy,
the Peninsula and at Waterloo

John Colborne

edited and with extensive
commentary by
G. C. Moore Smith

Colborne: A Singular Talent for War: The Napoleonic Wars Career of One of Wellington's Most Highly Valued Officers in Egypt, Holland, Italy, the Peninsula and at Waterloo
by John Colborne

edited and with extensive commentary by
G. C. Moore Smith

Adapted by the Leonaur editiors from the 1903 book
The Life of John Colborne, Field-Marshal Lord Seaton

Published by Leonaur Ltd

FIRST EDITION

Text in this form copyright © 2007 Leonaur Ltd

ISBN: 978-1-84677-346-4 (hardcover)
ISBN: 978-1-84677-345-7 (softcover)

http://www.leonaur.com

Publisher's Note

The opinions expressed in this book are those of the author and are not necessarily those of the publisher.

Contents

Publisher's Note	7
The Young Soldier	11
Minorca and Egypt	24
Malta	36
Battle of Maida	48
The General's Secretary	59
Sweden	73
Portugal	81
The Peninsula	93
Enter Wellington	113
Campaign of 1810	129
Campaign of 1811	144
Ciudad Rodrigo	157
Campaign of 1813	175
Into France—1814	188
Waterloo	202
March to Paris	223

Appendices

Colborne on Sir John Moore's Campaign in Spain	235
Colborne's Accounts of Waterloo	253

Publisher's Note

Sir William Napier is perhaps the most renowned and most quoted author and historian of Britain's conflict with Napoleon's French Army in Spain during the Peninsular War. Indeed, later readers and researchers would mourn that most subsequent accounts-both historical and personal written during the 19th century referenced his famous and monumental history so frequently that many despaired at finding a work not influenced by it or containing its assertions. Inevitably it also became the focus for detractors since those issues which were considered to be inaccurately recounted also appeared, uncorrected, in other accounts.

Nevertheless, Napier's was the first work of scholarship about that war and our understanding of it—some 200 years after the event—would be the poorer without his efforts. His research into the subject is unparalleled, but principally the quality of his work was drawn from the fact that he was an active participant in the events he later reported and analysed. Nothing guarantees an in depth understanding of a war more than first hand participation and an intimate association with those who were at the heart of events.

Napier did not only write about the subject of this book, he knew John Colborne personally. He marched on the same campaigns, fought in the same battles and served in the same regiments.

When considering the period immediately leading the

bloody battle at Albuera in 1811, Napier turned his attention to John Colborne's command—he held by that time the rank of Colonel—of a brigade from the Second Division as it harried French forces in Estramadura. The operation was a success, undertaken as usual with Colborne's customary vigour, aggression, imagination and sound judgement.

It led him to write—perhaps with no great emphasis—that here was a man 'with a singular talent for war'. The phrase was so apposite that it was not the last time it was applied to Colborne and it is used unreservedly in the title of the book you are now holding. Irrespective of who may have disagreed with Napier elsewhere, none have taken issue with him on this particular subject.

Colborne came from a comparatively humble background, but despite this his promotion was rapid for the times and was principally as a result of the universal appreciation of his military talents by his renowned superior officers from Sir John Moore to the Duke of Wellington himself. In Colborne they recognised not simply a reliable lieutenant, but an inspired natural soldier who could be left to his own devices and act upon his own initiative often with spectacular results.

Colborne learned and honed his craft during a period of almost continuous warfare during the wars with Revolutionary France and latterly with the First Empire under its charismatic Emperor. He campaigned in Egypt, the Low Countries, Italy, the Iberian Peninsula and finally on the immortal fields outside Waterloo in Belgium in 1815, where the last great battle of the Napoleonic era was fought.

On that day Colborne produced yet another stroke of tactical genius amply justifying—once again—Wellington's faith and high opinion of him. As the Imperial Guard laboured up the muddy slope to the British line in Napoleon's last desperate attack to sweep the Allies off the ridge, Colborne swung his brigade into a flank attack and poured musket fire into its side. The effect was crippling and instantaneous. The column crumpled, disintegrated and began to fall back. It was then that Maitland's Foot Guards completed the rout. Popular history has told a different story. The honour went to the Guards and one of their regiments was award the title of 'Grenadier' to mark their victory. Few now know that the *coup de grace* in the last act of perhaps the most famous battle in human history was devised and executed by John Colborne.

Colborne, with typical self effacement kept whatever disappointment he may have felt to himself and would not allow his subordinate officers to complain either. Such modesty was often not in his own best interests, but he would have it no other way and bore the consequences stoically. Perhaps inevitably, it also led to his reluctance to leave us with a comprehensive memoir.

This book was compiled by G. C Moore Smith from Colborne's letters, other writings and anecdotes told by him and recorded by his friends and associates. In a manner typical of the publishing traditions of its time, the original book embraced Colborne's entire career, from his days as a serving army officer to his elevation to the peerage, when, as Lord Seaton he undertook diplomatic roles including the Governor-Generalship of Canada.

This Leonaur edition has been edited so that it concentrates solely on Colborne's military career—during the campaigns against Napoleonic France.

In its original form the text was difficult to access with Colborne's own words often indistinguishable from those of Moore Smith and others. In an effort to make this important and riveting account more accessible for the modern reader we have used three text measures in the following pages. Colborne's own words, the most important here, are set to full text width; Moore Smith's commentary is inset and others quoted by him are further inset. By doing this, we hope we have created a version of Colborne's military life that is fresh and readable.

Chapter 1

The Young Soldier

John Colborne was only 16 when, on 10th July, 1794, he received a commission as Ensign in the 20th Regiment, by the interest of the Earl of Warwick. He left school immediately afterwards. He became Lieutenant on 10th September, 1795. The 20th did not return from the West Indies till the summer of 1796. Colborne, who had been assiduously devoting his time since he left school to the improvement of his education, joined his regiment in October, at Exeter, and served with it at Lichfield, Liverpool and Preston from 1796 to 1799. More than six feet high, and singularly handsome, he must have looked every inch a soldier.

Colborne has told us nothing of his earliest days in the service, but the following story:

I remember when I first joined, my Colonel, when speaking to me, pointed to an officer and said: 'There, sir, that officer was shot through the body, and was all the better for it; there's encouragement for you.'

In the summer of 1799 the 20th Regiment received orders to join the expedition to Holland, which was to be commanded by H.R.H. the Duke of York. It marched from Preston to Canterbury, where it was joined by 1,800 excellent soldiers, volunteers from the militia regiments of many counties. Before leaving Preston, Colborne wrote the following letter to his stepfather, who had left Winchester in 1798, on being presented by Mr. Peachey, afterwards Lord Selsey, to the living of Barkway, Herts, a village situated on the chalk hills a few miles south-east of Royston:

To The Rev. T. Bargus, Barkway

Preston
July 21st, 1799

Dear Sir,

I am this moment ordered to Windsor to receive the 1st Staffordshire Militia, who have volunteered into our regiment. The 20th Regiment marches tomorrow, and is destined for the second embarkation. Part of the 2nd Stafford and 3rd Lancashire have also volunteered for our regiment We shall soon be a thousand strong. Owing to the expense I shall be at in going to Windsor, and being ordered away at so short a notice, has induced me to do a thing not altogether proper. I have drawn on you for five-and-twenty pounds three days after sight, payable to Captain Thos. Hipkins. I could not do without it, I assure you, for although my expenses will finally be paid by Government, yet it will be some time before I shall receive the money. I shall be very much obliged to you if you will accept the bill, and beg you will deduct the amount from Mr. Lind's legacy.

I am, yours affectionately,
J. Colborne
To Rev. T. Bargus
Barkway

From Canterbury the 20th proceeded to the camp at Barham Downs, where it was divided into two battalions, Lieut. Colborne being appointed to the 1st, which was commanded by Lt.-Col. George Smyth. The main part of the intended force, amounting to about 15,000 men, left Barham Downs on August 8th, embarked on the 13th, and, landing at the Helder on the 27th, fought a successful action on the same day. On the following day a reinforcement of 5,000 men under Maj.-Gen. Don arrived. This included the 17th, 20th and 40th Regiments (two battalions each) and the 63rd Regiment, the two battalions of the 20th and the 63rd forming a brigade. The whole army, until the arrival of the Duke of York, was commanded by Sir Ralph Abercromby. Colborne said in later years:

We landed without our baggage on a cold, rainy night, and were on the bare sands with no food and no wood. General Don had a nice little cart with his things in, in which he was to sleep, and I recollect envying him when he said: 'Now, gentlemen, we halt here; make yourselves comfortable.' An officer I recollect shot a wildfowl and roasted it himself, and gave us all some.

Immediately on landing, the regiment formed in position on the sand hills a few miles south of Helder Town. It was afterwards moved to Zijp Dyke, and posted near the village of Crabbendam. The following narrative gives Colborne's reminiscences of his first campaigning days:

Eight days after our landing Colonel Smyth was given a separate employment by General Abercromby to take a dyke, I think. This was the first time I saw Sir John Moore, who rode up to us with General Abercromby. Colonel Smyth was exceedingly delighted, and I recollect his instruction was, 'March straight in, and if you see anything, don't fire, but push at them with the bayonet.' We pushed in accordingly, but saw no one. We took the dyke and a large farmhouse, in which I established myself very comfortably, and thought I was going to have a good night's rest, when I was suddenly ordered out on a picquet to inspect the road. I had not been there long when I heard a bugle sound. I was wondering what it could mean, when a sergeant said, 'Oh, sir, it must be for a truce.' However, a very smart French Dragoon officer came galloping clown with two led horses. He said he had brought General Don's horses, that General Don was detained by the French general, but the latter had sent back his horses, and the dragoon wanted a receipt for them. So I gave the receipt the first time I ever had occasion to write French. The fact was that General Don had gone with some despatches to the French camp. We were then trying to entice Holland back to allegiance to the Stadtholder, and we all wore Orange ribbon. General Don had several yards of Orange ribbon in his pocket, as well as some proclamations, and, being an absent-minded man, in taking out the despatches he pulled out the Orange ribbon too. They then searched him and found the proclamations. So the French general said, 'I think this is a very suspicious thing. You come here with despatches, and you have these things to corrupt the soldiers with. I shan't let you go until it is enquired into,' and he detained him for three or four days.

I sent round to my commanding officer, that he might receive the story from the Frenchman himself. The colonel talked to him a long time and extracted some valuable information from him, among other things that the road on which I was stationed with my picquet was the high road to Alkmaar. On discovering this the colonel said, 'This is of the utmost importance. There must be an entrenchment placed here.'

I was to remain with the picquets all night. At the grey of the morning the post was attacked, two men on my picquet were killed and some wounded. This was the first time I had been under fire, for at the disembarkation the 20th were in reserve.

As I expected an attack I had the men on the watch. There were some militia on the picquet who had only been embodied ten days. As they were throwing up a trench I heard one of them say to another, 'Well, I'll stand as long as the officer stands!' and all did behave remarkably well. The French soon went back when they found that we were prepared for them. Colonel Smyth next morning gave me great commendation for having first caused a trench to be thrown up in a very good position, and for having then repulsed the enemy very gallantly and defeated the design of the French officer.

Later that day Sir Ralph Abercromby came down himself to see all about it, and ask how far the enemy came, &c., and I was nervous and embarrassed, thinking it a very formidable thing to speak to the Commander-in-Chief: when an old Dutch General, Sontag, who had come with him (he was known in the camp as General Ney, on account of his long nose), came blustering out, 'Now, Sir, speak out, and tell the General all you have seen!' I was so angry with him I felt as if I could have knocked him down, but his words made me conquer my modesty and speak out directly.

On my returning to camp I was surrounded by all the officers of the 20th, and congratulated on having opened the ball.

On another occasion I was visiting a distant picquet near a dyke when I heard a sound in the water which I thought at first was a dog, but on going with a sergeant to reconnoitre, we discovered a Dutch officer in uniform measuring the depth of the dyke with a stick, and we captured him. The dyke was about three feet deep in water and three in mud. It was thought he was measuring with a view to an attack, and the surmise proved to be correct, for we were attacked two days afterwards. I was much complimented by my commanding officer for what I had done.

Before we went to Holland several soldiers from our regiment, as was then allowed, volunteered into the regiments ordered for service. However, a few months later we followed. I recollect two soldiers coming back to find their old regiment. I was lying half asleep on a sand bank, and I heard them coming along, and then one said to the other, 'Here, Tom, here's the old drum, I'll be hanged if it isn't,' recognising the drum of their old regiment, and very sorry they had ever left it.

The first man I ever saw shot was in Holland. There was a breach in the wall and the French were opposite. Several officers, and I among them, were standing round, when suddenly a shot came and carried off the leg of a poor artilleryman sitting on a cannon. The poor fellow screamed so, and seemed in such agony, that I hoped then I should never have my leg carried off.

On the 10th September the French and Dutch made a determined attack on the positions occupied by the British troops at the head of the Zijp Dyke. They gained some advantage on their right, but were met with determined resistance on their centre and left, especially from the 20th Regiment, who gallantly repelled the attack of their centre column on the entrenchments raised upon the dyke at Crabbendam. They were eventually driven back with a loss of nearly 1,000 men.

This affair (Schagen Brug) was John Colborne's first battle. He himself was among the wounded, as were, in his own battalion, Lieutenant-Colonel Smyth, Major Ross (afterwards 'Ross of Bladensburg'), Captain Powlett, and Lieutenants DesVoeux and Hamilton. The following letters were sent home by Colborne after the battle:

To The Rev. T. Bargus, Barkway

Vley
Zephyr

Dear Sir,

I have only time to say we were yesterday attacked by a very large force. Our regiment suffered particularly. I am wounded in the head, but not severely. Three thousand of the enemy were killed and wounded.

I am, yours affectionately,
J. Colborne

To Miss Delia Colborne

Heelder
13th September

My Dear Delia,

Of course you have heard of the action before this. I should have written to you immediately after it, but was so situated

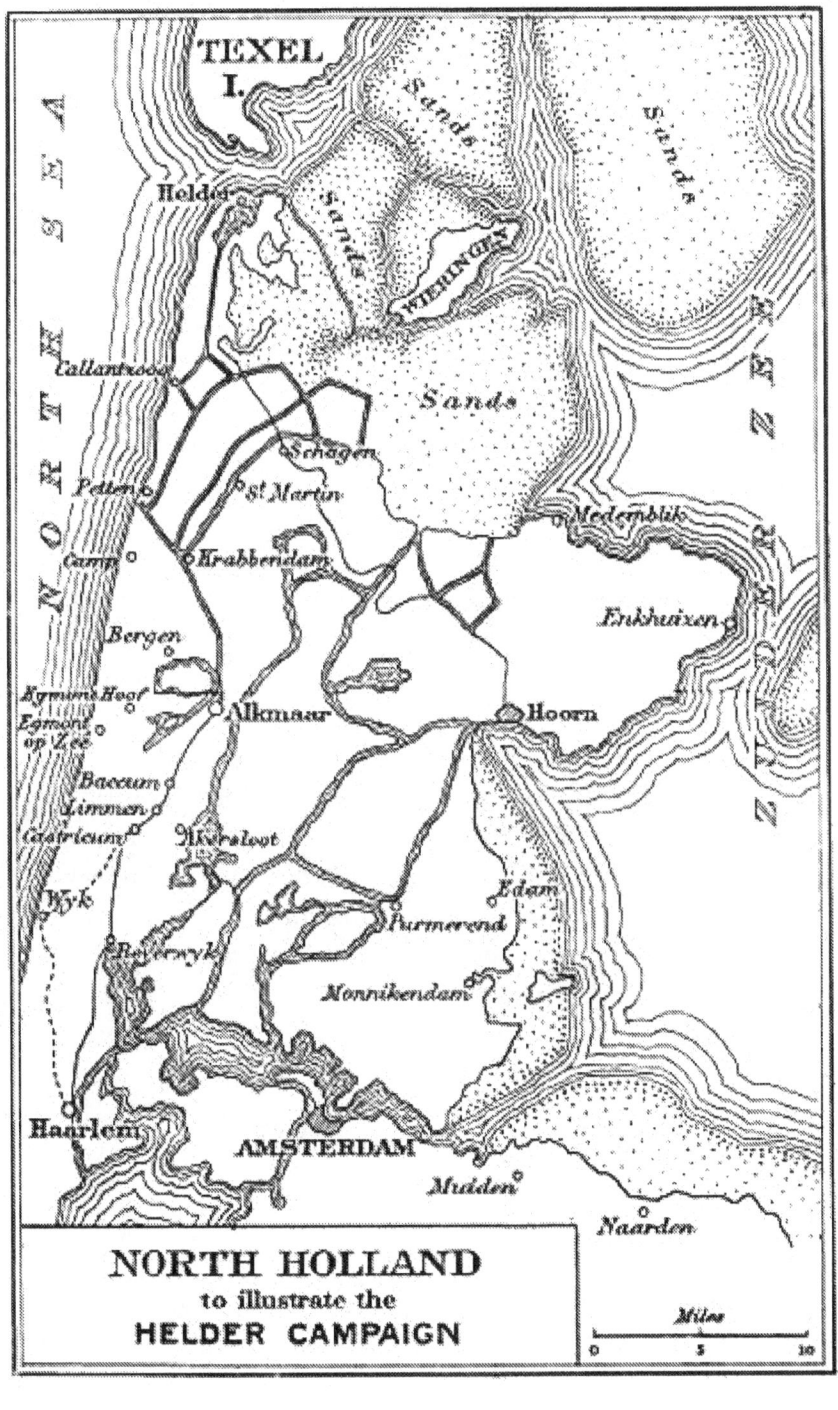

then, I could get but one sheet of paper before the packet sailed, which I sent to Mr. Bargus. I was wounded in the head, and feel no inconvenience, except from the violence of the blow and the sudden compression, which occasioned violent pains in the head. I have been bled twice, and find myself greatly relieved.

The 1st Battalion have had the advanced post ever since we have been here. On the 10th the Dutch and French made an attack on the whole line. They attacked the right and left first, but only as a diversion, and then advanced with nearly their whole force against the 1st Battalion of the 20th. They came down in three large columns with their riflemen in front, who soon spread themselves around us. The grenadiers of our regiment defended an outpost three hours, till all our ammunition was expended. We were then obliged to retire, as a company of the battalion had given way, placed on our right at a bridge. Neither the artillery nor our own men had any ammunition remaining. The enemy crossed the bridge. We then charged them with the 2nd Battalion, who came to our assistance, and drove them over the bridge. We charged twice in a village which they had taken. They then retired, leaving heaps of dead and wounded behind. Our regiment behaved uncommonly well. The first battalion had but six hundred men, as we left part of the regiment at the Texel Island. Our army is very much scattered No regiment but the 2nd Battalion came to our assistance till the action was over. It lasted from four till eleven a.m. I hope to join the regiment in two or three days again.

I am, yours affectionately,
J. Colborne

To The Rev. T. Bargus, Barkway

Heelder
13th September

Dear Sir,
Since we have been here the 1st Battalion of the 20th have had the honour of occupying the advanced post of

the whole army, consequently we have been but a few yards from the enemy for this last fortnight Our picquets have had frequent skirmishes; but on the 10th September the enemy made an attack on the whole line, advancing on the right and left as a diversion, but making their real attack on our battalion. Three large columns advanced on us in very good order with riflemen in front, who spread themselves on all sides in a few minutes, and came within eight or nine yards, picking out the officers to fire at. The grenadiers were advanced about a quarter of a mile in front of the battalion and defended the post until all their ammunition was expended, firing more than a hundred rounds. At this time a company in our rear, defending a bridge, was obliged to retire, the officer of the artillery being wounded and having no ammunition remaining; we then retreated with difficulty. The enemy passed the bridge and pressed on us. Part of the 1st and 2nd Battalions charged and drove them back; we then charged them twice in a village which they had taken; they retreated immediately, leaving heaps of dead and wounded on the field. Our army being so much scattered no regiment could come to our assistance till the enemy had retired. The action began between four and five, and ended about twelve. Sir Ralf was very much pleased with the conduct of the regiment; indeed, it was impossible for them to behave better. Six officers of the 1st Battalion were wounded out of eighteen who were engaged. The wounded are removed to this place. I hope in a few days to join the regiment again. The bullet took me on the side of my head just above the temple, but fortunately I had my hat on sideways, which prevented the ball from entering the skull; there is no fracture. I have been bled twice and find myself greatly relieved.

Remember me to Mrs. B. and the children.

J. Colborne

    Colborne referred to the action in later years as follows:

During the course of the battle General Abercromby came galloping among our artillery, exclaiming, 'Now fire one more round at them.'

The officer in command said, 'We have no ammunition left.'

'The first time I have ever seen the artillery ill served,' said the General, in vexation, and then, turning to the 20th, 'Now are there not forty or fifty of you who will charge with me into the village and drive the French back?' Immediately the whole regiment rushed forward, and a good many militia with them, who had only just come from England and had not had time even to change their militia uniforms. Sir Ralph, recognising this, called out, 'Come along! You are as safe here as if you were in Norfolk!'

General Hamilton lost his leg in the battle his first battle and my first battle, and so did Sir Charles DesVoeux. Hamilton did not care a bit about it, but Sir Charles was a very different person, of a low, nervous temperament. I recollect his saying, 'I have lost my leg, and on my birthday, too!' Hamilton was going soon after to Yorkshire to see a person very famous for making wooden legs, and on his way he met with a young lady with whom he fell in love. She turned out to have a large fortune, and he married her; so he found a wife and a wooden leg in one journey.

My own wound was caused by a bullet which grazed my head. I was taken to the house of a priest, who treated me very kindly. The doctors thought it a bad wound, but after being laid up for three weeks or a month, and fed on rice, I joined again; the wound was, however, still open.

> In the priest's house Colborne and his host, says Miss C. M. Yonge, had no common language save Latin, 'and this (as he used to tell) convinced him of the value of the classical studies which he had hitherto rather despised, and from that time, through all his stirring life, he set himself steadily to self improvement. He managed to acquire French, Italian, and Spanish, and even filled quires of paper with exercises of strokes to improve his handwriting.

In other respects, the time for reflection caused by the wound seems to have had a lasting influence on Colborne's character. In the early days of his service he was, as he used to say, a 'wild fellow,' but the wound 'sobered him.' From this time onwards he was conspicuous for his extreme abstemiousness, and for his refusal to follow the fashionable habit of swearing. 'I determined,' he said, 'to abjure it altogether.'

During the time that Colborne was laid up with his wound, the Duke of York landed at the Helder (13th September) with three brigades of British troops, and was followed by 17,000 Russian auxiliaries. Many of the Russian soldiers wore medals, which was astonishing to their British allies, as at that time no British medals were conferred on private soldiers.

The allied army attacked the enemy at Petten on 19th September, but without success, owing to the inconsiderate valour of the Russians, and on the 2nd October made another attack on the position occupied by the French and Dutch troops between Bergen and Egmont op Zee.

Colborne's presence in this action was an early proof of his courage and determination. It was only three weeks since he had received his wound in the head, and he had tasted nothing but rice since, but though his wound was by no means cured, and his physicians were afraid of the consequences of any exertion, he had determined on joining his regiment before the impending battle, and nothing could detain him. He desired to go in a commissariat wagon, but the commissary would not permit this, and the dispute grew so violent that they were both taken before Lieutenant-Colonel Smyth, of the 20th, who was then ill from wounds received on 10th September. Colborne, in a violent passion, exclaimed to the commissary, 'You actually think a bag of biscuits of more value than a British officer!' at which the Colonel laughed heartily, but said, 'Remember, Colborne, this won't do.' So, being refused the commissariat wagon, he had to do the twenty miles on foot. On the way he met Colonel MacDonald, who said, 'Well, Colborne, are you for England?' 'No,' he replied, 'I was wounded at Schagen Brug, and am on my way to join my regiment before the battle!' Colonel MacDonald expressed his delight at the spirit shown by the young lieutenant, and when he reached his regiment he was quite repaid for his long walk by the enthusiasm with which he was received by his brother officers.

During the early part of the action, the 20th (who were in Pulteney's column) were not engaged, but afterwards deployed and advanced among the sand hills, where they showed great gallantry in a fierce musketry battle lasting till nightfall, in which they had fifty soldiers killed and wounded. The regiment still bears 'Egmont op Zee' on its regimental colours. Colborne told a story of this battle:

At that time we had so little baggage, and there was so much difficulty in getting things, that we all wore our large cloaks strapped on to us. I had mine slung across my shoulders. I was standing with an old Scotch officer, a friend of mine, Captain Walker of the 20th, as the enemy were firing from a hill opposite to us, when a shot hit me, at least on the cloak, and when I took it off I found it had gone through and through every fold. Captain Walker said, 'Ah! I see they are determined to have you yet.' Captain Powlett, of the 20th, received a wound in his head, and putting up his hand, exclaimed, 'I'm done for!' on which I took the command of the company.

At this battle a militia officer named Musket, a very fierce-looking man, his face covered with black whiskers, &c., took fright almost at the first shot, set spurs to his horse, galloped for his life to the Helder, embarked for England, and was never afterwards heard of. Innumerable were the jokes and epigrams made in the army on this occasion. Colonel Mac-

Donald declared that the captain of the ship, seeing an officer arrive at full gallop, thought he was the bearer of despatches, and sent a boat off for him.

Cunningham, afterwards General Cunningham, was engaged to be married just before embarking for the campaign. At Egmont op Zee he was wounded, and dreadfully disfigured in the face. So, on his return, he offered to release the lady from her engagement, saying that he was not at all the same person as the man to whom she had engaged herself. However, she would not hear of it, and they were married immediately.

The result of the Battle of Egmont op Zee (or Alkmaar, or Bergen), in which the British loss amounted to 1,200 men, was the capture of Alkmaar and the retreat of the enemy on his last strong position at Beverwyk. But the enemy, on 6th October, again opposed the advance of the allies, and an indecisive battle took place near Castricum, or Egmont Binnen, in which the British lost 1,400 men, among the regiments which suffered most being the two battalions of the 20th. As the Dutch did not apparently reciprocate our desire that they should abandon their French friends and return to the allegiance of the House of Orange, the Duke of York again retired beyond the Zijp, and in consequence of a capitulation signed at Alkmaar on 18th October the allies re-embarked unmolested before the end of October, after restoring 8,000 prisoners.

Though the land war in Holland had thus proved a failure, we had obtained possession of the Dutch fleet and the island of Surinam, which had surrendered to our arms on 20th August.

John Colborne had been twice shot through the cap in the course of this campaign. On the return of the expedition to England, as he was sitting in a coffee-house at Yarmouth, he heard two officers say to each other. 'Impossible!' as they examined the bullet-holes at a little distance. They indeed testified to a narrow escape.

Chapter 2

Minorca and Egypt

Colborne thought himself ill-used at not receiving promotion for his services in Holland, merit in those days, as he held, being subordinated to interest. He called on the military secretary to the Commander-in-Chief to represent his case.

I was stammering, and feeling rather nervous, when he said, 'Come, Sir, speak up; my time is precious,' which so touched me up that I began to speak quite fluently and when he asked me 'How long have you been in the army?' it put me quite in a rage, and nothing makes a man speak so well as that.

So I said, 'How long have I been in the army? That's nothing to the purpose; look at that letter, and that.'

So then he said, 'Yes, Sir, yes, it is a very hard case; put in on paper, and I will give it to the Commander-in-Chief.'

He was sitting up at a desk like a clerk, and I recollect striking the desk with a little twig I had in my hand and saying, 'I do think it a confoundedly hard case, to use no other terms.'

The visit seems to have been not without effect, as on 12th January, Colborne, not yet 21, became brevet-captain.

Early in 1800 the 20th Regiment proceeded to Ireland and was stationed at Cork, where its numbers were increased by volunteers from several corps of Irish militia. In June the 20th was despatched with a small expedition against Belle Isle. According to Miss Yonge, Colborne used to tell the story that as he embarked at Cork an old Irish woman blessed him with the prophecy that he would come back commander-in-chief, a prophecy literally fulfilled fifty-five years later. The attack on Belle Isle having been abandoned, the troops were landed on the little isle of Houat, where for a week they had nothing to do but to gallop about on the rough ponies with which the island abounded. The regiment then proceeded to the island of Minorca, where it remained ten months.

The following letter was written soon after the disembarkation to his elder sister, Miss Colborne:

To Miss Delia Colborne

Fort George
10th September, 1800

Dear Delia,

Have you not been daily expecting a large quantity of Genoa velvet? I am sorry to say the velvet must now be changed into Minorca honey. I am *very much* disappointed. After our expectations had been raised with the idea of co-operating with the Austrian army, we find ourselves garrison troops at Minorca, with our light baggage only. My wardrobe consists of four shirts, as many stockings, and other necessaries in proportion *very agreeable* in a hot climate. Our original destination was Genoa but through the late arrival of Sir Ralph Abercrombie and the treachery of Melas' army[1] the grand expedition which has covered the seas for so long a time was rendered useless. Until *I am at the head of affairs* these expeditions never will be properly managed.

The battalions of the 20th, from the time of their entering the harbour of Mahon, voluntarily remained on board, hoping there would still be some expedition going on. Two days before Sir Ralph sailed we were ordered to disembark, as he

---

1. Melas was defeated by Napoleon at Marengo, 14th June, 1800.

had received orders from England to leave behind those regiments which received militia. The men, as much disappointed as their officers, and thinking the expedition might be going out of Europe, volunteered for general service. The Commander-in-Chief could not accept their services without an order from England.[2]

I am quartered at Fort George (formerly Fort St. Philip), remarkable for the siege in 1782. I send this by the *Guillaume Tell* one of the Nile fleet that escaped in Nelson's action. If you can steal a few old newspapers dated since the latter end of May (for I have not perused a paper from the time I left sweet Ireland), send them to me, and I shall be yours forever. You must learn Italian immediately, for I speak nothing but the *bella lingua Toscana*. I mean to make the Grand Tour as soon as the Governor and the dollars will permit. By the way, I must tell you that we are well paid in this island, and, what is more, I save money for the first time in my life. The sun has already made some impression on me, inasmuch as that I am getting very thin and, of course, genteel. The word *thin* reminds me of the garrison of Malta, who have entered the harbour this morning, starved out of the fortification of Valetta.[3]

As I am not to be actively employed, I prefer this place to England I can live on my pay comfortably, I have good rooms, and I have an opportunity now of spending (except when on duty) the greater part of the day in private. I assure you I am sensible of the number of days that I have lost, and am determined now, in a manner, to regain them. I am now astonished, on reflection, how I could have thrown away so much good time, and as activity of mind gives life to the most dreary desert, so I am willing to convert this dull fortress into a social

---

2. Militia-men were received in regiments of the line with the stipulation that they should not be employed out of Europe.
3. Malta surrendered to the British forces early in September, 1800, after an investment of nearly two years.

world; for the constant society of redcoats to a military man is no society. Female society we have none. The Minorca ladies are some of them pretty, but disfigure themselves much by their dress, wearing their hair down to their feet twisted in the form of a cow's tail, a close cap, and formidable stays with a peak as long as Tenerife. A strange custom and barbarous, the parents have, of sending their daughters that are pretty to a nunnery—the *uglies* are suffered to enjoy the pomps and vanities. The military are obliged to behave very reverently to the friars, and pay the greatest respect to the religions of the country. There are about nine monasteries and two nunneries in the island But one nun has been stolen from the convents since the arrival of the British. This holy sister was carried off by an officer of the 42nd Regiment, but was obliged to be sent back in faded splendour wan.

Fancy, how sublime, romantic, and picturesque, to see and hear the happy swains playing under the windows of their charming brunettes. This is the mode of making love. They are only allowed to see the fair for the first two years at the window, except at Mass. The third year they are admitted to kiss the hand, and the fourth, if agreeable to the parties, the courtship ends. As I think a month's attendance on these occasions is quite sufficient, I have no chance of marrying here. The society you would like, I have no doubt, and, when tired, you would have an opportunity of entering a very elegant nunnery, which is a place I would recommend to you if you would promise not to run away and bring disgrace on the sisterhood.

I am, yours affectionately,
J. Colborne

> At Minorca Colborne did indeed set himself as he hinted to 'redeem the time.'
>
> I used to ride at four o'clock every morning several miles to a man who taught me French, Italian and drawing. I used

to translate Latin into Italian. I used to ride back again by ten, and tie up my horse in the town and be in time for parade. My time in Minorca was a very happy one.

He adds one little trait:

We could get no vegetables in Minorca except pumpkins, and we used to have pies made of them, mashing them with pepper.

Meanwhile Lieutenant-General Sir Ralph Abercromby had proceeded with a British force to Egypt to force the French 'Army of the East' to evacuate that country. A landing was effected on the 8th March, and three engagements favourable to British arms followed; but on the 21st March Sir Ralph Abercromby was mortally wounded and the command devolved on Lieutenant-General. Hutchinson. Hutchinson advanced up the country to attack Cairo. Reinforcements were ordered to join the army in Egypt, and on the 24th June the 20th Regiment embarked from Minorca, and landing in Aboukir Bay on 24th July, took post on the east side of Alexandria. Lieutenant-General Hutchinson, having returned from Cairo, whose garrison had capitulated on 27th June, resolved to press the siege of Alexandria with vigour. This was the situation when Colborne wrote the following letter to his stepfather:

To The Rev. T. Bargus, Barkway

Camp before Alexandria
7th August, 1801

Dear Sir,

We arrived in the Bay of Aboukir the 17th of July, after a short passage from Minorca, and are now encamped about five miles from Alexandria on a sandy desert, the sea on our right and a large lake on our left, which has been cut so as to inundate a vast extent of country. I see Pompey's pillar at a distance, and probably in a few days shall have an opportunity of inspecting it nearer, as the attack is to be made on Menou's strong position before the town, as soon as the French that capitulated at Cairo are embarked. They consist of 9,000 effective Frenchmen, 4,000 auxiliaries, Greeks, Copts, &c, and 63 pieces of cannon. General Hutchinson is thought to have acted politically in getting so large a force out of the country without fighting his forces consisting but of 5,000 English, the rest being Turks, who are anything but soldiers, a mere undisciplined rabble, not to be depended on. General Coote commands the division before Alexandria, which has remained inactive since the 21st March. There is now an immense army here, in general healthy, sore eyes being the chief complaint, which occasions frequently loss of sight for a month or six weeks. There are but few instances of men going blind entirely. I prefer the climate to Minorca. Here you have a fine, steady breeze continually blowing from the north-west; there, during three months, not a breath of wind can be perceived. We have only to dread the Sirrock, or hot southerly wind, which has blown but twice since the arrival of the army. Sir Ralph was told by the Consul, Baldwin, that no water could be found, but fortunately we get water by digging under any palm tree, of which there are plenty indeed, Julius Caesar has shown us the way, who says he found *copia dulcis aquae* by digging near the sea. The leaves of the palm afford us shelter we make comfortable huts from them which enable us to enjoy the breeze, at the same time screening us from the burning sun.

Yours affectionately

J. C.

In after days Colborne told a story of the siege of Alexandria:

As I and another officer were walking round the walls, a French officer called out to us from the rampart and told us there was a friend of his whom we had taken prisoner to whom he wished to send a letter and some money. He then

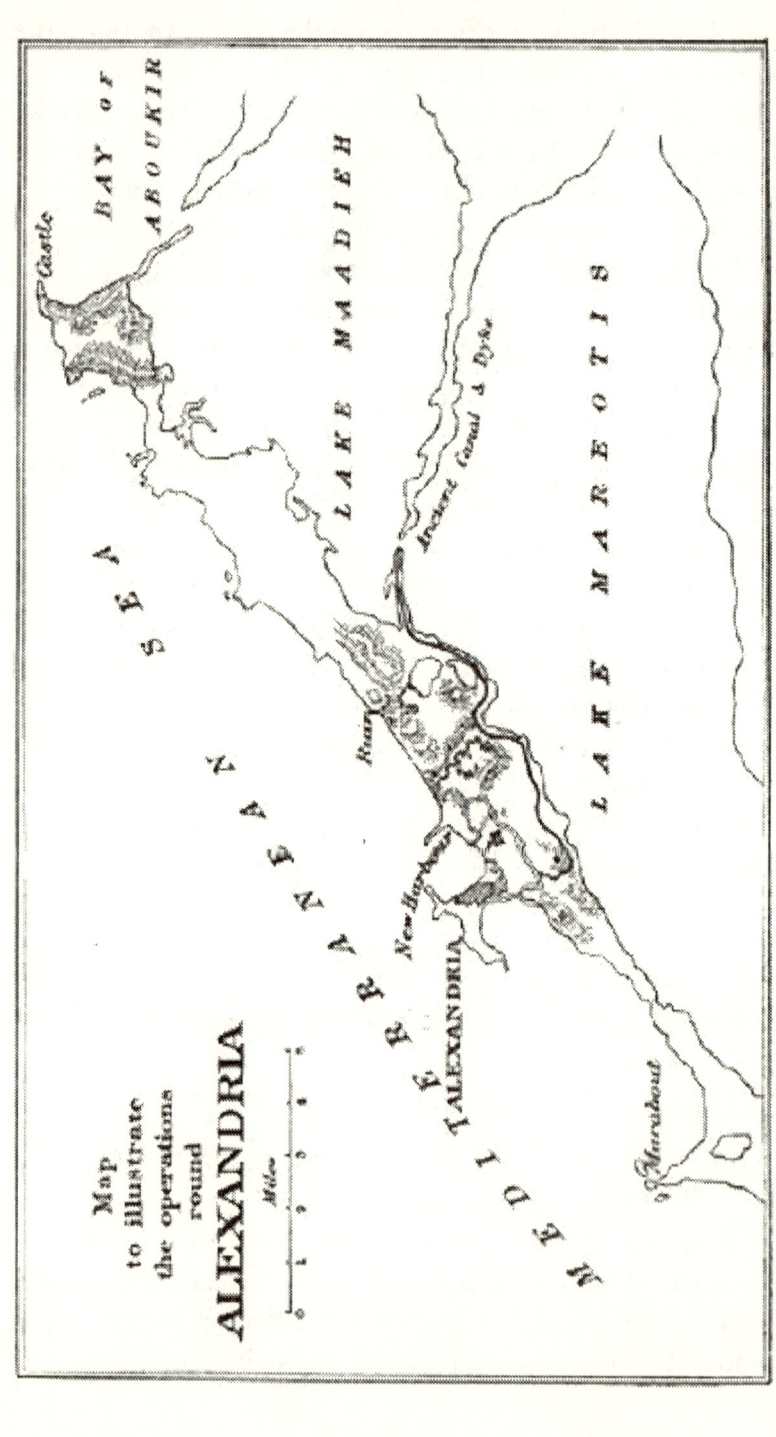

threw the letter and a purse over to us. I thought it showed great confidence in English officers. I inquired about the prisoner, who had been wounded, and sent him the money.

Before the date of the conclusion of the following letter Alexandria had fallen:

To The Rev. T. Bargus, Barkway

Camp near Alexandria
29th August

Dear Sir,

The army remained inactive till the 17th August, when General Coote sailed up the Lake Mareotis with 4,000 men, and landed without opposition near Marabou, westward of Alexandria. The same day General Hutchinson forced the enemy from a strong position on the east side. Coote advanced on the 21st three miles; the enemy retired in great confusion, leaving us seven pieces of cannon. We encamped within three quarters of a mile of Alexandria. Our camp was annoyed by shells from the French batteries previous to our attacking another of their positions on the night of the 27th (25th?) August, which was carried without any loss. The same night they endeavoured to make our picquets retire by firing at us about two hours. Next morning General Menou requested a cessation of hostilities in order to arrange the terms of capitulation.

2nd September. Our grenadiers this day marched into the principal forts of the enemy, agreeable to the Articles of Capitulation, which are much the same as those of Cairo. Thus has ended the Egyptian expedition, in which neither French or English generals have displayed great military talents. However, those who read the elegant letters of Hutchinson will be persuaded that he is one of the greatest generals of the age.

That part of the army which arrived at the commencement of the affair have suffered unexampled hardships with cheerfulness, and on every occasion shown courage and discipline.

Since the death of Sir Ralph,[4] Fortune has decidedly been Hutchinson's greatest friend in every instance. The French generals have either behaved treacherously or injudiciously. We are not permitted to enter Alexandria yet. The country immediately about us is much improved by the junction of the lakes Maadie and Mareotis,[5] lately stinking marshes. By the heaps of ruins, catacombs and baths (which, of course, are called Cleopatra's), it appears Alexandria extended as far as our encampment formerly.

Sir Sydney Smith is now off the Old Harbour, about to take possession of a Venetian 64 and two frigates, *L'Egyptienne* and *La Justice*, which are now in a fine basin near the town; the entrance is rendered difficult by shallows. The new harbour is on the east side of the town and separated from the old by a *presqu'isle*, at the end of which is Pharos. The harbourage is bad, and ships are exposed to the northerly winds. Pompey's Pillar rises majestically from amidst the sand hills, about half a mile from the town, composed of three pieces of granite, the base, shaft and capital. They say it is 94 feet high. I have not measured it. I have more than once trembled lest this vast work, which has so long withstood time, should be demolished or injured by the shot from our gunboats, whose fire was directed at a redoubt very near it. I am happy to find the balls have paid respect to this elegant column. General Coote made a regimental band play *God Save the King* round it this morning. There appears no historical proof why it should be called Pompey's Pillar, Damietta being the place where he fell. M. Sonnini is anxious it should be called hereafter Bonaparte's Pillar, or the Column of the French Republic, and says, 'Posterity will recollect that this was the headquarters from whence Bonaparte issued orders for the escalade, and it is not easy to determine whether of the two heroes, the Founder or Restorer, will excite most admiration in their eyes.'

---

4. On the 28th March preceding.
5. 12th and 13th April.

Were you to see the wretches whom the Restorer fought against, and the old towers that were taken by escalade, the point would easily be determined in your own mind. Alexandria, at that time, was only surrounded by the old walls erected by the Arabs on their invasion. This enclosure forms modern Alexandria. The Grand Vizier's army is composed of the most despicable rabble ever collected together. The annihilation of Turkey is at no great distance; not even a Belisarius would save this sinking state. These people, the proudest in the world without any reason, now condescend to shake an Englishman cordially by the hand and pass him with the greatest respect, repeating frequently, *'Buono Inglese.'* As for Bonaparte, they have curtailed his name, and now know him by no other than 'Parte.' The Indian army is at Rosetta they remain in Egypt for the present. So pleasant is the climate to me that should no other expedition take place I would rather remain also. The ophthalmia is much in the army, fevers are very common also., I never enjoyed better health, having had no complaint since my arrival. I intend going to Rosetta tomorrow on my way to the Pyramids.

It is most probable that we shall perform quarantine at Gozo, a small isle near Malta.

The climate in whose praise I have been so lavish has carried off in a few hours my most intimate friend, a young man respected by the whole regiment.

Yours affectionately and sincerely,

J. C.

The 20th was detained in Egypt for two months more.

To The Rev. T. Bargus, Barkway

Camp near Alexandria
5th November, 1801

Dear Sir,

We have been encamped since September on very unpleasant ground near Pompey's Pillar. The dust, in which there is a mixture of lime, annoys us perpetually. At present there are 240 men blind in the battalion. We expect to sail in a few days, Malta, it is supposed, will be our winter quarters. Five thousand men remain here, exclusive of the Indian army they consist of the Irish regiments and the Foreign Brigade. Alexandria is a most villainous town Cleopatra's Needles and a few baths are the only antiquities to be seen in this once splendid city, except some granite pillars which you frequently see adorning a mud-house.

I have been to Rosetta.[6] The streets are similar to those of Alexandria, but the eye is refreshed by the green fields of the Delta and the Nile running rapidly by them. From Rosetta we proceeded to Cairo. The Nile was at its height. It does not inundate the whole country like a sea, as travellers have represented, but seems perfectly under the control of the husbandmen, who, by canals and wheels, admit what quantity of water they think proper into their fields. We made our headquarters at Gizeh, a village where Murat Bey formerly resided, situated opposite Cairo on the left bank of the Nile. We set out from this place at 10 o'clock p.m., and managed to be on the top of one of the Pyramids before sunrise.

Cairo is a large, stinking, ill-built town. The streets are so exceedingly narrow that it requires some exertion to pass through the groups of Arabs, Mamaloucs and Turks, mules and loaded animals, which latter take up the whole breadth of the street. The only decent part to be seen is the Place d'Eau, a large square where Menou has built a house *a la Turque*.

---

6. While we were at Rosetta we met one or two parties and with one of them was an old brother officer of the 20th, Captain Colborne. He was very much teased with the musquitos one night when many of us were lying down to rest in a large room at one of the inns at Rosetta: he thought he would hit upon a plan to give the musquitos the slip, thinking they were on the walls of the room; he therefore shifted his bed to the middle of the room, and much to our amusement the musquitos attacked him worse than ever, and I believe few of us had any rest that night; we tried to smoke them out, but all would not do, and we arose in the morning very little refreshed. Lieut.-Col. Chas. Steevens, *Reminiscences of My Military Life*.

There happened a few days since a most horrid assassination, which now makes every Englishman ashamed to have acted with such detestable allies. The Mamalouc Beys, who have materially assisted in expelling the French, and whom the Commander-in-Chief promised to protect on the arrival of the army in Egypt, were invited by the Pacha to a magnificent breakfast. He afterwards persuaded seven of them to enter his boat on pretence of calling on Lord Cavan, the commandant of Alexandria. In a few minutes he changed his boat and went on shore, pretending a despatch had arrived from the Grand Vizier. Another boat came alongside of that which the Beys were in, filled with armed soldiers, and massacred Osman Bey and four others. General Hutchinson has behaved with spirit, and has acted like a soldier, if not as a politician.[7] The affair now detains us here.

The news of Peace has just reached us, but not officially.[8]

Yours affectionately,

J. C.

At the moment of the fall of Alexandria General Baird had arrived with an Indian army in fine order, but found nothing for him to do. Colborne had some idea of joining him on his return to India, but abandoned the intention. He said afterwards, 'It would have made a great change in my fortunes if I had gone.'

Colborne's love of knowledge often led him into rash escapades. One of these seems to have occupied his last days in Egypt. 'I rode a very foolish expedition by myself, day and night, all through the Turkish camps, and when I got back to Alexandria I found the army was to sail next day.'

---

7. Colborne told the story in 1847: General Hutchinson went to the Pacha's tent and upbraided him with it, and he said it was not his doing. 'I had received my orders what could I do?' We buried them with military honours, and it was a most impressive spectacle.

8. The *Lodi* brig carrying the official intimation entered Alexandria on November 15th.

Chapter 3

Malta

From Egypt the 20th was sent to Malta (disembarking on 9th December), which island, according to the terms of the Peace of Amiens, we were then to evacuate. However, owing to the ambiguous conduct of Bonaparte, the British Government determined to retain the island, and war soon broke out afresh. Colborne had not been long in Malta when, taking advantage of the interval of peace, he obtained leave to spend some months in an adventurous tour through Sicily and Calabria, and thus acquired a knowledge of those countries which was afterwards of much use. He found some brother officers ready to accompany him, among them Robert Ross, afterwards the victor of Bladensburg, and the Hon. William Lumley. One night at an inn, as Colborne used to relate, the people came round and began firing into the windows at them. He knew no reason, unless it was that one of his companions had given some offence in the town during their visit. On another occasion they lost their way late one night and got into a river, after which they were shown to a gentleman's house, who received them very kindly and entertained them for several days. Strange to say, four years later, this casual acquaintance was renewed, the British force being encamped, after the battle of Maida, in the neighbourhood of this gentleman's house. Some other incidents of the tour we may give in Colborne's own words:

In Sicily a tailor once sent in a bill about four times as much as it should have been, so we agreed to pay each £3 and present it on the points of our swords. The tailor, thus treated, would not take the money, so we went on presenting it till he was driven into a corner, and every time the sword touched him, screamed out *'O Signori!'* At last he snatched the money from each of the swords and ran off as hard as he could. Afterwards, on our tour, whenever they brought us a bill which we thought too much, Ross, a very funny fellow, always said, 'I think we must prick this man.'

None of us could speak Italian, but we had an Italian grammar with us, and we had learnt a list of adjectives and expletives. So at one place where the man charged too much we went on calling him one term of abuse after another, the man quite surprised where we could have got them all, till we came to *Boja* (hangman), which made him very angry. Afterwards, when we were coming back, we stopped a night at the same place and called at the inn. The man looked out, recognized us, and shouting, *'Io non sono Boja'* slammed the door in our faces.

To The Rev. T. Bargus, Barkway

Malta
20th April, 1802

Dear Sir,

I am lately returned from Sicily. The description of it by Brydone is poetry. I was much disappointed in this renowned island. We landed at Syracuse, a miserable hole, and then proceeded to Catania, slept at a village on the mountain, and ascended to the crater early in the morning, a dangerous experiment at this time of the year. The effect of the cold we did not recover (from) for many hours.

Messina was our next stage, from which place we crossed to the town of Scylla. The current is amazingly rapid, and our Messinese mariners were as much frightened at it as their forefathers could have been at Scylla and Charybdis.

We experienced many difficulties in passing through Calabria to Naples the greatest obstacles were rivers swollen by the rains. I found my swimming of use to me. The Calabrian gentlemen were very polite, and we made it an invariable rule to enter the best house in the town (where) we halted. We travelled in uniform, and being English officers, it was a sufficient introduction to the inhabitants. Having seen Vesuvius, Naples and all the lions, we returned by Palermo, where we saw his Sicilian majesty, whose chief employment is making butter. Although his amusements are so innocent, yet he is a detested tyrant It is a most miserable government that these Neapolitans and Sicilians live under, and they are such wretches *aprincipio* that they deserve no better.

The second battalion is about to be reduced. I stand seemingly, with or without a company. On the battalions being consolidated we shall have about 1,000 men for general service. We evacuate this island in two months, and then to the West Indies it is reported we go. Eighty of our men are sent home blind, who I think will never recover their sight.

Yours affectionately,
J. Colborne

To Miss Delia Colborne

29th April, 1802

Dear Delia,

I have heard nothing of you for an age. You either do not pay the inland postage or never write. One letter only have I received from you in Egypt, although I have expended a quire of paper in writing to you. We expect to evacuate Malta in a month. It is reported that we are destined for the West Indies. If that be really our destination, you may expect me to return in the course of three or four years, not with the fat cheeks that you were wont to see, but emaciated, scorched and shrivelled beneath the burning zone. You will be unable to trace my unmeaning features.

Garstin, of the 20th Regiment, your coz, has been here a long time sick. I recollect you once mentioned that he was a handsome man, from which speech I must infer that either your eyes deceived you or that the poor animal is miserably fallen away.

Meagre and very rueful were his looks,
Sharp misery had worn him to the bones.
Famine is in his cheeks.
(Otway, hem!)[1]

'I am not exactly certain whether it is sharp misery that has made the man such an object, but at present I am at a loss whether to compare him to the Apothecary in *Caius Marius*, or Lismahago.[2] He was very attentive and polite to me in Egypt.

Charles Greville passed this place on his way to England. He is not a *great* coxcomb, only the poor man can't open his mouth. 'Will you dine with me today, Greville?' Three times was I obliged to repeat the question before I could discover whether he said *yes* or *no*. At last, by a certain motion of his head, I conceived that he answered in the affirmative. He certainly is a very fine young man.

I have been three months in Sicily and Naples, experienced many difficulties in passing through the most romantic country in the world, Calabria saw Herculaneum, Pompeii, Pozzoli, Baiae and Cumae, and ascended the two mountains Etna and Vesuvius—and am returned, perfect master of Italian, speak it fluently, much better than a Neapolitan and full as well as a Roman—never praise yourself. I shall not attempt giving a description of these countries, the history of which, both ancient and modern, you are so well acquainted with. Besides, any poetical descriptions would swell my letter too

---

1. Colborne is quoting from Otway's *History and Fall of Caius Marius*, a classicized version of *Romeo and Juliet*. All that is Otway's in these lines is the addition, 'and very rueful'; the rest is Shakespeare's, though Colborne was perhaps unaware of it.
2. In Smollett's *Humphry Clinker*.

much. I presume you have read Brydone. I have discovered that his volumes are poesy, that is, fiction, the greatest part; he deserves praise for his ingenuity. I doubt whether he ever visited Sicily.

I am afraid now my chance for a company is not great, unless we go to the West Indies, where, if we go, I would not compound for a majority.

You will say this is a strange hand he writes now, but know, this is a pattern for you to copy I think there are more words in one page of this than in any letter I have ever received from you. Your words are in general so stretched, that even if you had news or inclination to fill your epistle, no common sheet of paper would contain your thoughts.

I see by the paper my Uncle Colborne is dead, the last of the family that was good for anything (present company excepted).

As for Mrs. G—, I will never call on her if I should be in London for a year. I recollect that woman opened a letter of yours about six years ago. It has made an impression on my mind. She must be an old sinner, for a woman or a man that would commit the above-mentioned action would not scruple at any mischief. Am sorry you called on her.

Yours affectionately,
J. Colborne

The following reminiscences relate to this time:

When I was in Sicily, on my return from Calabria, an officer at Malta in order to escape marrying a lady or being assassinated by her brother, set off in a tremendous storm in a little shironata, and sailed to Syracuse. It was a great wonder that he was not swamped. We were all watching her in. After he had arrived and told his story, an American sea captain who was present said to him, 'Sir, I would rather have married *the vilest woman on earth* than have set out in such a storm as this!'

This American captain was a very ugly fellow, the ugliest man

I ever saw. At Gibraltar there was an officer, I forget his name but he was always called Ugly Jack. One day, when this American captain was on the parade ground, he went up to this officer, and pulling out a snuff-box, said, 'There, Sir, that's yours!'

'How mine? What do you mean?'

'Why, that snuff-box was given me to give to any man that I found uglier than myself, and I think I've found him!'

The same man once said to me, 'The President asked me what I thought of having chaplains on board every ship, and I said, "I don't like it at all, I have sailed in six or seven British ships and only met one respectable chaplain."'

He said at another time, 'Your navy will be much better than ours; there are very few of us old fellows left in our navy, and when we are gone it will be worth nothing!'

He once gave a ball at Naples, and borrowed a beautiful band, and after the ball was over he sailed away and took the band off to America, as a present to the President. For this he was dismissed the service.

During the 20th's long stay in Malta, from 1802 to 1805, it was quartered first at Vittoriosa, later, from May, 1803, at Valetta.[3] Colborne remained still zealous for self-improvement. He once said, 'At Malta I was learning several things, and wanted all the time I could get, so I had a bell fixed to my bed and gave a man a dollar or so a month to ring it at four every morning when he went to ring the bell of the neighbouring church; and I used to get up immediately. I found, after the first two or three mornings, that I awoke before the bell rang. Among other things, as it was the time that the French gave up the Ionian Islands, and there was some chance of our going there, I got a Greek master and set to work to learn Greek, and soon knew a good deal of it.'

---

3. From April, 1804, to September, 1805, Colborne's schoolfellow, S. T. Coleridge, was living in Malta as secretary to the Governor. Did Colborne meet him, one wonders.

Late in life it was Colborne's lot, as Lord Seaton, to govern the Ionian Islands, but he had then forgotten his early attainments in Modern Greek.

Colborne was not, however, merely a student himself; he encouraged his subalterns to study also. In a memoir of Colonel T. F. Wade, C.B.,[4] we are told:

> On joining the regiment (at Malta, 21st July, 1805), Ensign Wade had the good fortune to be posted to the company of Captain John Colborne; and by this great soldier he was instructed, not only in his duties as a subaltern, but in much beside, especially in foreign languages.

But the time at Malta was one of play as well as work. On one occasion Colborne formed one of a party who, at a masquerade at the palace, were to represent Silenus and his crew:[5]

> We took the colonel's donkey, and after we had stolen him, the difficulty was to get him upstairs. However, we carried him up. On entering the room the first person we saw was the colonel himself. He came up, looking very hard at the donkey, and said, 'Why, I do believe that is my donkey!'
>
> I was dressed as a Bacchanal attending Silenus. An intimate friend of mine was dressed as a town crier, and had papers, 'Lost such and such a thing,' which he read out, and when he saw someone laughing at the allusion to someone else, he pulled out another paper which reflected on him. He offended nearly everyone in the room, and no one could find out who he was.
>
> On another occasion, when some private theatricals were being arranged, two friends of mine, to play a joke, sent another person to request me to be

---

4. Lancashire Fusiliers' Annual for 1893.
5. Cp. C. Steevens, *Reminiscences*.

manager. It was just at a time when I was working hard and occupied all day. So, when this person was shown in to me, and made his request, I was as angry as possible, received him in the most formal manner, and said, 'Certainly not.' He went out quite confused, and I heard afterwards that he said he would never have been induced to go if he had known what sort of a person I was.

The rain at Malta in the winter is very violent indeed. I remember once when we were there, after a few days' rain, such a torrent came down a street against the gate of a guard-room that it was broken open, and a sergeant and two soldiers of the guard were washed away. It was near the sea, and the sergeant was washed into it and drowned, but the two men saved themselves.

During part of the time of Colborne's stay in Malta, H.R.H. the Duke of Kent was Governor of Gibraltar. Colborne used to tell stories of the Duke's extraordinary attention to small points of dress.

When the Duke of Kent was at Gibraltar, as soon as a ship arrived, he used to send on board a tailor and a hairdresser to measure the men's cuffs and collars and hair, lest they should not be according to regulation. He was so particular, that I remember when we were at Malta, if an officer arrived from Gibraltar, the whole garrison used to turn out to see the Gibraltar dress. The Duke was once cleverly out-manoeuvred. As he was riding out with his staff he saw a man in a fatigue dress and immediately gave him chase, but the man disappeared, and they could not find him. However, the Duke had a capital eye, and next morning at parade he recognized the man. So he called him out and said, 'Now, I'll forgive you if you'll tell me how you escaped?'

'Why, Sir,' was the reply, 'I saw a fatigue party coming along, and I took up step and joined them, and you passed me.'

So the Duke had been beaten through the man's presence of mind!

Once, at a review of Russian troops, after getting Prince W— to bring out his best regiment and go through some manoeuvres, he said, 'Well, that was well done, and I ought to be a judge, for for twelve years (or whatever the number was) I have never one single day missed a parade!'

The following letters of Colborne's date from these years in Malta:

TO THE REV. T. BARGUS, BARKWAY

Malta,
13th October, 1802

Dear Sir,

As there are no tidings of the Grand Master, I shall recommence a correspondence which has been interrupted for several months by the appearance of a speedy evacuation of Malta. It is generally believed that the English garrison will remain here till the summer. Two thousand Neapolitan soldiers have been sent to us, rather prematurely. The French envoy is arrived, a major-general, possessing, to a great degree, all the impudence peculiar to his nation. His aide-de-camp has already caused some disturbance at the theatre. Thinking it beneath the duty of a Republican to conform to English customs, he refused to stand up while *God save the King* was played; in consequence of which he was turned out, not in the politest manner, apparently by the universal consent of the audience. Alexandria is still in our possession, and there are no preparations for the departure of our troops. A French frigate has been dispatched there to ascertain the cause of the delay in conforming to the definite treaty. The Mamelukes are killing the Turks without mercy; the former are victorious in every action. The 20th Regiment will probably revisit Egypt before England.

We have had *dira febris* among us, which has been more destructive than battles or sieges; but the climate is now become mild and agreeable, and, of course, more healthy. The heat for three months was intolerable. Our two battalions are consolidated.

Yours affectionately,
J. Colborne

Malta
9th December, 1802

Dear Sir,

I am sure it will give you great pleasure to hear of my appointment to a company. My commission is dated 20th May.[6] I esteem myself most fortunate, as there is not another instance of promotion going in a regiment where the vacancy has been caused by duelling. Had it not been for this step I might probably have remained many years in my former situation, as the vacancies now are generally filled up by the half-pay.

Yours affectionately,
J. Colborne

Writing to Mr. Bargus, in July, 1804, Colborne says he has sent a bracelet for his sister and slippers for Mr. Bargus. He comments on the engagement of his sister, Miss Colborne, to the Rev. Duke Yonge, and continues:

The French are in full march to Naples, a Neapolitan frigate has been dispatched to Lord Nelson for assistance. I hope it may be productive of some active service. Ten thousand men might be employed advantageously in Sicily, and would save many a broken head. The French will be there before us; to drive them out when they have possession of Syracuse and Messina will be very difficult.

We are all delighted that the reign of the Addingtons is ended. Their abilities seem to have (been) useful to a few bishops and the Addington family; the loss of them to the country will not be very great. We have an imperfect account

---

6. Colborne had been a Brevet-Captain since 12th January, 1800.

of another monstrous coalition, Pitt and Fox, etc. The dread of an invasion will never cease. You are as safe in England as we are in this impregnable Malta. The new Emperor will not land a man in England, neither will he attempt it. Let him have a million gunboats, still he will never use them. Ireland is certainly the vulnerable heel, but to wound it he must hazard much. Politicians think he has a deeper scheme. There has been an insurrection at Tripoli incited by *la republique imperiale*. It is reported the Emperor means to occupy the whole of the African coast in the Mediterranean.

Yours affectionately,
J. Colborne

Writing from Malta on 15th September, 1804, to his half-sister, Miss Alethea Bargus, he acknowledges the gift of a pin containing her hair, and continues:

To Miss Alethea Bargus

As your hair becomes darker, so mine on the contrary takes a lighter shade, and I fear before we meet it will be a beautiful grey.

Do not forget to collect all the laughable family anecdotes, as I am become very grave and my mouth now resembles that of the parish clerk of Barkway. I am quite tired of Malta, and half roasted by the heat of last summer. I will not invite you to pay me a visit here, but I shall be happy to see you when we are at Naples.

Your affectionate brother,
J. *Colborne*

To The Rev. T. Bargus, Barkway

Malta
18th October, 1804

Dear Sir,

Thank God the hot weather is passed and we are again in our own climate. We have lost too many of our men in the hot months, owing to their sacrificing so frequently to Bacchus. We are now about 800 bayonets, and in the highest order. I really think there is no regiment in the service that has so much *esprit de corps* as the 20th.

Transports are ordered to be ready to receive 4,500 men, but for whom we are ignorant. The order has caused a variety of speculations some say they are for the Russians, who have already 12,000 men assembled at Corfu, others say the garrison is going on an expedition. I am of opinion we shall not be idle in the spring.

They have not yet given us a 2nd battalion. His Royal Highness the Duke ought to consider that our two battalions last war were Egyptian volunteers, the only regiment of that description in Egypt. I speak feelingly, for a 2nd battalion would probably make me 2nd captain. Colonel Oliphant is about to sell out; the step will pass over me as the four senior captains are too poor to purchase. It is a hard case to see a junior captain, almost blind and quite unfit for a field officer, leap over all our heads. I have no reason to complain, for I believe there is not a more fortunate man than myself.

I should like to see your improvements at Barkway, and hope to pay you a visit when we have Peace, provided the French do not plunder the parsonage.

Yours affectionately,
J. Colborne

To The Rev. T. Bargus, Barkway

Malta
10th February, 1805

Dear Sir,

Lord Nelson was off Messina on the 30th January. The French left Toulon on 18th January. They have passed the island for Egypt a second expedition must be the consequence.

Yours affectionately,
J. C.

Chapter 4
Battle of Maida

During the campaign, which ended on 2nd December with the battle of Austerlitz, Russia and England agreed each to send a force into the kingdom of Naples, although the King of Naples committed a breach of faith by countenancing the project, as he had bound himself not to admit into his ports or territories the fleets or armies of any power at war with France. As the 20th Regiment formed part of the British force under Lieutenant-General Sir James Craig, it at last 'escaped from Malta,' as the following letters of Colborne show. The first letter, it may be noted, was written eleven days after Trafalgar, but the great victory remained unknown to the force till after its arrival at Naples. It would seem that even then only the bare news of the victory arrived at first, as Colborne used to relate that the Queen of Naples said she was sure Nelson must have been killed or he would have written to her.

To The Rev. T. Bargus, Barkway

Malta
1st November, 1805

My Dear Sir,

We embarked yesterday and sail tomorrow for Syracuse to unite with the Russians thence we proceed to Italy.

Yours affectionately,

J. Colborne

At sea
14th November, 1805

My Dear Sir,

I was very fortunate in receiving your letter of the 11th August the day we sailed from Malta, whence we escaped 3rd November. Harassed by perpetual contrary winds, we beat about Cape Passaro till the 10th, and were unable to join the Russians before that day.

We are now standing towards Maretimo on our passage to Naples.

The expedition should have arrived there early in the present month, but these democratic winds have so long delayed us that a salute from the French on our landing will probably be the consequence. Commodore Gregg commands the Russian squadron, consisting of four sail of the line, two frigates, and troopships carrying 14,000 hardy barbarians.

The whole combined army is commanded by Field-Marshal Lacy, about 22,000. The French force at Terracina, about three days' march from Naples, amounts to 23,000, commanded by St. Cyr. Nature has not been lavish in her gifts to the English generals on the expedition, they are men of very limited capacities and no experience, but I trust this defect in our army will be remedied by the conduct of the excellent regiments that compose it.

The service for which we are destined will more tend to form good soldiers, and improve us in the knowledge of our profession, than any that British troops have lately been employed on. I have already planned the campaign.

The Austrians that occupy the position on the Adige between Verona and Legnago are to attack that of the French extending from Peschiera to Mantua. Another Austrian army will then cross the Po and advance towards Genoa, which motion will render the situation of the army, which we mean to beat very, dangerous, and should they not make a rapid retreat, will probably be cut off.

Provided your humble servant is not a head minus, you shall have a correct account of our operations, and am,

Your truly affectionate,

J. C.

Alas, the star of Austerlitz was in the ascendant, and the hopes of the young British strategist were quickly belied!

Baola
13th January, 1806

My Dear Sir,

Nothing of importance having occurred, I have not written to you since our disembarking at Castel a Mare; but little did I think that my next letter would inform you of a retrograde movement without firing a shot. The combined army was cantoned in the vicinity of Naples till the 11th of December, when it moved forward, passed the Volturno at Capua, and providentially arrived in good order as far as the Massic Mountains, an extraordinary circumstance considering the talents of our generals.

The headquarters of the Russians were fixed at Teano, those of the English at Sessa. In these cantonments we remained till the 10th of January, anxiously expecting to cross the Garigliano. But how great was our surprise at the British troops being ordered to re-cross the Volturno! It was intended that we should have occupied the pass at Fondi, the Russians that of Ponte Corvo, and 30,000 Neapolitans were to have defended our right near Sulmona, extending our line from the Mediterranean to the Pescara, but the defection of the Russians has been the cause of Sir James Craig making a most inglorious, ridiculous retreat, and so dangerous was our situation thought that he ordered the regiment which had advanced as far as Itri to retire 36 miles in one day and burn the bridge over the Garigliano in its retreat.

Possibly these precautions were necessary, yet the enemy was not within forty leagues of us, and might have penetrated the Neapolitan dominions by Ponte Corvo had he been inclined to interrupt us in our retreat. This disgraceful haste, added to the slovenly, confused manner of our march, increased the alarm of the peasantry who thought themselves abandoned, and the cause desperate. Admitting that our force scarcely deserved the name of army, and was incapable of resisting any considerable number of the enemy, and that ultimately we must have evacuated the country, yet our remaining in it to the last moment would have checked that democratic spirit so prevalent here.

Gaeta, a strong fortress, was open to us, and we might have retired there or into Calabria, had we been hard pressed. The Calabrians, who are well affected, might have been raised *en masse*. We are now in full march to Castel a Mare to re-embark. Our precipitate retreat has given the Neapolitans a very unfavourable impression of the spirit of English soldiers. You may easily conceive with what regret I shall leave the *campania felice*, and how vexed and disappointed I am at the conclusion of this expedition, after speculating so much on the success of the campaign.

Acting with large armies is the only method of obtaining a knowledge of our profession, and even this short affair has pointed out many defects among us, which will exist as long as inactive old men are selected to command. The Commander-in-Chief is at present afflicted with the dropsy, or some other disease that renders him unfit for active service. There are five generals with us, one of them alone can speak the language of the country to which they were sent.

The sudden transition from a sterile, parched-up rock to a fertile, picturesque country, from a sickly hot climate to one cold and bracing, might be compared to a passage from the dismal regions to Elysium. Remaining so long at Malta, one's ideas became as contracted as the island. Thus the delightful scenery of the Bay of Naples, the immense hills covered with oaks, olives and vineyards and the many grand objects that were presented to our view on entering it, formed a most striking contrast to the country we had lately left, and had a double effect on us Maltese. While I was at Nocera I had an opportunity of revisiting the ruins of Herculaneum, Pompeii and Pestura.

The farther we advanced the more beautiful was the appearance of the country, but the misery of the inhabitants and infamy of the government are but too conspicuous.

Your affectionate,

J. Colborne

The retreat, which caused Colborne so much disappointment, requires a few words of explanation.

The triumphant Emperor of the French, on the morning after the signing of the Treaty of Pressburg, issued a proclamation that as a punishment for its perfidy, 'the Neapolitan dynasty had ceased to reign,' and soon afterwards despatched an army of 50,000 men, under Massena and his brother Joseph, to take possession of Naples. Such an army could not be withstood by the Russian and English forces now in the Peninsula. On the 7th January the Russians received orders to retire, and the British, being freed from any further obligation, re-embarked at Castellamare with the intention, however, not of returning to Malta, but of holding Sicily for King Ferdinand. The king, however, who had himself fled to Palermo, was so much irritated by the British desertion of the mainland that though the force arrived in the harbour of Messina on 22nd January, for four weeks he would not allow it to be landed. Eventually, on 17th February, it was permitted to land and occupy Messina. On 15th February Joseph Bonaparte had entered Naples amid popular rejoicings, and two months later, by his brother's decree, he was created King of the Two Sicilies.

Meanwhile the Prince of Hesse Philippsthal still held the citadel of Gaeta against the French, and Major-General Stuart, who had succeeded Sir J. Craig in the command of the British forces, thought a fresh venture might be

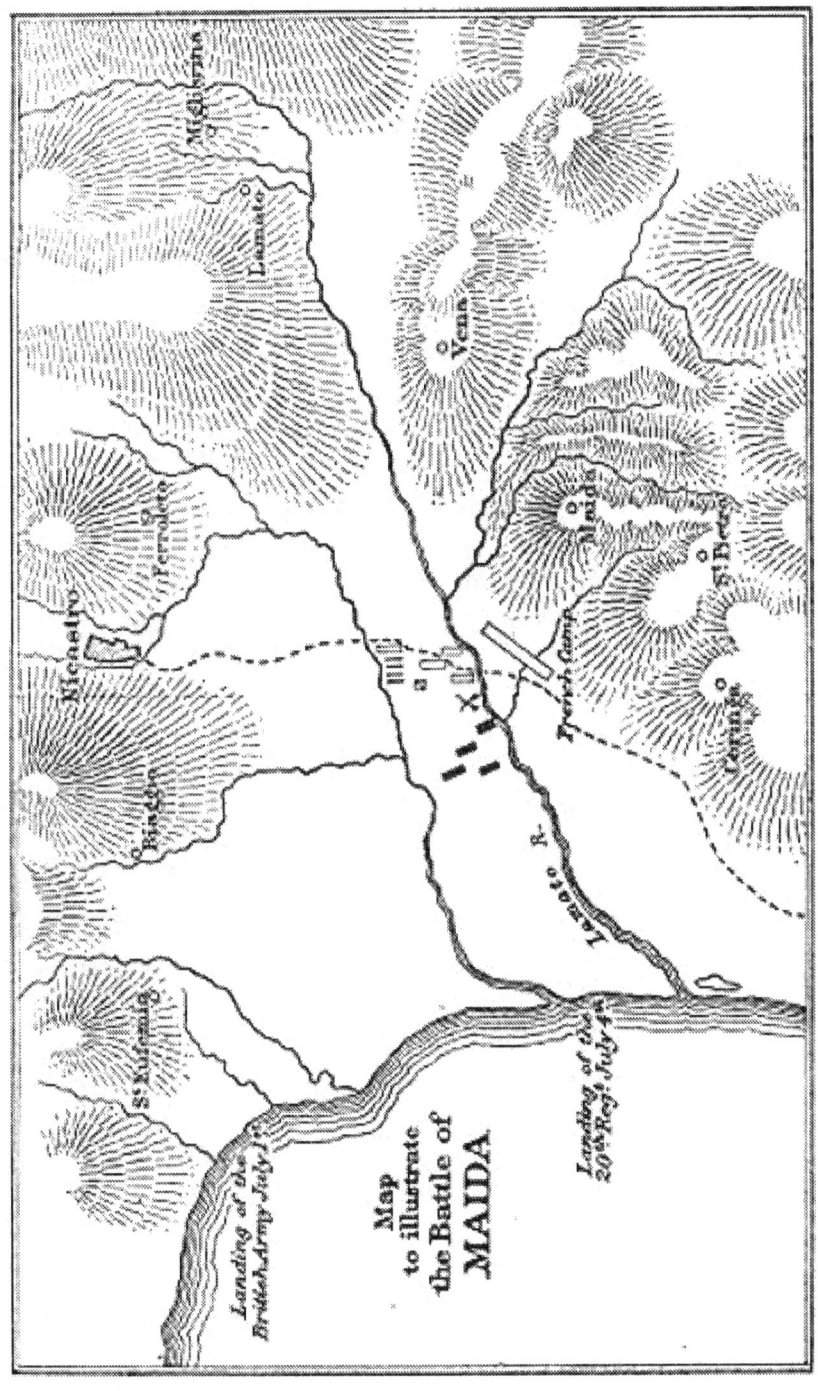

tried, and a French design of invading Sicily anticipated. Accordingly a force was collected and landed in the Bay of St. Eufemia on 1st July. One company of the 20th, under Captain McLean, was included in the Light Infantry Brigade under Lieutenant-Colonel Kempt, another company of the 20th was included in the Grenadier Battalion, which with the 27th Regiment formed Cole's Brigade. The battalion companies of the 20th Regiment, under Lieutenant-Colonel Ross, were not despatched with the main force, but were ordered, before landing, to make a diversion on different points of the coast. Accordingly they landed only on 4th July, when Colonel Ross, hearing that the main army was about to be engaged with the French, hurried his regiment forward partly at a running pace, and succeeded in arriving on the plain of Maida just at the moment to decide the issue of the day.

Colborne's account of the battle, given in the following letter, is another instance of his singular modesty, as he says nothing whatever about himself, and we are left uncertain whether he came on the field with Ross or had been present from the beginning of the action. If the latter, as his account seems to imply, he had probably commanded the grenadier company of the 20th.

To The Rev. T. Bargus, Barkway

Camp near Monteleone
11th July, 1806

My Dear Sir,

This sheet of paper you will perceive bears strong marks of active service, and as all my baggage is contained in my pocket it has, of course, been considerably damaged. I have not time to give you a detailed account of one of the most glorious battles that an English army has ever fought.

The expedition sailed from Messina, and arrived in the Bay of St. Euphemia on the 1st of July. On the 4th Sir John Stuart moved on to attack the French army under the command of Regnier, who occupied an excellent position in a wood above the plain of Maida, but confident in his own genius, the superiority in numbers both cavalry and infantry, and despising us too much, he advanced to the plain to meet us. The right was first engaged, and some of the best regiments of the enemy charged us with the greatest intrepidity, nor were our men less forward to meet them. Reserving our fire till we came within a short distance, the astonished invincibles were mowed down by a well-directed fire, and the right of our line passed through their left. Few of them escaped. Their dead and wounded marked the original line. In this affair our light infantry distinguished themselves.

All the force of the enemy was now directed to the left, endeavouring frequently to turn it, but owing to the cool and gallant conduct of Lieutenant-Colonel Smith and the 27th Regiment under his command, who penetrated the design of General Regnier, this attack succeeded as the one on the right. The 20th, coming up at this critical moment in echelon, and forming on the left of the 27th, the enemy retired in the greatest confusion, and had we had cavalry, every man of them would have been a prisoner. The loss in our regiment has been chiefly confined to the flank companies, above five and thirty privates and one captain (McLean), a particular and intimate friend of mine and the only officer killed in the field. He was shot through the heart at the commencement of the action.

The field of battle after the action was a horrid sight. The loss of the French in killed, wounded and prisoners is almost incredible, nearly 2,000. Our army entered the field with 4,600, the enemy had 7,200 bayonets and 300 cavalry. Fortunate it is for us that the spectators were numerous. I now begin to think, as our ancestors did, that one Englishman is equal to two Frenchmen.

Yours affectionately,
J. C.

The action is excellently described by Sir H. E. Bunbury. He tells us that after McLean's death Colborne succeeded to the command of the light company of the regiment. He was possibly selected for the duty on account of his knowledge of Italian. Colborne related afterwards that at Maida two Swiss regiments, but for an accident, would have been actually opposed to one another.

Colonel Claval, one of the Swiss with the French, was wounded and taken prisoner. I went to see him with a Swiss officer from a regiment which had always been in our service. After we left, the Swiss with me said, 'I know that man perfectly well, we are from the same canton, but he did not recognize me.'

On the day after the battle, as Bunbury tells us, the army marched to the little town of Maida, where Sir John Stuart devoted the day to writing his despatch.

In the meantime, Colonel Kempt had advanced some distance along the hills and detached the light company of the 20th (under Captain Colborne) to follow the track of the enemy and gather information. It pressed forward, expecting that our army was advancing in the same direction, and it overtook the rear of the French column, which was marching in great confusion; but discovering to his mortification, at the end of the second day, that he was entirely without support, Captain Colborne found it necessary to fall back on his battalion.

The following represents Colborne's account of this business as he gave it in conversation towards the end of his life:

It was after the battle of Maida, and we were going on towards a town called Borgia, and were not at all certain where the French were. I commanded the advanced guard about 87 soldiers and two dragoons (these were my cavalry). I had only one other officer with me. The column was some way behind us, and my guide was getting frightened, so I said, 'Well, I can't help it; if you don't show us the way, or get another guide, you must be hanged.' So he went with two or three soldiers and tried to knock up somebody in a cottage. At last a man was found who said he would lead us if we would let him go when we were within a hundred yards of the town. When we were within sight of the town he took care to put us in mind of our engagement, and we let him go. Then I had not the least idea whether the French were there or not. Just at the entrance to the town I saw a man, so I said, 'There, catch him! Make haste!' We ran after him and tried to catch him, but he ran into his cottage, and the same thing happened with two or three others, until we actually found ourselves halfway up the town. At last we got a man who happened to be the *Capo Genti*, the head of the town; so I said, *'Dove sono i Francesi?'*

'Oh, they passed through five or six hours ago, and are encamped a few miles further on.'

Then all the people, when they found we were English, came flocking round us, and I had begun to take lodgings for us all, when a message came from our column that it had retreated. Hearing rockets and fireworks they thought it must be the enemy, when really it was the people in the town firing for joy of our arrival. This retreat of our column was a great pity. The French retired still further the next day, and the people of the town were very angry with us, because, in my expectation of the column, I had ordered 4,000 rations. They all turned out and reproached us, and I was anxious as to what would happen. I said, 'It is not my fault. I am very sorry indeed to go back.' But they were very angry all the same.

So after marching all day and all night, at four o'clock we had to march back again. I had a bad fever afterwards, but I do not know if that was the reason. Great numbers had fever owing to the carelessness of the Quartermaster-General's department, who took up our quarters close to a marsh; although you are sure to get malaria if you sleep anywhere where there is stagnant water and the thermometer between 80 and 90. About sixteen in a company died of it, and the doctors did not know how to treat it, and bled for it, so it was nearly a year before the army was free of it. I was bled for it, and had all my hair shaved and went over to Messina.

Of the moral effect produced on Englishmen by the battle of Maida, Alison speaks in terms which recall the last sentence of Colborne's letter. 'It was a duel between France and England, and France had fallen in the conflict . . . people no longer hesitated to speak of Cressy and Azincour.' Even the local results were for the moment considerable. The French forces hastily retreated, leaving artillery, stores, ammunition, and every town or fort in Calabria to the victors. But on the 18th July Massena took Gaeta, and his army of 18,000 men was free to assist Reynier. Sir John Stuart had no course before him but to re-embark his forces for Palermo, though by doing so he was forced to incur the reproach of abandoning the peasantry whom he had stirred up to war.

Chapter 5

The General's Secretary

To Colborne himself the Calabrian expedition resulted in good; in fact, it laid the foundations of his future fortunes. General Fox, brother of the Minister, having been sent to Sicily to supersede Sir John Stuart in the command of the British forces in the Mediterranean, Colborne became his military secretary,[1] and was thus brought into close contact with Sir John Moore, who, nominally Fox's second in command, was practically, as a more vigorous and experienced soldier, his adviser and equal. When Fox was recalled, and Moore succeeded to his command, Colborne still remained military secretary, and acquired a devotion to his master which lasted beyond the dark hour at Corunna and became the inspiration of his life.

But if Moore's friendship and protection were valuable to Colborne, we do not doubt that they were well earned by Colborne's own qualities. Even in the criticisms which he passes on others in the following letters we see the fruits of native military genius improved by years of serious study and dauntless adventure.

---

1. It is said that in making the appointment General Fox wrote: 'You owe your appointment to the reputation and name you have acquired in the Army.'

To The Rev. T. Bargus, Barkway

Messina
31st August, 1806

My Dear Sir,

I have had a very narrow escape, and have been very ill with a violent fever contracted in Calabria, but, however, it has been a fortunate expedition to me, and by a lucky accident I have acquired some good friends. General Fox has appointed me his military secretary, a confidential post, and thirty shillings per diem in addition to my pay as captain but it is no sinecure. I have not had a single moment to myself, but General Fox goes to Palermo tonight and I shall have time to write to you.

Yours affectionately,
J. Colborne

Messina
23rd June, 1807

My Dear Sir,

The few letters you have lately received from me, I am afraid, will make me appear to you a most ungrateful fellow. The fact is, I have nothing to say in my defence, except that procrastination has generally been the cause of my not writing. I do not mean to offer this as a tolerable excuse, as one can always find time to write, if determined.

I received your letter of the 1st of November, and am much obliged to you for it. The Fox's have always been very attentive and civil to me.

I work excessively hard, and in truth it is a most laborious office; the confinement does not agree with me, activity in the open air being more congenial with my disposition.

I have acquired some very good friends since the Calabrian expedition. General Sir J. Moore has behaved to me in a most friendly manner, and I am under great obligation to him. Being now the senior captain in my regiment, I have some chance of getting a majority; at least, I shall be much disappointed if I do not succeed. The senior major has memorialed to succeed to a lieutenant-colonelcy now vacant. If this promotion does take place I have every reason to expect the majority from a letter Sir J. Moore has been good enough to write home about me. General Fox did not know I was the senior captain, and I thought it would be impudent to remind him.

You will have heard of our disasters in Egypt. A more foolish expedition never was planned, and I am sorry to say the misfortunes that have happened to our force there since its arrival can only be attributed to the incapacity of the chiefs; 1,400 men have been lost to the service in a most provoking manner. The British troops are now at Alexandria, and in perfect security. If 3,000 men had been sent with Admiral Duckworth to the Dardanelles, it would have given quite a different turn to affairs in that quarter.

England and Russia are now very anxious for peace with the Porte; this war has been the cause of Austria hanging back. Our army here has been mutilated by the different detachments sent from it to Egypt and Malta; without reinforcements we can do nothing.

The Prince of Hesse has had the folly to undertake an expedition in Calabria, and mistaking the falling back of the French outposts for the retreat of their army, he advanced to Mileto, near Monteleone, where he was *culbuté* in a most complete manner, and his army, upon the first discharge, ran 25 miles without looking behind them. We remain silent and inactive spectators, and, *I* think, make a most ridiculous figure. I should not be surprised were General Fox to be recalled, he is too honest to be employed in such a corrupt country as this, and by a corrupt ⸺.

You have no idea of the imbecility of your Ministry, I mean, both parties, for, believe me, there is very little difference in their conduct. The bad information they have of all this part of the world is incredible. The people they employ on what they call secret missions or embassies are quite children, all theory, waiting for orders, and take up half their lives in communicating with England.

This army has dwindled into nothing by the neglect of the late Ministers; no orders, no instructions for those in command how to act have been received from them. We are looked upon here as the supporters of an oppressive government, and I can venture to say, a more infamous one never existed. We have lost our popularity here altogether, for the Sicilians expect nothing from us. This army, had it been kept afloat (leaving garrisons in the fortified towns of this island), ready to act in the north of Italy, or Dalmatia, might have annoyed the enemy greatly, and assisted our allies. We might have destroyed every Frenchman in Italy, and prevented them reinforcing their Armies from that part. . . .

Your most obliged and faithful,
J. Colborne

Messina
2nd August, 1807

My Dear Sir,

In my last letter I mentioned to you that I should not be surprised at General Fox being recalled; and in a few days after the date of it, a communication from the Duke of York unexpectedly arrived, begging him to attribute his recall to the fear of His Majesty's Ministers that he would not be able to support the fatigue of an active campaign, from bad health; and expressing a wish that he should give up the command of the army in the Mediterranean to the person to whom the executive part must ultimately fall, General Sir John Moore.

Now, as General Fox has not enjoyed better health for many years, and had received directions from Ministers relative to active operations a few days previous to the receipt of the duke's letter, he is (not without reason) much mortified at leaving this command.

Mrs. Fox is good enough to say she will forward this to you. They embark tomorrow on board the *Intrepid*.

I might have easily obtained leave to go to England, and perhaps with some advantage, but much as I wish to see you again, I could not quit this part of the world, foreseeing an active campaign, and not being a little flattered at Sir John Moore's asking me a few hours after he knew of General Fox's recall whether I had any objection to remain with him in the same situation.

Sir John Moore is one of the best generals we have (that, you will say, is not much to his credit), an active, acute, intelligent officer, about 43 years of age, and full of that coolness in action and difficult situations, so necessary to those who command. He is one of those determined and independent characters who act and speak what they think just and proper, without paying the least regard to the opinion of persons of interest or in power. If he have a fair opportunity, I conceive he will prove a most excellent general.

Considering my unfitness for an office of the kind which I occupy, both from disposition and habit, I have got through the business of it tolerably well, but not without infinite labour, and have been harassed almost every hour for these last twelve months. The particular situation of General Fox's command in Sicily has involved him in a most extensive and important correspondence;[2] this, added to the detail and routine of the army here, has allowed me but few leisure moments.

You may easily conceive that I shall part with General Fox with the greatest regret. He is an honest, good-hearted man. Having been now acquainted with his family so long, I feel quite hurt at the thoughts of separating from them. Mrs. Fox is an amiable woman, and one of the best and most ladylike characters I have ever met with.

Yesterday we were alarmed with the report of a peace be-

---

2. General Fox was not only in military command, but British Minister to the Neapolitan court.

tween Russia and France. I believe it; and am afraid the Battle of Friedland has been but too decisive. Things cannot be worse with us. We shall have soon enough to do in this part of the world. . . .

Yours truly and affectionately,
J. Colborne

P.S. I have sent by Mrs. Fox a few silks for gowns or anything else for Mrs. R, Delia, Alethea, Fanny and Maria. They tell me they are at present fashionable.

In Sicily Colborne was still training himself for war.

I remember at that time I thought it was the best way to prepare for active service by sleeping and eating as you would in the field; a bad plan in some respects, for I found afterwards that the more you saved yourself the more you could bear after, but not altogether. It is very bad to sleep on a feather bed, for example a good hard mattress is the thing. Now, I had a very thin one, scarcely enough to save my bones from the boards; a sort of truss! I do not suppose there was one officer in a hundred did as I did, and it occasioned a good deal of joking among them. At Palermo, being military secretary, I had a very fine house, and I remember some officers passing through my room being struck with my luxury, and the contrast between my bed and the magnificence of the house. However, it was a very good thing, all that. I kept myself in good health and good habit of body, without which I should never have got over my wound afterwards. I mean I was quite strong, but not fat or soft. After Sicily, when I went into active service I had very little baggage, all in a very small compass, and I tried placing my mattress on boards, but I found I was too near the ground. If I had slept on the ground in a tent I should have got ill, you know. Then I got a very nice little iron bed which answered exactly; it folded up and took up very little room, and scarcely weighed six pounds.

He tells the story of a practical joke played at this time in Sicily.

The 20th invited the 52nd to dinner. I was away at the time with General Fox. Poor Diggle of the 52nd was seated between two funny young officers of the 20th, who persuaded him, when they got to the toasts, that it was the custom of the regiment always to propose a toast 'Confusion to all General Officers.' So up he got, and with Colonel Ross seated at the head of the table, said, 'President, I have a toast to propose, D—n all General Officers!' The officers of the 52nd at that time were a most proper set, all very anxious to please Sir John Moore, and the Colonel was so scandalized at this behaviour that at a meeting of the officers they almost agreed to turn Diggle out of the regiment. One of the officers wrote to me to tell me so. However, Colonel Ross understood how the whole thing had happened, and begged the colonel of the 52nd not to take any notice of it, as it was all a joke. Their great alarm was that it should come to Sir John Moore's ears, but I don't think he ever heard of it.

He tells the following stories of Sir John Moore and of General Fox:

Sir John Moore once, in 1806, in the presence of Mr. Drummond, our Minister Plenipotentiary, and General Fox, said jokingly, with reference to the Queen of Naples, 'Oh, we can easily ship her off to Trieste.'

This, Mr. Drummond most mischievously and unwarrantably repeated to an associate of Her Majesty. Sir John Moore was told that he had done so, and from that time conceived a bad opinion of Mr. Drummond, so much so, that when the queen came to Sicily, he held an interview with her without first asking Mr. Drummond to present him. The queen said to him, 'Well, Sir John, so I find you are a Jacobin.'

'Not more than Lord Nelson,' he replied. When Mr. Drummond remonstrated with him on what he called his 'very irregular proceeding,' Sir John replied, 'I am well aware, Mr. Drummond, of your irregular proceeding that you have repeated a private conversation.' Mr. Drummond had the effrontery to deny that he had done so, though the fact is undoubted. However, Sir John, owing to this, did not get on well with the queen. The British Government expected that she would entrust her forces to the British general.

General Charles O'Hara, who was Lieutenant-Governor of Gibraltar in 1792-3,[3] when Sir John Moore was serving there with the 51st Regiment, was very anxious that Moore should disguise himself as a sailor with a red cap, and make some observations on the French at Ceuta, but Sir John said, 'No, thank you, general. I have no objection to go in my uniform, but I have no wish to be taken and hung as a spy.' It is, of course, allowable to hang anyone as a spy who goes in disguise, but an officer taken in uniform would not be hung, although he were engaged in the same occupation.

O'Hara was a very agreeable man, very talented and witty in fact, a specimen of a well-bred Irish gentleman. He was very angry when the army and navy had to cut their tails off. Gibraltar was a great place for soldiering in those days. Four or five hundred men mounted guard every day, and all the officers on guard used to stand behind the general on the parade ground. O'Hara was in a great rage one day when Moore appeared on parade without his tail. He said, 'I should not have been surprised if it had been one of the other officers, but Moore, who has been brought up under my own eye, I never expected him to do such a ridiculous thing!' They used to tell a story that when he was introduced to Colonel England, who was a man of very large proportions, he said aside to the officer who introduced him, 'England, indeed! Great Britain, Ireland and France!' He was a very good officer, and had seen a great deal of service.

At the time I was military secretary to General Fox he

---

3. He was full Governor from 1795 to 1802.

was thought an old officer; he was about fifty. He had a great objection to anything in the shape of display, and I recollect once, in making the tour of Sicily, he desired that no salutes should be fired for him. When, however, we came by Fort Auguste, they began to roar out a tremendous salute. So old Fox turned round very angrily and said, 'Really, this is treating me very badly,' and sent off his aides-de-camp scampering right and left to stop the salute.

In Sicily they always have a quantity of bells hung round their mules' necks, and they can tell by the sound if the mule is lazy or going well. General Fox, being tired and unwell, was once ending a day's journey in a sort of covered sedan chair drawn by mules, and he told his aide-de-camp to desire the man to take the bells off the mules because the noise disturbed him. The man made great objections and said, 'Why, they would think I was carrying a dead person!'

So the aide-de-camp said, 'Why, if he were dead, then you might have the bells, because he would not mind,' which tickled the fancy of the bystanders, and they laughed so much that the man was obliged to take off the bells.

A merchant named Warrington, who lived at Naples, told me that at the time when everybody was expecting that the king and queen were going to leave (December, 1798), he thought the best way was to go and watch the palace himself. So he went, and actually met the king and queen and Lord Nelson and Lady Hamilton coming downstairs, and he overheard Lady Hamilton say to Lord Nelson, 'You did not forget the watch, did you?' He concluded directly from that that it was a regular flight, and hastened home as hard as he could and told his wife to pack up for Sicily. He proved to be right. The king and queen went on board the fleet that day.

Colborne used to tell another story in connexion with Lord Nelson. Once at a ball at Sir William Hamilton's, Josiah Nisbet, Nelson's stepson, after drinking too much wine, pointed at Lady Hamilton and Nelson, and said,

'That woman is ruining that man.' Lady Hamilton went into hysterics, and Nisbet, as he was being dragged away, shouted, 'Clap a swab to her neck; that will bring her to!'

In the autumn of 1807, Napoleon having sent a large army under Junot to take possession of Lisbon, Sir John Moore received orders to sail from Sicily with the 20th and other regiments to support the Portuguese government.

We received the order to embark, without being told where we were going. I was military secretary to Sir John Moore at the time, and Colonel Ross, a very great friend of mine, came to me and said, 'Can you tell me where we are going, or give me the least hint, whether east or west? It is of the greatest consequence to me, for if we go east, I shall leave Mrs. Ross here, but if west, we may be off anywhere, and in that case I should see her off for England directly.'

I said, 'Of course, I know where we are going, but I cannot give you the least hint; however, I will go and ask Sir John Moore if I may tell you.' So I asked Sir John Moore, and he said, 'Well, Ross is an honourable man, you may tell him.' We were going to Portugal.

The next letters were written on the voyage to Gibraltar.

To Miss Alathea Bargus

Queen, off Sardinia
7th November, 1807

My Dearest Alethea,

We are now fighting with an ill tempered westerly wind, which will not permit us to weather Sardinia seven days blowing from the same quarter it really is enough to irritate even a greater philosopher than myself.

On the 24th of October we embarked on board the *Chiffone* frigate at Messina, and proceeded to Syracuse, where we changed to the *Queen* a three-decker, and, the convoy being collected, set sail to the southward and passed Sicily with a fair wind after being driven considerably to the eastward by a contrary gale.

If you chance to have a quarter of an hour to yourself, collect the news quickly, and let me hear from you during the time I remain at Gibraltar. You must be quick, or possibly I may be a thousand miles further.

Your last letter is dated on the 18th of June, in which you tell me you expect a copy of a poem from me. Now, although they say I am extremely flighty, yet I have a most unpoetical head, but, be assured, had I been inspired, the muse would have sent forth at least a sonnet by every packet to you and Fanny. Instead of subscribing to my poem, I must insist on your taking two copies of a print designed by a particular friend of mine, Captain Pierrepont, of the 20th Regiment I have not seen it in its finished state, but I believe Loutherbourg has improved it and made it a very good picture. The subject, the battle of Maida.

I hope Richard Bargus has escaped the danger which seemed to threaten him. I am always sorry to hear of a military man being so foolish as to marry.

The conclusion of your last letter amused me very much. 'Your dutiful and loving sister, Rebecca Bargus.' How infinitely better Rebecca sounds at the end of the sentence than Alethea. Deborah or Tabitha might have been still more respectable.

Believe me, your most affectionate, but unwillingly I am obliged to add, your most undutiful brother,

J. Colborne

To The Rev. T. Bargus, Barkway

H.M.S. *Queen*, off Sardinia,
8th November, 1807

My Dear Sir,

Thus far we are, on our passage to Gibraltar, with about 7,000 men, which it is supposed will be considerably increased on our arrival there. Our final destination is as yet a secret We have been so long with an unfavourable wind, I fear the object of the expedition will be known before our force is concentrated.

The Twentieth Regiment is in the fleet. I am in the same ship with Sir J. Moore and almost too comfortable. You may conceive that changing from a small transport to a three-decker is not much against my inclination.

The troops, I am sorry to say, are not abundantly supplied with provisions.

The more I see of the general, the better I like him; and most sincerely hope he will be successful in the service for which he is intended.

Enclosed is a bill of exchange for £247-10s. on the Lords of the Treasury, which sum, on settling my accounts at Messina, I found due to me. I ought to have saved more, but horses and other unavoidable expenses, and having no time to attend to my own affairs, prevented me from being very economical.

You must allow that the Ministry are endeavouring to be active, and indeed had not some unlooked for circumstance occurred which prevented the evacuation of Egypt from taking place sooner, a respectable force would have been collected in Sicily four months ago. The great disadvantage in not being able to circulate orders quick is the cause of many difficulties.

The details of the affair at Buenos Ayres, as we hear it through the French papers, are most disgraceful, and from the notorious bad character of Whitelock we are inclined to believe the whole of them.

Most sincerely yours,
J. Colborne

> Things having advanced so far in Portugal that nothing could be done there Lisbon having fallen into the hands of the French, and the royal family having fled to the Brazils—Sir John Moore was obliged to bring his force home to England. Accordingly, Colborne saw his native shores for the first time since June, 1800.

To The Rev. T. Bargus, Barkway

Gibraltar,
4th December, 1807

My Dear Sir,

We arrived here on the 1st inst, after a most tedious passage. I am now only waiting for a fair wind to take a cruise in the *Chiffone* with Sir John Moore; and it will soon be decided in what manner we are to be disposed of. If no military operation takes place (which is very probable), I shall have the pleasure of seeing you in a few weeks or months.

Most affectionately yours,
J. Colborne

Gibraltar
12th December, 1807

My Dear Sir,

We returned this morning from off the Tagus, and having found that the Prince of Brazils, the Court, and the nobility came out to Sir Sidney Smith about ten days ago, with nine sail of the line, intending to proceed to the Brazils, we are preparing to sail for England with the greater part of the force under Sir J. Moore's command; the service for which we were intended is now at an end.

I am very much pleased that the 20th return to England, as I believe I shall not join again as captain.

It is very probable we may arrive by the latter end of January. The French marched into Lisbon, the 4th, 14,000 men.

Yours most affectionately,
J. Colborne

Euryalus
St. Helen's (Isle of Wight)
29th December, 1807

My Dear Sir,

After a passage of only thirteen days the whole of the convoy, consisting of forty sail of transports, came to an anchor yesterday evening. We have not yet had any communication with the shore, but suppose we must remain in quarantine two or three days.

It is Sir J. Moore's intention to remain here until he receives orders from London. I hope to have the pleasure of seeing you at Barkway in eight or nine days. Yours most affectionately,
  J. Colborne

To Miss Alethea Bargus

Euryalus
St. Helen's
29th December, 1807

I beg leave to announce to you the following important intelligence: 'Yesterday, arrived at St. Helen's, thirteen days from Gibraltar, Captain Colborne, 20th Regiment. The captain is very fat and having slept during the greatest part of the passage most profoundly, is supposed to have thriven exceedingly on board. Upon the whole, considering an absence of nearly eight years from his native land, he looks tolerably well.'

Chapter 6
Sweden

Colborne announced his arrival in London in the following note to his stepfather:

To The Rev. T. Bargus, Barkway

Ibbotson's Hotel
Vere Street
5th January, 1808

My Dear Sir,

I arrived here last night, but am afraid it will not be in my power to see you before Friday. I have seen Sir John Moore this morning, but cannot yet tell what is to become of us. I rather think we shall soon be afloat again. I shall be very happy to accompany General Moore, whatever part of the world may be his destination.

Yours most affectionately,

J. Colborne

On 21st January, 1808, Colborne gained the rank of major in the army. He was now nearly 30.

The following letter shows that he was anxious to obtain also a regimental majority. Colborne had no doubt already visited his stepfather and family at Barkway, and the strengthening of old ties of affection is marked by the fact that his letters henceforth are no longer addressed 'My Dear Sir,' but 'My Dear Mr. Bargus.' Preparations for a new expedition were as will be seen already being made.

Ibbotson's Hotel
17th March

My Dear Mr. Bargus,

On my arrival here I found that Colonel Clephane had nearly concluded a bargain with a Major Campbell, of the 41st Regiment, relative to the disposal of his commission, the final arrangement was to take place on Thursday. I immediately, therefore, set off to General Moore and mentioned the state of the case. He received me very kindly, and assured me that should Wallace decline in my favour, he would do everything in his power to assist me. I went down to Brabourne Lees and explained the nature of my visit to Major Wallace. I was not long in ascertaining his determination, for after a short conversation he fairly told me he would much rather see a stranger come into the regiment than allow a junior officer to pass over his head. So thus ends the affair, and perhaps it may yet turn out better for me, should we be employed in the spring.

I found it necessary to return to London; my old friends at Brabourne seemed all very happy to see me, and had I not lately been at Barkway, I could have fancied my regiment another home.

Will you have the goodness to despatch Kingsley with my horse to London, so that he may arrive at the Foundling Hospital by six o'clock tomorrow evening? I merely mention that place because it is probable he may know it I will meet him there. It is my intention to ride to Brabourne, and I shall leave town on Saturday morning. The horse I have at the regiment is so hot and unsteady that it will be some time before I shall be able to mount him at a parade.

Notwithstanding all you see in the newspaper, I have reason to think that no commander is yet fixed on for the expedition, nor any regiment appointed, but believe that most of the regular regiments will be employed in two months.

General Whitelock's trial[1] is finished. The paper gives a very imperfect account of it He read part of his defence on Monday, beginning with an ill-judged attack on the Judge-Advocate, Mr. Ryder, accusing him with tampering with his aides-de-camp. He endeavoured to prove that General Gore[2] caused the failure of the expedition, and said that General Craufurd did not execute his orders. General Craufurd was present and Colonel Birch opposite to him, enjoying the charge against him. Whitelock looked angrily and in a very significant manner at General Moore, whenever he thought he had answered any of his questions. He called on General White for a character, the very person who must have been acquainted with his conduct at St. Domingo,[3] He wept exceedingly, but the tears appeared to proceed from passion, and being exhausted he was obliged to sit down. Lewis, his brother-in-law, and General Maude read the rest of his defence. People think he has not refuted a single charge. The judge-advocate's observations when the defence was finished were excellent, and must have been very cutting to General Whitelock. He stated that if ever there was a time that called for the Commander-in-Chief exposing his own person, it was during that attack, but that he, instead of using any exertion, remained in a situation where the tops of the nearest houses could scarcely be seen, and slunk back half a mile to the rear in the evening. If I can procure a pamphlet of the trial I will send it you.

Believe me, most affectionately yours,
J. Colborne

---

1. For misconduct at Buenos Ayres.
2. Leweson-Gower.
3. In San Domingo in 1794 Whitelocke tried to gain Port de la Paix by bribing its commander, who indignantly challenged him to single combat. See Annual Register, 1794, pp. 174, 175. Shortly afterwards Whitelocke was superseded by Brigadier-General Whyte.

Brabourne Lees
28th March, 1808

My Dear Mr. Bargus,

I like this quarter very much, but am singular in my opinion. We are completely separated from the non-combatants the nearest town is Ashford, five miles from us; Hythe is seven. They could not have chosen a more proper situation to inure troops to the more northern climate of Sweden, should we be intended for that service. It is extremely cold, but the old bones of our men seem to bear the change well; I have not seen them look better for many years. We have been obliged to discharge fifty, totally unfit for service.

Yesterday I had a letter from Sir John Moore. No news. The Sicilian mail has arrived and has brought me some letters; our popularity in Sicily becomes less and less daily. The few friends we had have deserted us since the Russian war. Scylla, I am afraid, is taken.

Yours most affectionately,
J. Colborne

From Brabourne Lees Miss Alethea Bargus received an Italian letter from her half-brother, dated *'28 di Marzo'* and signed *'Vostro fratello affettuosissimo. J. Colborne.'*

In his letter to Mr. Bargus of 28th March, Colborne had mentioned Sweden as the destination of the new expedition. The British Government, with the intention of assisting the King of Sweden against a Russian invasion, collected some 10,000 troops, which sailed from Yarmouth Roads on 10th May, under Sir John Moore's command. Colborne was again military secretary to the general, who had as an aide-de-camp Colonel Graham, afterwards Lord Lynedoch. The fleet reached Gottenburgh between the 17th and 20th May. General Moore and most of his staff resided on shore, but the King of Sweden refused to allow the troops to land, and claimed that they should be at his own disposal. After communicating with England, Sir

John Moore started for Stockholm on the 12th June. Colborne, who accompanied him, wrote the following letter soon after his arrival in the capital:

To Miss Alethea Bargus

Stockholm
19th June

My Dear Alethea,

I have but a few minutes to write to you, but as a messenger is about to be despatched direct to England, I will just say that I have not suffered much from our arduous campaign.

What a pleasant way of travelling! without trouble or expense. General Moore is at present residing in this capital, where he was obliged to come on business. The army is still at Gottenburgh.

I am much pleased with every part of Sweden I have seen. We travelled in an open chaise from Gottenburgh to Stockholm in fifty-nine hours. The roads are excellent, the country covered with beautiful woods.

We passed several large lakes, the Winer and Malar, &c. The peasants are the best people I have seen in any country; strictly honest and very civil. They are all dressed in the old costume such as might have been worn in England about two centuries ago.

At Gottenburgh I was acquainted with a very pleasant family. The ladies in it were so beautiful that I really believe I am smitten, so instead of returning covered with wounds from a hard campaign, should you not be surprised to see me groaning with *une Suedoise*, and hobbling from the load of a wife instead of the spoils taken from the enemy?

Stockholm is the most quiet metropolis in the world you would conceive yourself in a village on entering it, but its situation is different from any other town I have seen. The Old Town is on an island and the suburb is the most fashionable quarter to reside in. It is a most delightful scene all around us

I have not time to describe its beauties but what has above all repaid me for my journey is that I have grasped the swords of Gustavus Vasa and Gustavus Adolphus, and worn the hat of Charles the 12th. This is an honour which I never expected to have had. It is light enough to read the whole of the night. I am now very anxious to get as far as Tornea, where the sun is seen nearly the whole 24 hours. I wish much to be frozen up here the winter, but am afraid it will not be the case.

Most affectionately yours,

J. Colborne

Colborne apparently did not succeed in making the journey to Tornea. In later years he gave the following particulars of his time in Stockholm, which show that his zeal for improving every occasion had not abated:

As we thought we should stay in Sweden for some time I worked hard at Swedish. I used to get up at four o'clock to study it. My teacher was a young man named Anderson, who was living in the same house. I did not find it very difficult. I liked Stockholm very much. It was a very gay capital.

The whole business, however, degenerated into farce. The King of Sweden, who was all but a madman, wished to employ Moore on wild schemes of his own, and when Moore declared that he was compelled by his instructions to return to England, the king practically put him under arrest. Sir John, leaving Colborne behind him, then escaped incognito to his fleet, which he reached on 29th June. Colonel Murray left Stockholm later, on the 27th. The fleet sailed from Gottenburgh on 3rd July. Colborne had succeeded in joining it the day before,[4] having left Stockholm on the 29th. They anchored in the Downs on the 15th, and next morning were ordered to proceed to Portsmouth on another service. Colborne told this story in later years:

---

4. Colborne's diary shows that Sir G. Napier is wrong in saying that Colborne overtook the fleet at sea. *Early Military Life of Sir G. N.*

When we were in Sweden, the king sent an invitation to Sir G. Murray to dinner. As the king had insulted Sir John Moore he was going to decline, but the aide-de-camp said, 'The king said if Colonel Murray did not come he would send a file of soldiers to make him; and you may be sure he will do it!'[5]

To The Rev. T. Bargus, Barkway

H.M.S. *Audacious*
16th July

My Dear Sir,

Once more we are in a British port. General Moore is going this moment to town. We all go round to Portsmouth, and are now getting under weigh. We expect to be in Spain in a few weeks. I have a long story to tell you about Sweden. We were very near being detained prisoners at Stockholm.

Most affectionately yours,
J. Colborne

To Miss Alethea Bargus

H.M.S. *Audacious*
Dover Roads
17th July

My Dear Alethea,

We arrived in the Downs from Gottenburgh on the 15th. We found orders for us to go to Portsmouth, from whence we shall sail, I believe, as soon as the transports can be victualled. General Moore is gone to town, but I expect to find him at Portsmouth by the time the fleet reaches that place.

I hope you received my short letter from Stockholm. My adventures in that part of the world, after I had written to

---

5. Colonel Murray (afterwards Sir George Murray) was invited by the king on the 26th June. The invitation was declined, but Colonel Murray did see the king the same day. See *An Historical Sketch of the Last Years of Gustavus IV.*, Adolphus, London, 1812, which contains the correspondence and accounts of the interviews between Moore and the king.

you, were numerous and extraordinary, and I look on myself as very fortunate in getting away. You will have seen by the paper some account of Sir John Moore's leaving Stockholm; part of it is true, and as I remained a few days after him at Stockholm, it was thought probable that the foolish King of Sweden would have been ridiculous enough to have stopped the suite of the general, but we managed to get away without being discovered.

I am afraid we shall not meet before I leave England. This first expedition has finished but badly; indeed, there was nothing to be done in the Baltic, so perhaps it is better that this force still remains entire.

Yours affectionately,
J. Colborne

CHAPTER 7

Portugal

On his return from Sweden Sir John Moore learnt that he was to carry his troops at once to Portugal, the British Government having determined to assist the Spaniards and Portuguese to throw off the yoke of Napoleon. But in this expedition Moore was not to be in supreme command, but to serve under Sir Hew Dalrymple and Sir Harry Burrard. Moore protested against this 'unworthy treatment,' but submitted to it like a soldier.

What Colborne thought of it we see in the following letter, undated, but evidently written from Spithead between 25th July, when General Burrard arrived, and 31st July, when the fleet sailed from St. Helen's:

To The Rev. T. Bargus, Barkway

My Dear Mr. Bargus,

I must write to you before I leave England to inform you of the changes that have taken place. Sir John Moore, from the intrigues and dirty cabals of Ministers, is not thought worthy to be entrusted with the chief command, nor even to be second in command. Sir Hew Dalrymple is to command the army when united, Sir H. Burrard is second in command. The Ministry have treated Sir John in an infamous manner, and have tried to vex him in order that he may not go out with us, but he has conducted himself in a temperate and dignified manner, telling them that he thought his former services entitled him to some respect, that he had raised himself by his own exertions to the rank he held without mixing in any party or intrigues, that he would go cheerfully on the service he was ordered, and would exert himself with the same zeal and activity in the service of his country and King as he had always done when employed.

The Cabinet sent him a menace that 'had not the military arrangements been so far advanced that they could not change them without detriment to the service, they would relieve him from the unpleasant situation in which he must be placed at present, and that the Cabinet would take the first opportunity of relating to His Majesty the conversation which took place between Sir John Moore and Lord Castlereagh in London,' (for he had told him his sentiments and what he felt).

Sir John answered that he had already fully expressed his sentiments to Lord Castlereagh, that a repetition would be needless, that he should proceed on the service he was ordered without the least objection, but that it gave him great pleasure that it was the intention of the Ministry to lay the whole before His Majesty, as he should be in most perfect security in the justice of the King, and had the firmest reliance in trusting his honour, conduct, and reputation in His Majesty's hands. This cuts short the correspondence; they are afraid to recall him, for he had documents that would make them tremble, were he to produce them. The fact is, no man has more merit and none more enemies, even among the generals of high rank. They have not the sense to hold their tongues, but you may be assured Sir John Moore is the only soldier good for anything amongst the whole set, with very few exceptions.

Sir John, immediately he knew his situation, offered to get me in the Quartermaster-General's department or the Adjutant-General's, but I thought it best to refuse both and join my regiment, which is on the passage to Portugal or Spain.

The former would have been a more comfortable and easy situation, and a much more profitable one as to pay but the latter more honourable, I think, particularly as I belong to such a regiment as the Twentieth. Sir John was pleased with my choice, and hoped I should be a lieutenant-colonel the sooner for it. I certainly shall learn more as a major, and have no doubt but that I shall do very well. We meet with fewer competitors in the field than in the office, and I have never found many candidates offer when any real service is going on. I am convinced Sir J. Moore will be my friend as long as he lives, and I do not wish a better, for he must rise again in spite of their cabals. I go with him on board the *Audacious* and shall join the regiment where I find it.

Sir Harry Burrard sent for me today and begged I would carry on the business until Sir H. Dalrymple took the command. I told him that my object was to join my regiment, and there could not be much business until we arrived, but if it would facilitate business or be any convenience to him, I should be happy to remain in the situation until I fell in with the regiment. I was anxious to explain to him that it was doing me no sort of favour, but merely for his convenience. Indeed, if it had not been so, I do not suppose that it would have been offered to me. But, however, it is settled that I embark with him and Sir J. Moore, and for the present I remain.

We go to Portugal to attack Junot first. If the business has been executed by Sir A. Wellesley previous to our arrival, we proceed to Spain and act according to circumstances. The Spaniards, I am sorry to say, have been beaten with the loss of thirteen pieces of cannon near Benevente.

We are to sail tomorrow, they say. I do not think we shall. You may venture to write to me the same directions as usual, 'Mil. Sec. to Sir John Moore, H.M.S. *Audacious*.'

I took a walk the other night after dinner to Fareham and called on Dr. Bogue. Miss Bargus made her appearance; she said I was very much like Delia. As it was quite dark (about half-past nine o'clock) she might have imagined it, so I agreed with her that everyone thought so. They were all very civil and attentive, John Bogue as erect as a bed-post, but full of fine speeches and compliments.

Yours most affectionately,
J. Colborne

The fleet sailed from St. Helen's on 31st July. On 16th August Sir Harry Burrard went on, ordering Moore to lay to till he received further orders. Meanwhile, another portion of the expedition, under Sir Arthur Wellesley, having left Cork on 12th July, had already landed (6th August) in Mondego Bay. This force fought the battle of Rolica on 17th August and that of Vimiero on the 21st. Sir Harry Burrard arrived at Vimiero in time to witness Wellesley's defeat of Junot, though his first act of interposition was to forbid any pursuit. Next day he was himself superseded by the arrival of Sir Hew Dalrymple. Sir Hew, with the concurrence of Burrard and Wellesley, now concluded with Junot the Convention of Cintra, by which the French were embarked with their arms and baggage and sent home, and Portugal was restored to independence. The Convention excited a storm of indignation in England and in Portugal. Sir Hew, Sir Harry and Sir Arthur all went home in consequence, and Moore received a despatch, dated 25th September, by which he was put in chief command of the army to be employed in Spain.

Colborne's next letter gives his impressions of the battle of Vimiero and of the Convention that followed it. His regiment, the 20th, had arrived in Mondego Bay on 19th August, too late for the combat of Rolica, but in time to play its part at Vimiero on the 21st, where it attacked the enemy's flank with great gallantry. Colborne, who had sailed with Sir Harry Burrard and Sir John Moore, had unfortunately not been able to join it before the battle.

Whether he arrived on the field with Sir Harry Burrard in the course of the action, or had been left in the fleet with Sir John Moore, is not clear.

To The Rev. T. Bargus, Barkway

Camp, near Veimira
3rd September, 1808

My Dear Mr. Bargus,

We are now on the march towards Lisbon, where it is said the army will remain until the whole of the French are embarked. It seems to be the general opinion that they have let them off too easily. Sir A. Wellesley advanced as far as Leiyra without opposition. On the 17th ult. his march was opposed by 4,000 men posted at a strong pass (Rolica), many officers think that our army might have forced it with less loss. The bull was taken by the horns, and more bravery than generalship was shown. However, the French lost near 1,500 men.

Sir Arthur halted at Veimira. His army was posted on some rugged hills forming nearly a half circle, the centre considerably advanced, and his two flanks inclining towards the sea. It was the intention of Sir A. to have advanced himself that morning and attacked the enemy at Torres Vedras, but the arrival of Sir H. Burrard in the bay prevented him. Junot having left his position in the night, arrived in the woods about Veimira early in the morning. His army having halted to breakfast, he commenced a furious attack on the centre and left about 9 a.m., but the conduct of our men was so steady and spirited that neither of the columns of the enemy gained an inch at any part of the action.

He was repulsed with great loss, some say 4,000, leaving 16 or 17 pieces of cannon on the field. This was the time to have destroyed his whole army, our right had not fired a shot; indeed there were 7,000 men not engaged. Sir Arthur, seeing the enemy retiring in confusion, wished to have advanced his right, intending to cut off their retreat (this is what people say and I believe it, for almost any general would have done so), but the evil genius of the army sent Sir H. B. on the field during the action, and although he did not interfere while the battle was going on, yet he would not agree to any pursuit. The next day the enemy requested a suspension of hostilities.

We are ignorant of the terms of the capitulation, but the French are allowed to return to France; they should have all been sent to England. The Russians, of course, become prisoners, with seven sail of the line and four or five frigates. I presume the lenity of our general will be ascribed to his wish to employ this army immediately in another quarter. I hope there will be no delay.

The weather has been unfavourable, very hot during the day and heavy rain at night. We have no camp equipage, but the country being woody, we erect huts, which answer very well when it does not rain.

I will write to you from Lisbon.

Most affectionately yours,

J. C.

> Colborne had a story in later years in regard to the Convention of Cintra. Before it was signed, Sir Hew Dalrymple was discussing its terms with General Kellermann, at Coimbra, and, to obtain better terms, was insisting that the fleet containing Sir Harry Burrard's army was already in sight off Oporto. At this moment Sir James Douglas rushed into the room, and to Sir Hew's infinite annoyance, exclaimed, very *mal a propos*, 'I have been looking out for the last two hours and the fleet is nowhere in sight.'
>
> General Kellermann related this story on the ship on which he was afterwards conveyed to France, and said that Sir James Douglas's speech had enabled him to rise considerably in his demands. General Kellermann suffered dreadfully from sea sickness on that voyage, and one of the navy officers used to say to him in the midst of his par-

oxysms, 'Ah, General, if I only had you now at Coimbra, I should get better terms from you.' The following stories relate to the same time:

General Hervey, at Lisbon, asked Junot if the famous anecdote was true, that when he was acting as secretary to Napoleon, and a shell burst near him, he quietly remarked, *'Voila de la poudre'* (*i.e.*, 'There's powder for blotting the ink.').

Junot replied, 'The emperor wanted to write an order, and called out, "What, is there no one here who can write?" I came forward, and it is true that as I was writing a shell burst very near us, and I may have said, *'Voila de la poudre!'*

When Lord Paget was presented to Junot he was in a general officer's uniform, at that time a very unbecoming dress, and Junot, going up to Graham, said, *'J'ai toujours supposé que Lord Paget etait le plus beau garcon d'Angleterre, mais je ne le crois pas du tout.'* However, when next day he came to dine in his splendid Hussar uniform, Junot changed his mind. *'Ah, il faut avouer a present quil est iresbeau.'*

After the conclusion of the Convention I was selected to carry to Elvas General Kellermann's order for the surrender of that important fortress. I rode with it night and day, Elvas being 130 miles from Lisbon. At Estremoz, about 30 miles from Elvas, I was surprised, at a turn of the road, to see a number of armed men just before me, my orderly riding up at the same time and saying, ' I don't like the looks of these men, Sir.' The people had mistaken me for a Frenchman as they saw me approaching, and had ridden out to capture me. Resistance was useless, and I was led in triumph into the town, hooted and pelted at, and only thankful to escape without a pistol ball through my head. The mere loss of time was most provoking. Fortunately there was a French emigre officer in the town, attached to the Spanish army. He immediately saw the mistake, and called out from a balcony, 'This is not a Frenchman, my friends; this is an English officer.' I informed this friend-in-need of the object of my mission; and the anger of the

Spaniards was converted into friendship. I was taken up into the Governor's house and regaled with coffee and cake, and a body of Spaniards escorted me to Elvas.

The Spanish army was lying encamped round Elvas. When I requested an escort the Spanish general was delighted to grant it, assuring me that it was *'con mucho gusto'* that he heard that Elvas was to be given up. The fort of Elvas was situated on a hill, very much like Fort Abraham, a glacis sloping away regularly and fortified at the corners. It was the most beautiful work in Europe.[1] As I advanced with my flag of truce I was seen from the fortress, but as a matter of form a party was sent to meet me with pointed muskets, and I was marched blindfold up a steep hill into the presence of the governor, or commandant, an engineer officer named Girod. A Swiss officer, who was second in command, was sitting in the same room.

This Swiss said to me, 'Directly I saw you I was sure the French had had the worst of it. However, whatever misfortunes occur, I shall remain faithful to the emperor, though not obliged to be so.' On which Girod remarked to me in an aside, *'Quelle bete!'*

When I showed General Girod the paper in General Kellermann's hand ordering him to give up the. town, he looked at it and said, *'Il faut penser deux fois* before giving up a fortress of this importance.'

So I was in a great rage, and said, 'Why, look there, don't you see General Kellermann's hand and seal?'

'Oh, yes, I see that, but these things are sometimes forged.'

So at last I said, 'Well, will you let me go into the town of Elvas, and get post-horses, and I will take any officer you like

---

1. Sir W. Gomm wrote Aug. 4th, 1810: The fortification of Elvas is the most interesting thing I have ever seen. There are three hills; upon the centre one stands Elvas and its castle; on the right, looking towards Badajos, stands a fort which commands great part of the works of Elvas; and on the other side, upon much higher ground and commanding everything, stands the impregnable Fort La Lippe. Nothing but starvation ought to dispossess a garrison of Elvas.' Carr-Gomm's *Letters, &c. of Sir W. Gomm*, 1881.

down to Lisbon to judge for you?' He said he would let me do that, and accordingly the gates were opened and I went in, and was kissed and embraced by every lady (and gentleman too) whom I met. They were delighted to see an Englishman; it was a sign to them that their troubles were over. So I had a very good breakfast, and then, in two hours' time, set off again to ride back to Lisbon to obtain confirmation of Kellermann's order. It is astonishing how one gets used to riding all day; one feels as if one would never wish to sleep. Though I had already ridden a great distance, now, in going back, I was keeping up the same pace.

The poor French officer, after being so long shut up in a besieged town, was soon knocked up, and did not at all approve of the rapid rate at which I travelled. He was constantly wanting to stop for rest and refreshments, but I was determined he should not; I was determined to work him. I myself, as was usual with me on such journeys, partook of nothing but tea, which I carried in my pocket, and bread which I obtained in the villages.

The French officer said, 'You do not exemplify the proverb, *Boire comme un anglais!*'

'I always thought the proverb was *Boire comme un allemand!*' I replied.

How well I remember the scene at Kellermann's when we reached Lisbon! He was in such a rage at the scrupulousness of M. Girod.'

'What, did he not see my handwriting? I'll have none of his tricks. His folly will detain us here five or six days longer than necessary. Go back, sir, directly with this officer, and ask him to give up the town immediately.' I made no hesitation about returning, but the French officer, on being ordered to accompany me, begged to be excused.

'*Monsieur, je suis si fatigué.*'

'How is it this English officer can ride double the distance without being tired?' exclaimed Kellermann, in anger.

'*Oh, il est anglais?*'

'Go, then, and desire a cavalry officer to get ready to go.'

I had again only two hours' rest.

When I reached Elvas a new difficulty had arisen. The Spaniards claimed that the fortress should be surrendered to them, and not to us, and they were now blockading it. *Before*, the French would not come out; now, the Spaniards would not let them. (The Portuguese said afterwards that the Spaniards did it in order that they might destroy the works.) I had to ride back to Lisbon for fresh orders. At Lisbon I was instructed to ride to Badajos, to obtain from Galluzzo, the Spanish general there, the order that Elvas was to surrender to the British. This time I had the company of Colonel Thomas Graham (afterwards Lord Lynedoch). It was the first time I ever saw Badajos.

> Lynedoch's diary supplies some additional details. They started on 24th September, travelled all night, but met with delays at every post. For one stage they were so badly mounted that they had eleven falls between them, which created great merriment. On the 25th, for want of horses, they had to make a stop at Estremoz till 4 a.m. on the 26th. They breakfasted at Elvas, and were supplied by the postmaster with fine horses, which they found afterwards belonged to French officers. They arrived at Badajos very wet at 2 p.m. They saw General Galluzzo twice, and after hearing from him 'the most absurd language on the subject of his pretensions as a besieger,' obtained the order and took it next day to Elvas, where they obtained the surrender of Fort La Lippe. The town itself had been previously surrendered to the Spaniards.
>
> From Elvas Colonel Graham went on to Madrid, while Colborne obtained leave of absence from his regiment, now at Elvas, and started alone on a romantic ride towards Calahorra, the headquarters of the Spanish army of General Castanos. From this characteristic adventure he was recalled

by Sir John Moore when the latter succeeded to the supreme command. On his return he wrote the letter which follows:

To The Rev. T. Bargus, Barkway

Lisbon
17th October, 1808

My Dear Mr. Bargus,

I am as usual in a violent hurry. We are to commence our march towards Spain in two days. Behold me once more a knight of the quill. Sir John Moore, you will have heard, is appointed to command 40,000 men in Spain. This appointment has given great satisfaction to the army, and it certainly must be highly flattering to himself, for you must well know that Ministers have been certainly driven to it; and why? Because they could find no one else fit for the situation. We have a long march before us to Burgos and Vittoria.

I had proceeded as far as Canaveral on my way to Salamanca, and in consequence of having had several very narrow escapes and many adventures (for I was pursued through every village and constantly taken for a Frenchman whether there was anything in my appearance against me, or that the ugly face of my servant did not please the peasants, I know not, but I conceived it must be the latter), I determined to return to the frontiers of Portugal, to leave him at Elvas, and take a Spanish peasant acquainted with the roads as my squire. On my going through a town called Albuquerque I met an officer who brought me Sir John Moore's letter relating to the extraordinary change that has taken place. I managed to arrive at Lisbon forty-eight hours afterwards. You may now direct to me 'Military Secretary, &c.'

The enthusiasm prevalent in Spain is beyond what I expected. I really do not think a Frenchman will be able to pass through that country for many years, either in peace or war.

Most affectionately yours,

J. C.

Some further details of Colborne's ride in quest of Castanos are given in the following extract from a letter (to Miss Townsend) of the 9th March, 1809:

To Miss Townsend

Immediately after the Convention I obtained leave of absence, and putting on the Helmet of Mambrino, entered Spain unshackled, for the first time completely independent, chief in command; in fact, my own master. I was resolved not to be traced, and pushed straight across the country for Calhorra, the headquarters of Castanos. I proceeded about 50 leagues, but met with so many interruptions from the ignorant and inquisitive peasantry, and either my own physiognomy or that of my servant was so much against us, that we scarce passed through a village unmolested, and were daily examined by the *curé* of the parish, or *corregidor*, amidst a barbarous mob. This was intolerable, and I returned to Elvas, determined to leave my servant and take a Spaniard as *compagnon de voyage*. It was there I received a note from my unfortunate friend that he was appointed to the command, and wishing me to join him at Lisbon. Although at the time he received the appointment nothing was prepared, yet the different columns were in motion in seven days.

Colborne seems to have resumed his duties as military secretary to Sir John on the 17th October.

CHAPTER 8

The Peninsula

Moore waited at Lisbon till the 27th October, when the several divisions of his army had moved off. On the 8th November he was at Almeida, on the 11th at Ciudad Rodrigo, on the 13th at Salamanca, where he halted, intending that place to be the rendezvous of all his forces. Even now he wrote:

> The moment is a critical one: my own situation is particularly so: I have never seen it otherwise; but I have pushed into Spain at all hazards: this was the order of my Government, and it was the will of the people of England.[1]

He had then only three brigades of infantry with him; the rest would take ten days to assemble, and Burgos and Valladolid, at three days' march distance, were occupied or menaced by the French army. He at once sent orders to Baird and Hope to march with all speed to Salamanca, the former from Corunna, the latter from Madrid.

Colborne used to contrast Moore's behaviour during his stay at Salamanca with that of Kellermann when he was staying at Lisbon.

At Salamanca, Moore was in the house of a very rich man, but he desired his own *major domo* to provide everything he

---
1. *Moore's Campaign.*

required. When the gentleman heard this he said he would not allow it; if they stayed in his house he would provide everything.

Sir John Moore said, 'Impossible! I am going to have people with me every day. I cannot think of putting you to so much expense.'

'Well, if you will not let me give you everything,' he replied, 'you shall not stay in my house,' and Sir John Moore was forced to submit.

It was the custom of the French generals, when they were in a town, to quarter themselves on someone, and make him supply everything, even wine. At the time of the Convention of Cintra, Kellermann was living in Lisbon in a man's house, and the man, hearing of the Convention, had locked up his cellar and gone out. Kellermann had asked Paget and myself to dine, and after dinner no wine was forthcoming, and Kellermann was told the reason the master of the house had locked up the cellar.

'*Quon force la porte?*' he said. Perhaps the servants then found the key. At any rate, we had plenty of good wine.

To return to the story. Moore, as has been said, had ordered Baird and Hope to join him with all speed at Salamanca. But as one Spanish army after another was defeated, and it was plainly hopeless for the British army alone, even if united, to withstand the vastly greater forces of Napoleon, Moore and his staff came to see no way before them but retreat. In this gloomy situation Colborne wrote the following letters:

TO THE REV. T. BARGUS, BARKWAY

Salamanca
26th November, 1808

My Dear Mr. Bargus,

We have been here about a week, collecting our force. Owing to the badness of the roads, the cavalry and artillery were obliged to march by a different route,[2] and we are very much separated.

Take your map. We have 14,000 men at Salamanca, 4,000 at Escorial, and Sir David Baird at Astorga. The French are at Valladolid, and they have beat General Blake, dispersed his army, and have defeated the Estremadura army. I am afraid they will attack us before we are united. They have about 80,000 men in Spain, or more.

Remember me to Mrs. B., Alethea, Fanny and Maria, and believe me, my dear Mr. Bargus, yours affectionately,

J. Colborne

Salamanca
27th November, 1808

My Dear Mr. Bargus,

Since my last letter a third army has been defeated, the Aragoneese.[3] I fear we shall not be able to unite. The Spaniards are a fine people, but have fallen into bad hands, not a person fit to direct them. I rather think we must retire on Portugal. We expect to be attacked in our turn. Nothing can be more unfortunate.

Remember me to Mrs. Bargus, and Fanny and Maria. I remain, most affectionately yours,

J. C.

To Miss Alethea Bargus

Dear Alethea,

I am quite ashamed I have not written to you, but in better times you shall hear from me.

Yours most affectionately.

J. Colborne

Next day arrived the news of the defeat of Castafios' army. This made Moore's course plain to him. He wrote on

---

2. i.e., Hope's force, which marched by Madrid.
3. Palafox's.

the 28th to Baird that he had determined to retreat upon Portugal with his own corps and with Hope's, if Hope could join him by forced marches, and he directed Baird to fall back on Corunna and thence to sail to the Tagus. But, deceived by information of growing enthusiasm in Madrid, on 6th December (when Madrid, though he knew it not, had already fallen) he countermanded his former order,[4] and bade Baird return to Astorga. Hope was now in the neighbourhood of Salamanca, so Moore's position was altogether more secure. On 7th December Moore was joined by Hope's division; on the 20th, having advanced to Mayorga, he effected a junction with Baird's. He had now 24,000 men, and moved against Soult with the intention of drawing Napoleon after him. His plan succeeded. Napoleon, who had taken Madrid on 4th December, on hearing of Moore's advance, made against him with 180,000 men. Having gained his point, Moore commenced his famous retreat, which ended, after innumerable hardships, with the successful stand against Soult at Corunna on 16th January, and Sir John Moore's own death. Colborne told the following stories of the retreat:

On the morning of the cavalry affair at Benavente (29th December) I happened to be detained behind the staff. My horse was already at the tent door, and my servant packing, when a dragoon came galloping by with his sword drawn. My servant went out to inquire the reason, and returned saying, 'The French are crossing the ford, Sir!' So, instead of following the staff, I immediately galloped to the scene of action.

---

4. This change of plans was due in part to finding that the French had not already taken Valladolid, as he had been informed. Gomm, who was sent there to find out the truth, brought back this comparatively cheering news. 'By evening I was entering Sir John Moore's quarters with the report. Colonel Colborne, then military secretary, looking half incredulous and something more at first of the fact of Valladolid having been really reached (by me), but hastening with the letter to his anxious chief, secured him a balmier rest through its contents than he had for many a night enjoyed.' Carr-Gomm's *Letters, &c., of Sir W. Gomm* (1881).

'It was an immense plain. The French were crossing the river and our cavalry waiting to receive them. Lord Paget, who commanded, galloped up twirling his mustachios, and said, 'You see, there are not many of them.' I remained by his side during the action, which lasted some hours and ended in the repulse of the French without much loss on our side.

After the action, when Lord Paget was reporting the affair to Sir John Moore, he suddenly turned round and said, 'But there's your military secretary; he was there, and knows all about it,' to Sir John Moore's astonishment, who had not the least idea of the manner in which his military secretary had been employed.

Graham said, 'You must have the gift of second sight, Colborne, and that was the reason you stayed behind; you knew what was going to happen.'

I received a clasp for the action.

In this fight near Benavente the French general, Lefebvre Desnouettes, was taken. I was consulted by Sir John Moore as to whether it would be right to ask him for a written promise not to escape. I advised not, as I remembered a French officer in Sicily being much affronted at such a request. Sir John Moore said, 'I am glad you told me this. Of course, I will not ask,' and as Lefebvre had surrendered his sword Sir John courteously presented him with his own. However, after Moore's death, Lefebvre broke his parole by escaping from England.

Once, during a halt on the retreat, Sir John Moore had no book, and said to me, 'Come, Colborne, have you no book to amuse me with?' I happened to have a copy of Lord Lyttelton's *Memoirs*[5] with me, and the book greatly entertained him.

On 3rd January, near Villafranca, Colonel Graham (afterwards Lord Lynedoch) had an almost miraculous escape from death. Colborne tells the tale thus:

---

5. *The Letters of Thomas Lord Lyttelton?*

A narrow road ran through a ravine, on one side of which was a precipice with a river at the bottom. There was scarcely room for a horse to walk, and the night being very dark, Graham's horse stumbled and fell over. I was riding behind him, and thought he was gone, but fancied I heard a noise, and told a sergeant to put down a pike and sash, and so we dragged him up, six or seven of us. With great presence of mind he had extricated himself from his horse and supported himself by some bushes on the side of the precipice. He said afterwards he heard someone say, 'Put down a pike and sash to him.'[6]

The following story of Colonel Graham probably relates to this retreat:

Lord Lynedoch, though near fifty when he entered the army, had as much activity and spirit as the youngest officer. One day, towards evening, after a very fatiguing march, I and one or two other staff officers were bringing up the rear, endeavouring to keep the men together as we were descending a hill. We knew that the French must be very close on our heels, but men and horses were too much exhausted to ride back and ascertain how close they were. Presently Lord Lynedoch rode up to me and said, 'Now, Colborne, should not you like to ride up to the top of the hill and see exactly where the French are?'

'No, thank you,' said I, 'I am much obliged to you, but even if I wished it, my horse really could not do it.' The words were hardly out of my mouth before Lord Lynedoch was nearly at the top of the hill.

'What a regular old fox-hunter!' said Sir H. Clinton to me.

Colborne told another story of Lynedoch's energy.

---

6. Delavoye's *Life of Lord Lynedoch*.

Lord Lynedoch was a man who had a pleasure in doing anything for anybody, and he was a most active, energetic man. Once when he was a member of Parliament, he was in Dublin on an occasion when it was of great consequence to have every possible vote, and they were saying it would be quite impossible for him to arrive in time. So Mr. Dundas, who was a great friend of his, said, 'Tell him he can't do it, and you will be sure to have him in time.' They did so, and Graham arrived with his watch out about a quarter of an hour within the time; and a journey from Dublin was a longer affair then by a good deal than it is now.

On 8th January, at Lugo, the British army took up a position and expected a French attack, which, however, was not made.

Sir John and his staff were sitting together in their tent, and Colonel Graham, who was always eager for enterprise, said, 'Well, Sir John, after you have beaten them you will take us on in pursuit of them for a few days, won't you?'

'No,' said Sir John, 'I have had enough of Galicia.'

'Oh, just for a few days!'

On the morning of the battle of Corunna Sir John was not aware that the French were so close, or that they would venture to attack. He said to me only ten minutes before the battle, 'Now, if there is no bungling, I hope we shall get away in a few hours.'

A few minutes after Sir John Hope came with the news that the French were advancing in great force, and they soon opened a furious cannonade on us from the heights.

So many attacks have been made on Moore's generalship, from 1809 to the present time, that it is worth while to show that Colborne, no less than the historian Napier, for whose history of Moore's campaign Colborne supplied much information, was among Moore's most thorough admirers.[7] In an unpublished review of Southey's History of the Peninsular War he thus writes, in 1827, of his revered commander:

It is our intention to demonstrate, with the aid of many valuable documents, that the reputation of Sir John Moore was basely sacrificed to party spirit, and that the attacks with which his character has been continually assailed, are as inconsiderate as they are unmerited. We, who have followed him from early youth and cannot forget his professional zeal and devotion to his country, and the estimation in which he was held by the army of Holland and of Egypt, may not enter on his defence with the coolness of an historian who compiles from gazettes and periodical publications sent forth in the midst of tumult and party but we pledge ourselves for the accuracy of the statements made.

This General appears to have been visited with the extraordinary bad fortune of being placed in a series of embarrassing situations, so that he had no sooner extricated himself from one than he was thrown into another. The first command that was offered to him would, had he accepted it, have given him the charge of that very absurd operation, the taking possession of Alexandria in 1807. The second to which he was named involved him in an unpleasant affair with the Queen of Naples and the British Minister at Palermo; the third made him responsible for the assembling of a force dispersed between Egypt, Sicily and Gibraltar, depending for its union on the result of Russian and Turkish treaties, but which had in view a service that admitted of little delay in execution. The fourth sent him to Sweden with 10,000 men, on an expedition some degrees less ridiculous

---

7. Colborne wrote from Brussels, 30th August, 1814, indignantly to refute a statement that he had compared Sir John Moore unfavourably with Wellington. 'I never have stated or thought that Sir John Moore was less decided or less qualified for the command of a large army than Lord Wellington.' Yet, as will be seen, he lauded Wellington's generalship to the full.

than the Egyptian one planned by the Whig administration, and which brought him in collision with the ex-King of Sweden. The fifth appears to have been hopeless from the first moment of his appointment.

From the same article we give Colborne's account of the close of the campaign:

When the army had passed the Esla, and the convoy of artillery stores which returned from the Ford of St. Juan had reached Benevente, the continuation of the retreat could be no longer delayed. Two divisions had marched on La Baneza and Astorga on the 26th December. Napoleon was within a few leagues of the Esla on the 28th, and Soult, having received orders to move to Leon, his advanced guard appeared in front of the Spaniards at Mansilla on that day.

The inferiority of the British army, and its critical position, would have induced Sir John Moore to retire sooner on Astorga than he did, if the ammunition and stores could have proceeded on the route by which it was intended they should be conveyed. But the officer in charge of the convoy had been driven off from his first route, and had, in consequence of the heavy rains having rendered the river impassable, so increased his march that a halt at Benevente became necessary.

Sir David Baird left Valencia on the 29th, and the reserve retired from Benevente the same day. Several arches of the bridge of Castro de Gonzalo were blown up, and the cavalry occupied Benevente with their picquets extended along the right bank of the river.

A few days after Sir John Moore and the reserve had marched from Benevente, General Lefebvre Desnouettes, with the chasseurs of the Imperial Guard, arrived on the high ground near Castro de Gonzalo, and observing the picquets on the plain below apparently unsupported, imagined that only a rearguard of cavalry might be left in Benevente. The peasants having shown him a ford, he determined to press on.

He passed the river rapidly, formed on the right bank, and advanced in echelon towards the town.

The picquets, which had assembled on the first alarm, opposed his march by disputing the ground with his leading squadron, and reinforced by a part of the hussars of the German Legion, retarded his progress. Lord Paget, who arrived on the plain soon after the Imperial Guards had passed the river, ordered the picquets to retire slowly in order to draw the enemy on towards the town till the 10th Hussars could be brought up.

Without any means of ascertaining what supporting force might be preparing to cross from the left bank of the Esla, it appeared no easy matter to decide how far the enemy should be allowed to advance. The 10th Hussars, however, were formed in line not 100 yards from his left flank before Lefebvre discovered his error, and that he had been drawn on skilfully by his opponent till the interval between the 10th and the picquets and the leading squadron of the chasseurs was so much diminished that their escape was scarcely possible. At this moment Lord Paget charged with the whole of the 10th. Lefebvre, perceiving the force against him, had just time to wheel about and to retire at full speed.

The race was so equal that for a few minutes it was doubtful whether the enemy's mass gained distance or not, but fortunately for the chasseurs, the left of the pursuing squadrons, in endeavouring to get on their flank, passed over less favourable ground for the charge than that on which the former moved. This circumstance alone prevented the entire capture of the chasseurs. All that were badly mounted, and among them General Lefebvre, were overtaken and made prisoners. The greater part forded the river in confusion and made an effort to form up on the left bank, but after a few rounds from our horse artillery they retreated. The cavalry remained at Benevente till the evening. The reserve marched in two days to Astorga, which the cavalry reached on the 31st.

The 30th the bridge over the Esla was made passable, and the enemy occupied Benevente in force. The corps, under Soult's orders, marched from Palencia and Paredes on Mansilla to join the troops moving from the Carrion.

The branches of the Asturian Mountains which project to the southward run behind Astorga, and thence form a chain to the westward with the Sierra Segundera and De Mamed. This barrier and the mountains of Galicia are formidable to an enemy, but had we attempted to defend the passes and Galicia in the winter by placing a regular army in position without cover or supplies in a country exhausted by the continual passage of troops, it must have been exposed to such fatigue and privations as would have occasioned its destruction.

Near Astorga the ground is not sufficiently favourable to induce an inferior army to wait the attack of an accumulating force or risk an action. At Foncebadon, one of the points of defence of this mountainous district, an enemy might be opposed with advantage; but no important object was to be gained by halting there and defending that pass. The Galicias may be penetrated by roads from Zamora, Benevente and Braganza to Puebla de Sanabria, and thence by the Val de Jares and the valley of the Sil to Lugo. Magazines and cover for the troops would have been required had Sir John Moore halted, and the enemy, being able to choose his time of attack, would have compelled him to abandon the mountains, when his combinations might have rendered a retreat impracticable.

The Marquis de Romana proposed to defend Astorga. He was without provisions, he had but 5,000 men fit for service, and no means of procuring supplies, and if he had remained near the British army would have proved only an encumbrance.

Thrown back on an accidental line of operations, without being able to fix precisely his base and what kind of defensive movements should be followed, depending on the efforts of the enemy and his demonstrations of force, Sir John Moore was persuaded that he could not maintain himself in Galicia with advantage to the Spaniards or without risking the destruction of his army. To defend a pass a considerable corps must be posted near it, prepared to meet the mass of the enemy. Therefore the only question to be considered was whether, if the enemy followed in great numbers, it would not be more advisable to outmarch him, and embark the army before he could interrupt that operation, or whether a corps should be sacrificed in opposing him on the march.

'It was for the interests of Spain that Sir John Moore should endeavour to divide and isolate the French forces by drawing them into the mountains till the enemy's line might become dangerously extended.

He decided, then, to continue his retreat, and if he should be forced into Galicia, to embark the army, after which operation it could be moved to any point where the Spaniards or Portuguese required its support.

On this principle his movements were guided, and on it he continued to act, regardless of the common fame he might acquire by fighting a battle without an object. The safety of his army and the ultimate effect of his operations alone influenced his decisions.

It is true that his army had been disappointed, and that various were the opinions of officers of rank respecting his movements. But neither in advance nor in retreat did one single breach of discipline take place in consequence of these opinions, and it is absurd to suppose that he paid any attention to them. Officers talked and discussed the views of the general, as they always do; but beyond that, no symptom of disapprobation or the reverse was shown or heard of. His orders, in which the term 'disorganization' was used, referred to the stragglers, and the supposed want of exertion in some corps in preventing their soldiers from halting and falling out in villages.

Sir John Moore has been accused of not fighting in Galicia, but the principles on which he conducted his retreat and his character will show that it is not possible that he would be actuated by the frivolous motive of engaging with the enemy for the mere purpose of increasing the reputation of the army which had driven the French out of Portugal the year before.

To suppose otherwise would be a great injustice to his character. I know of no other general who was more qualified to command. He had firmness, resolution, activity, courage and prudence, and from a long service with his troops, and his being the principal in the operations of the landings in Holland and Egypt, he was perfectly acquainted with the superiority of the British soldier to any other. His judgment of ground and the advantages of a position was unrivalled.

Before we listen to clamour, the unexpected position in which he was placed must be considered, the unprepared state of the Portuguese, and, for instance, the great diversion he did effect for the recovery of the cause, and through his judicious action the French lost by allowing themselves to be drawn into Galicia and by the separation of their corps.

The retiring of Bonaparte from Astorga to prosecute his Austrian war was never known to Sir John Moore. He had only to judge what was most probable to happen, that the whole disposable force would be brought to Galicia. Having been driven into it by superior force, the sooner he could get out of it, the better for the Spaniards.

If the French had made the great attack on Portugal in 1809 with their whole force, no general would have been warranted in risking his army at that time in its defence.

His disinterestedness, his great value in all the preceding operations, were fully known, and his last hours fully corresponded with his former conduct. So nothing could be more impressive than his death—his anxious enquiries as to the result of the battle—solicitude for his country's opinion and interest in his friends; and his exclamation, 'You know I always wished to die thus,' is such a picture of the man's mind, that there was not a man who witnessed his death, the serenity of his countenance . . .

The rest of the passage is lost. But a letter written by Colborne to Miss Townsend on 9th March, 1809, more than completes the sentence:

To Miss Townsend

You have, of course, heard various reports which have been spread with uncommon assiduity by the malicious and ignorant, to injure his reputation. His movements can be fully justified. Fortune never smiled. He was soon aware of his situation, but never discovered the true state of things until he had actually entered Spain. He was disgusted at the infamous conduct of the soldiers, and the inattention of inexperienced officers. We cannot endure hardships; we have not the military patience with which our enemies are gifted. We can stand to be shot at as well, or better than, most people, but this quality, although essential, is not sufficient for a military nation. What unheard of difficulties, hardship and labours! living on turnips! no sleep!' All this frightens mama, but do not believe the quarter that you hear. John Bull is as fond of the marvellous as an Italian or a Spaniard.

I was not present when Sir John received his wound. About a quarter of an hour after the firing had commenced he sent me with a message to General Paget. On my return with the answer, I could not find him, but heard he had lost his arm. At this time I had no idea the wound was mortal, and therefore did not return to Corunna till dark. On my entering the room where he was you may conceive my situation. I saw that all was over. The surgeons were examining the mangled wound. It is impossible to imagine a more horrid one; the ball had carried away his left breast, broken two ribs, shattered the shoulder, and the arm was scarcely attached to it—the whole of his left side lacerated. One would have supposed that the first gushing out of the blood would have instantly caused his death, or made him insensible—the most resolute minds and firmest nerves when thus assailed sink under pain, and Nature, exhausted, yields, but he, cool and collected, continued talking, recollecting the most minute and trifling circumstances till the last moment. His lungs were affected, and his voice from this was rather hoarse. He knew everyone, and while conversing was suddenly suffocated by internal bleeding, and who would not have wished to be him at that instant? No distorted countenance, no sign of anguish, the picture of the mind could be traced by the serenity of the face, the one calm and dignified as the other was pure and heroic.

On falling from his horse no alteration in his countenance took place. They wished to take off his sword, but he said as it was not in the way he begged it might remain on. A most extraordinary man. The nearer you saw him, the more he was admired. He was superior by many degrees to everyone I have seen: he had a magnificent mind. A most perfect gentleman. A determined enemy to the corrupt, corruption, and jobs, he never spared where he thought it his duty to inflict. A man of this cast must create a host of enemies, and he certainly had his share of them.

To pursue melancholy subjects. We never heard of the death of poor Mrs. Fox until a short time before our arrival at Corunna. He thought her the most valuable and excellent woman with whom he ever was acquainted. He received General Fox's letter the day before the action. I beg to be kindly remembered to the General and Miss Fox. Most sincerely yours,

J. Colborne

> It is worth while even to add to Colborne's narrative a fuller account of Moore's last hours, because if Colborne's name had been remembered in no other connection, this ever-moving story, preserved by the pious affection of Colonel Anderson, must have kept it alive:
>
> As the soldiers were carrying the wounded general from the battlefield. . . .

. . . . he repeatedly made them turn round to view the battle and to listen to the firing, the sound of which becoming gradually fainter, indicated that the French were retreating. Before he reached Corunna it was almost dark, and Colonel Anderson met him, who, seeing his general borne from the field of battle for the third and last time, and steeped in blood, became speechless with anguish. Moore pressed his hand and said in a low tone, 'Anderson, don't leave me.' As he was carried into the house, his faithful servant François came out and stood aghast with horror; but his master, to console him, said, smiling, 'My friend, this is nothing.'

He was then placed on a mattress on the floor and supported by Anderson, who had saved his life at St. Lucia; and some of the gentlemen of his staff came into the room by turns. He asked each as they entered if the French were beaten, and was answered affirmatively. They stood around; the pain of his wound became excessive, and deadly paleness overspread his fine features. Yet, with unsubdued fortitude, he said at intervals, 'Anderson, you know that I have always wished to die this way. I hope the people of England will be satisfied. I hope my country will do me justice!

'Anderson, you will see my friends as soon as you can. Tell them everything. Say to my mother ———!' Here his voice faltered, he became excessively agitated, and not being able to proceed, changed the subject.

'Hope! Hope! I have much to say to him but cannot get it out. Are Colonel Graham and all my aides-de-camp safe?' (At this question Anderson, who knew the warm regard of the general towards the officers of his staff, made a private sign not to mention that Captain Burrard was mortally wounded.) He then continued: 'I have made my will, and have remembered my servants. Colborne has my will and all my papers.' As he spoke these words Major Colborne, his military secretary, entered the room. He addressed him with his wonted kindness; then, turning to Anderson, said,

'Remember you go to Willoughby Gordon[8] and tell him it is my request, and that I expect he will give a lieutenant-colonelcy to Major Colborne; he has been long with me and I know him to be most worthy of it.'[9]

He then asked the major, who had come last from the field, 'Have the French been beaten?' He assured them they had, on every point. 'It's a great satisfaction,' he said, 'for me to know that we have beat the French. Is Paget[10] in the room?' On being told he was not, he resumed, 'Remember me to him; he is a fine fellow.'

Though visibly sinking, he then said, 'I feel myself so strong I fear I shall be long dying it's great uneasiness it's great pain! Everything François says is right. I have great confidence in him!' He thanked the surgeons for their attendance. Then, seeing Captains Percy and Stanhope, two of his aides-de-camp, enter, he spoke to them kindly, and repeated to them the question, 'If all his aides-de-camp were safe?' and was pleased on being told they were.

After a pause Stanhope caught his eye, and he said to him, 'Stanhope, remember me to your sister.'[11] He then became silent. Death, undreaded, approached, and the spirit departed.[12]

---

8. Military Secretary to the Duke of York.
9. It is very characteristic of Colborne's character that he was reluctant to allow this testimony to his merits borne by his dying general to be published. Captain Graham Moore writes to him on the 29th May, 1809: 'The purport of my letter is ... chiefly at this moment (when) James is employed in an attempt to have justice done to our brave brother's memory, to endeavour to prevail upon you to give up your objection to making public every particular circumstance in the last scene of his life.... To every candid and liberal mind it must appear honourable to you, as well as to himself, the strong interest he felt that you should have justice done you, and as it is certainly a strong characteristic trait of the General, I do hope and request of you, in the name of my mother and all our family, that you will give up your objection to the whole of what he said on that sad occasion being made public.'
10. The Hon. Edward Paget, who commanded the reserve.
11. Lady Hester Stanhope, whose warm attachment to Moore is well known. A seal which she gave him was cut off Moore's fob after death by Colborne. He gave it to Mr. Carrick Moore, who (continued on next page)

The story is continued by George Napier, who had been Moore's aide-de-camp from the beginning of the campaign.

With a heavy heart I turned my sorrowful steps to the headquarter house. On entering I saw no light; I heard no sound, no movement all was silent as the grave. A cold, dread chill struck upon my heart as I ascended the gloomy stairs and opened the opposite door, from whence I imagined I heard the half-stifled sob of grief.

Oh God! what was my horror, my misery, my agony! Sir John Moore lay stretched on a mattress; a dreadful wound bared the cavity of the chest; he had just breathed his last...... Never shall I forget the scene that room displayed on that fatal night. Colonel Anderson, who had been from youth the tried friend and companion of his general, was kneeling with his arm supporting Sir John Moore's head, with blanched cheeks, half parted, colourless lips, and his eyes intently fixed on that face, whose smile of approbation and affection had been his pride and his delight for years; but the look of keen anguish that Anderson's countenance expressed is far beyond my powers of description.

Next in this group stood Colborne, whose firm and manly countenance was relaxed and overcast with thoughtful grief, as though he pondered more on his country's than on private sorrow, for he felt and deeply mourned the amount of England's loss. Then high-spirited, guileless Harry Percy, pouring forth in convulsive sobs the overflowing of his warm and generous heart, and poor James Stanhope completely struck down and overwhelmed by the

---

however returned it to Colborne, saying, 'You have the better right to it.' It is now in the possession of the Hon. Lady Montgomery-Moore.
12. Moore's Life of Sir J. Moore.

double loss of his brother[13] and his friend. Although last in this imperfect sketch, not least absorbed in the deep anguish of despair stood his faithful and devoted servant, François, bending over his master's mangled body, his hands clasped in speechless agony, his face as pale as the calm countenance he wildly gazed upon. That eye, which was wont to penetrate the inmost soul, was glazed in death. That manly, graceful form, the admiration of the army, lay stretched a bloody lifeless corpse; the great spirit had quitted its earthly habitation; all around was sad and gloomy. Moore was dead![14]

At midnight on the 16th January Sir John Moore's body was removed by torchlight from the house on the quay, where he had died, to the quarters of his friend Colonel Graham in the citadel of Corunna. An entry in Graham's diary of 17th January gives us the last scene of the story.

A grave was dug[15] in the centre of the flat bastion of the citadel where poor Anstruther[16] lay, and there, at eight o'clock in the morning,[17] the general's body, without a coffin, was interred. Anderson, Colborne, Percy and Stanhope were present only,[18] Napier and I being joined to General Hope's staff; and, some firing from the point having taken place, they hurried it over.[19]

---

13. Charles Stanhope, who had been killed, was second to Charles Napier in command of the 50th. Charles Napier, who had been taken prisoner, was believed at this moment by his brother to have been killed also.
14. Early Military Life of Sir G. T. Napier.
15. Apparently by the 9th Foot. See Earlier Letters of Sir W. Gomm.
16. Brig. General Anstruther, a great friend of Moore's, had died on reaching Corunna.
17. Wolfe's famous lines say 'at dead of night,' and Sir W. Napier writes: 'The battle was scarcely ended' when Moore was buried. But Graham's statement is the true one.
18. The service was read by the Rev. H. J. Symons.
19. Delavoye's Life of Lord Lynedoch.

It was still early, as George Napier writes:

> .... when 'Colonel (Major) Colborne[20] and myself went on board the *Audacious*, 74 gun ship, Captain Gosling, having with much difficulty reached her, as in consequence of the enemy bringing some guns to the heights, which in fact commanded the bay, and opening a fire on the transports, they were cutting away their cables and were in much confusion, and it was a service of danger to get through them.[21]

In the following note from Falmouth Colborne announces to his stepfather his return to England:

TO THE REV. T. BARGUS, BARKWAY

25th January, 1809

My Dear Mr. Bargus,

I have only time to say that I am well. You will know the loss we have sustained.[22] I shall soon see you.

Yours most affectionately,

J. Colborne

---

20. Should Napier have written *Colonel Graham*?
21. *Early Military Life of Sir G. T. Napier.*
22. Miss Yonge says that fifty years later Lord Seaton's voice trembled as he spoke of Moore. (Miss Coleridge's *C. M. Yonge.*)

CHAPTER 9

Enter Wellington

The following letters show that Colborne, after reaching London, had much work on hand in settling the accounts of the late expedition with the Commissary. He was in frequent communication with Sir John Moore's family, and warmly interested in defending his military character against the attacks which were made on it. In his own case, the General's dying request had been complied with. He was appointed to a lieutenant-colonelcy in the 5th Garrison Battalion on 2nd February, 1809.

These garrison battalions were corps of old soldiers formed to remain in England, but Colborne obtained permission to return to the Peninsula.

To Mrs Yonge (Delia Colborne)

London
Ibbotson's
Vere Street
January (25?), 1809

My Dear Delia,

Knowing that you would be uneasy, I sent you a short note immediately after the action. I hope it arrived before the public news reached you, as the officer who carried the dispatch put it in the post-office Falmouth. *I ought* to have been sent with General Hope's letter, but Sir D. Baird preferred one of his own aides-de-camp.

General Hope sent me to London as soon as we arrived at Portsmouth with a copy of his dispatch, and I only reached this place a few hours after the original.[1]

It seems a dream I can scarcely believe that I am in England. Indeed, this is the first day since the action I have had time to reflect and lament my friend. He was a noble fellow had I not seen him die I should have thought it impossible for the firmest mind to have endured bodily pain with such indifference, with such calm serenity for although when in health, and sound, one conceives a possibility of bearing every ill, yet the stoutest hearts yield to nature and sink under the pain of a mutilated body.

General Moore was struck on his left breast and shoulder by a cannon shot which broke his ribs, his arm, lacerated his shoulder and the whole of his left side and lungs. From the gushing out of the blood I should have thought he would have instantly expired. His voice was rather hoarse from inward bleeding. When knocked off his horse he did not say anything, nor did the shot make him change countenance. He was carried away in a blanket, and spoke to everyone as he passed. I remained out until the action was over, and when dark rode to Corunna. On my entering the room the General knew me, and spoke most kindly to me and said, 'Colborne, have we beaten the French?'

I replied, 'Yes, we have repulsed them in every point'

'Well,' says he, 'that is a satisfaction. I hope my country will do me justice.' He then said to Colonel Anderson, 'Go to Colonel Gordon when you arrive in England, tell him it is my wish remember, I request that Colborne gets a lieutenant-colonelcy.' He then said, 'Remember me to General Paget—General Edward Paget—he is a fine fellow.' He asked everyone that came into the room about the enemy, and died in a moment after he had spoken, without the least symptom of pain. He was buried by his own aides-de-camp and myself, on a bastion at Corunna.

---

1. Captain Hope, who brought the original, arrived in London late on the 23rd.

The Duke of York received me with great kindness, and was much affected on reading General Hope's dispatch.

I can tell you nothing certain about myself. The greater part of the fleet is not come in, but I have yet much business to finish, if possible. I need not assure you how happy I shall be to pay Duke and little Delia a visit. Remember me to them, and believe me most affectionately yours,

J. Colborne

To The Rev. T. Bargus, Barkway

London
27th January, 1809

My Dear Mr. Bargus,

I arrived in London about one. I have seen General Hope; as yet he knows nothing, but appears very anxious to get away.

I found a note from F. Moore,[2] begging me to defer my visit to Richmond until tomorrow. This I was not sorry for, as I find that only 7,000 men are arrived at Portsmouth, and until the Commissary and Paymaster-General arrive, or that General Hope returns to Portsmouth, it will be useless my going there.

I cannot tell you how long I shall be obliged to remain here. Government find themselves exceedingly encouraged about this *letter*.[3] General Stewart has blundered, and said it was General Moore's wish to have it published. I can assert that this is not the fact.

They talk of an immense force being sent to Spain. If so, I can safely say it will not be ready for six weeks or two months.

My wish is to get the command of a regiment on the new expedition, but I fear this is impossible.

---

2. Francis Moore, who was in the War Office, was a younger brother of Sir John Moore. Their father Dr. Moore, had died at Richmond in 1802.
3. General Moore's letter to Lord Castlereagh of 13th January. General Stewart had been sent to England with it before the battle. It was printed by Order of the House of Commons, though Sir J. Moore says, 'My letter, written so carelessly, can only be considered as private.' See Annual Register, 1809.

I find some people have been making enquiries where I am to be found. I have reason to suppose they wish to sound me about General Moore's dispatch. However, they will get nothing from me, to whatever Party they may belong.

Yours affectionately,

J. Colborne

14, Chapel Place
Vere Street
30th January

My Dear Mr. Bargus,

I have just received your letter. You seem to have formed a great notion of my merit. I only wish I deserved half as much as you think or wished.

They have behaved very handsomely in giving me the first vacancy, and you will be surprised when I tell you it pleases me. My promotion is in a garrison battalion. There are hundreds who like to be idle, and will exchange. Therefore I shall have time to look about me, and get into a good regiment perhaps the Twentieth, for it is in vain to look to command a regiment immediately most regiments have two battalions and two lieutenant-colonels.

An office will be opened in London where all my business must be arranged.

The Wellesleys will have the command of the new expedition.

Most affectionately yours,

J. Colborne

To Miss Alethea Bargus

14, Chapel Place,
Vere Street
8th February, 1809

My Dear Alethea,

.... Friday it will be necessary to call on the Duke to thank him for my promotion. I was gazetted last night. You may now give me my rank.... I have called several times on Lord Castlereagh, and had an interview this morning.

J. Colborne

  In a letter to Mr. Bargus, dated London, 21st February, 1809, Colborne says 'I begin my work tomorrow morning.'

To The Rev. T. Bargus, Barkway

London
1st March, 1809

My Dear Mr. Bargus,

I have nearly settled all my business, but the Commissary with whom I must finish my account is not in town, nor will be here until Monday. I am determined not to leave things half settled, therefore you will not see me before Wednesday.

Colonel Ross called on me yesterday, previous to his going down to the Twentieth. He means to push Colonel Campbell for an immediate answer.[4] Should it not be favourable, I have my application ready for Colonel Gordon, which I am convinced will not be refused. I saw the Duke the day before yesterday. I was resolved not to forsake him while under a cloud.[4] The parading at the levee of the King is by no means necessary, the only advantage to be reaped from such a ceremony consists in reading one's own name in the newspaper the next morning. I must defer taking Lady Selsey's[6] advice till I return from Spain, or till I have achieved some grand exploit.

---

4. Colborne desired to exchange back into his old regiment.
5. The conduct of the Duke of York had been impugned in the House of Commons on 27th January. He resigned the office of Commander-in-Chief on 18th March.
6. Hester Elizabeth (Jennings), in her own right, Lady of the Manor of Barkway, wife of Hon. John Peachey, who became second Baron Selsey in 1808. She and her husband had presented Mr. Bargus to the vicarage of Barkway on 28th November, 1798.

'I went to the House on Friday, and remained till five in the morning. I was disgusted with the impudent falsehoods on the part of Canning.[7]

The Ministers had the advantage, for the opposition attacked in the dark. Had I been in the front row, I really believe the spirit would have moved me to have given the Ministers the lie direct.

They all speak very bad; Windham's is the most disagreeable voice I ever heard; Canning affected to put himself in a passion, but made no impression on the House, at least, if I can judge by my own feelings. Tierney speaks like a country gentleman, blunt, and sometimes even eloquent; Perceval both speaks and looks like an apothecary. The minor orators, if they can be called orators, are worse than could be found in the meanest spouting club of a country school: the few words they uttered were sputtered out with *I wish, sir, I conceive, sir, I hope, sir, my right honourable friend, the gallant general* and *the right honourable lord* squeezed in, almost in every sentence, so as to make them unintelligible to us that are not in the habit of attending the House. Of this class were Brigadier-General Stewart, Lord Milton, a Major Allen, and many others. I forgot Lord H. Petty. He speaks very clear and distinct, but there is a monotony in his harangues which offends my ear exceedingly. I sat in the midst of newspaper reporters, who frequently put down (when

---

7. 'Lord Castlereagh and Lord Liverpool paid an honourable tribute to the merits of the commander; but Mr. Canning, unscrupulously resolute to screen Mr. Frere, assented to all the erroneous statements of the opposition, and endeavoured with malignant dexterity to convert them into charges against the fallen general. Sir John Moore was, he said, answerable for the events of the campaign . . . for he had kept the Ministers ignorant of his proceedings. . . . Not long afterwards Sir John Moore's letters, written almost daily and furnishing exact and copious information of all that was passing in the Peninsula, were laid before the House.' (Napier, Bk. V., chap, i.) The debate Colborne attended was that held on 24th February, when Mr. Ponsonby moved for an inquiry into the circumstances of the late campaign, and was defeated by 220 to 127.

they cannot hear) anything to make up a sentence. Not one of the speeches appeared in the papers correct, or even like the originals.

Yesterday I walked to Richmond and dined with F. Moore, and returned in the evening. I was not more than an hour and a (half) going and about an hour and three quarters on my return. I spoke to him seriously about publishing certain letters.

It is reported that the Brest fleet are now in Rochefort.

Most affectionately yours,

J. Colborne

P.S. I am much obliged to Mrs. B. for Miss Law's letter. I mean to write to General Fox or some part of his family.

To Miss Alethea Bargus

London
7th March, 1809

My Dear Alethea,

Most heartily tired I am of accounts and claims. By way of exercise after the fatigues of the morning I have frequently walked to Richmond and back the same night. Sunday I slept there, and returned early on Monday morning.

Antonio,[8] I am afraid, is very troublesome. Let him be made useful, if possible; he is very idle. Is there anything that you or Maria wish from this gay city? Was it *Mordaunt* or *Edward*[9] that Maria wished to have?

The party to Mr. M's is inevitable is it not? Were I to live with you two months I certainly should be thought the greatest brute in the county of Herts. Instance the first. Here is a man, hospitable to a degree unknown amongst the good people of England in general: rides through snow, over hedge and ditch, to see me, and yet I am such an ungrateful, unsociable and extraordinary animal that I do not feel the least inclination to partake of his good cheer. More silly than

---

8. A Calabrian servant whom Colborne had left at Barkway.
9. Both novels written by Dr. Moore, Sir John Moore's father.

mad, you will say, but such is the nature of the beast *la societá non mi piaca affatto*.

Adieu, my sweet old maid, and believe me, with kind remembrance to all the family, your very humble servant and brother to command,

J. Colborne

Miss Townsend, to whom the following letter is addressed, was apparently a member of General Fox's family who had lived in his house in Sicily. Colonel Bunbury had married the eldest Miss Fox.

To Miss Townsend

14, Chapel Place
Vere Street
9th March, 1809

My Dear Miss Townsend,

If I had been cudgelled for a month, there is not one hour out of the many days since I had the pleasure of seeing you that I could have sat down deliberately with the intention of writing to any of my own correspondents. I have heard of people composing elegant stanzas and writing very pretty letters during the deepest distress, but I confess, when I am disappointed, vexed or afflicted, I am one of those who can neither write nor read. I resign the appellation with which you or Colonel Bunbury[10] honoured me, *the Philosopher*.

I promised to write to you from Sweden, and much there was in that country to describe, for a most delightful one it is, but the foolish errand on which we were sent put me out of humour not a little.

Away we go to Portugal, where I once more joined my old regiment.[11]

---

10. Colonel H. E. Bunbury, the author of *Narrative of some Passages in the Great War*, was Quartermaster-General to the British forces in the Mediterranean.
11. The rest of this interesting letter has been given already.

To Miss Alethea Bargus

14, Chapel Place
London
9th March, 1809

My Dear Alethea,

I shall ruin you in postage. It will be impossible to close my business before Saturday; therefore I cannot be with you till Sunday or Monday. Nothing shall prevent me from leaving town on Monday, I may probably get away before.

Whether the climate, the wind or the smoke of London affects the nerves of your melancholy brother, I cannot say; but most certain it is that I never felt so strong an inclination to hang myself at times. This is only *façon de parler*, for I should think twice and look at my garters a long time before I exalted myself. But I am really miserable and what is more extraordinary, I cannot find out the cause; this is very provoking. Pouring out the tea with one hand and my letter in the other, I think I see you much inclined to read this letter to the public. If I find you proclaiming my secrets, I shall not write to you.

The Duke of York will, I think, keep his place; the Ministry support him. Last night the debate was adjourned.

Most affectionately yours,

J. Colborne

P. S. I have just heard but I cannot vouch for its authenticity, that Lord Paget went off a few days ago with Mr. Henry Wellesley's wife, sister of Lord Cadogan, and that Sir Arthur Wellesley called out Lord Paget and killed him in the first fire. The first part of the story is certainly true.

Circumstances prevented Colborne from leaving England as soon as he intended. On the 27th March his stepfather, Mr. Bargus, was seized with convulsive spasms while officiating as Justice of the Peace for Herts, and died in a few hours, and Colborne was called upon to give his filial assistance to the widow of his stepfather.

He had, at the same time, the pleasure of hearing from Mr. Bargus' old friend, Dr. Goddard of Winchester, the esteem which Mr. Bargus entertained for him. Dr. Goddard wrote on the 2nd April:

> I feel true satisfaction in assuring you that he has often expressed himself to me as amply repaid for the care and anxiety he had experienced on your account by your exemplary conduct, and the estimation in which you were held by those who were most intimately acquainted with your character.

On the following day Sir George Murray wrote to say that he had mentioned Colborne to Sir Arthur Wellesley for the post of military secretary. This post he declined at the price, it is said, of some displeasure on the part of Sir Arthur and being greatly occupied with his private affairs and those of Sir John Moore, he found himself unable to join the army till three months after Sir Arthur's landing at Oporto (22nd April).

It was in this interval that Colborne first met the fair lady who was destined to be his wife, Miss Elizabeth Yonge, called 'the beauty of Devonshire.' She was the eldest daughter of the Rev. James Yonge, squire of Puslinch, Devon, and rector of Newton Ferrers. Her cousin, the Rev. Duke Yonge, of Antony, near Plymouth, had married Miss Cordelia Colborne on the 14th May, 1806. Miss Yonge writes in her diary under the date 21st June, 1809: 'Duke Yonge and Colonel Colborne called at Puslinch,' to which she added, some time later, 'The first time we ever met, and this day four years we were married; not aware, for some time, of its being the same month and day.' Colonel Colborne called at Puslinch again with his brother-in-law on the 29th, but a few days later, when his business was done, he took his passage to the Peninsula to see further service. The following letter testifies to his warm affection for his half-sister, Miss Alethea Bargus, and to his desire as far as possible to take the place of the father she had lost.

To Miss Alethea Bargus

Falmouth
21st July, 1809

My Dear Alethea,

I arrived here yesterday. I intend to proceed to Cadiz in the packet, but we are detained by the embargo. I remained one night with Delia. I expect you will be a first-rate performer when I return. Two hours at drawing, two at music and three at history *savete qualche cosa*—then, provided you will rise at 7 you will have three hours for other employments. Read by yourself every day, and recollect what you have read at the end of the week; that is, make an abridgment. Always continue your chain of reading, even if it is but half an hour each day.

I must beg of you to buy another of Moore's books and send it to Mr. Sisson, with my compliments.[12] Never were there materials so mangled as by that stupid doctor, and the publication is full of errors. However, the letters are well selected, and certainly do honour to Sir John Moore.

Have you determined on a house?

Most affectionately yours,

J. Colborne

> Colborne reached the Peninsula too late to take part in the passage of the Douro (12th May) and the battle of Talavera (28th July), but in his conversations in later years he told some stories of these feats of arms:

The Duke was occasionally not above writing in his despatches to please the aristocracy. At the passage of the Douro, Hervey made a very brilliant charge with his regiment, something like the Balaclava charge, right through the French, and Sir Charles Stewart, who was riding with him, waved his hat, but had nothing whatever to do with it. Hervey was obliged

---

12. *A Narrative of the Campaign of the British Army in Spain commanded by* . . . *Sir John Moore*. By James Moore, 1809.

to retire again across the river, and when among the infantry had his arm shot off. In the despatch all the credit was given by the Duke to Stewart.[13]

Poor Hervey said to me when he was wounded, 'Now, did you ever see anything like that? I wanted some little puff of that kind, and Stewart could get on without it; besides, it was my affair.'

I don't mean to say this was peculiar to the Duke; it used to be a common thing with general officers. Old Admiral Duckworth, after the passage of the Dardanelles, during which Lord Burghersh was present on the deck of his ship, wrote home in his despatch, 'and among the most animated on the deck was Lord Burghersh.' The different captains who had carried their ships through it all were very indignant, and said, 'What a shame of the old fellow diverting the attention of the public to a man who had nothing to do with it!'

After Hervey had lost his arm he was attacked by a Frenchman, sword in hand, but directly the Frenchman saw that Hervey had but one arm, he put up his sword, made him a courteous bow, and left him!

The Duke made a great mistake in fighting the battle of Talavera. Owing to false information, he was not aware of the overwhelming force against him, and he did not know that besides the army in the field there were three immense *corps d'armeé* behind. It was entirely owing to disunion and jealousy between Victor and the other French generals that we were not completely annihilated. As it was, we lost one third of our army, and though we remained master of the field, we were obliged to retire into Portugal. The Duke as much as owned his error to me in discussing the affair afterwards. He said, 'The fact is, they had too many men for us.'

---

13. 'Brig.-General the Hon. C. Stewart then directed a charge by a squadron of the 14th Dragoons, under the command of Major Hervey, who made a successful attack on the enemy's rear-guard.' Despatch of 12th May, 1809, Oporto.

Colborne, after landing at Cadiz, seems to have arrived at Sir Arthur Wellesley's headquarters at Jaraicejo about 11th August, and to have been at once despatched to the Spanish army commanded by Cuesta, with instructions to follow its movements and report on them. On his arrival, he found that Cuesta[14] had just been superseded by General Eguia (12th August). The latter took great umbrage that Sir Arthur Wellesley's letter had been addressed to Cuesta and not to himself, and professed to see in this a personal insult. As Colborne related in after years:

On reaching the Spanish headquarters I was shown into a room completely filled with despatches intercepted from the French army. The Spaniards, with characteristic negligence, left them lying about for anyone to do as he liked with them, but made no real use of them. Lord Wellington frequently complained, even after this, that he was never sent important information, even if the Spaniards had intercepted any. I made use of my time to select the cream of the correspondence and send it to Sir George Murray. One of the despatches which I sent to headquarters was one from Soult, regretting that he had not besieged Ciudad Rodrigo according to his first intention. This first informed Sir Arthur Wellesley that such had been Soult's intention, and caused him to march north instead of south. Sir George Murray accordingly wrote back to me that Sir Arthur was much pleased, and wished much that I would 'send more of such despatches,' and for that purpose would attach myself to the staff of the Spanish army. I was unwilling to do this, as it would interfere with my prospects in the British army, but as long as I remained in La Mancha I said I was willing to make myself useful.

Soon after joining the Spaniards Colborne wrote the following letter to the widow of his stepfather:

---

14. Colborne is made to say that he arrived at the moment when Venegas was superseded by Eguia. But I think for Venegas we should read Cuesta. See Napier, Bk. VIII., ch. III.

To The Rev. T. Bargus, Barkway

Merida
1st September, 1809

My Dear Mrs. Bargus,

I arrived at Cadiz the beginning of last month, and proceeded by way of Seville to the army in Estremadura. The battle of Talavera and the position of the French armies since that affair have changed the appearance of things in this country, I mean, considerably for the worse. The British army is retiring on Portugal, and has suffered so much from the campaign that I doubt whether it will be fit for any service of importance for several months; the sick amount to ten thousand. The French will not molest the British army until they receive reinforcements.

I intend returning to the south in a few days. The country through which I have passed seems tired of war, and the central and provincial *juntas* are disputing with each other respecting the appointment of an officer to command their armies. Amidst so much discord and stupidity, I am afraid the French will not find many obstacles opposed to them, should the affairs in Austria be finally settled.

My friends, the Spaniards, have behaved very ill in the battle of Talavera. Cuesta is a perverse, stupid old blockhead. To him most of the misfortunes must be attributed.

Sir John Moore's letters, after what has happened, are quoted by every person who has been in Spain as a faithful picture of the country. I am sadly vexed they have been brought before the public by James Moore. His work is a most miserable performance, and the language coarse and vulgar, but notwithstanding these disadvantages attending the letters of Sir John Moore, they will convince the world that he possessed more foresight and judgment than those who abused him, whilst the manly spirit that runs through the whole of them must be admired by even the most prejudiced. As things have turned out, I regret that I did not accept the offer of General Abercrombie to accompany him to India.... *(remainder lost).*

Colborne remained with the army of La Mancha for three months. At the end of October General Eguia was replaced in the command by General Areizaga, who entered on operations of extraordinary rashness, which ended with the complete destruction of his army by Soult, at Oçaña, on 19th November.[15]

Colborne describes the battle in the following letter, in which he also announces that he has been appointed to the 66th Regiment,[16] To get a regiment was no doubt very gratifying to him, for the last few months had been a time of great expense.

To Miss Alethea Bargus

Badajos
5th December, 1809

My Dear Alethea,

On my return to Badajos from the Spanish army of La Mancha (which has been completely defeated and dispersed) I found that I was appointed to the 66th Regiment. The 2nd Battalion being here, I have taken the command of it, so you may direct to me in future in Portugal, where we are about to proceed in two or three days.

Thanks to a good horse and fortune I have arrived safe and in excellent preservation at the British army.

You may easily conceive the confusion[17] when I tell you we had 46,100 infantry and 6,000 cavalry drawn out in a very bad position. The French attacked with about 27,000, and having turned the right of the first line of the Spaniards, my friends were thrown into confusion, and retired to an olive wood, where, the Spanish cavalry pressing in upon the infantry, the confusion was completed.

The French pushed on their cavalry, and in about a quar-

---

15. Napier, Bk. IX., chap.V.
16. His appointment was dated 2nd November.
17. Battle of Oçaña, 19th November.

ter of an hour the whole Spanish army dispersed, leaving guns, equipage, &c., to the enemy, who pursued us about 4 leagues.

I have received two letters from you, and am glad to hear you have at last taken a house. I am afraid you will be soon tired of Sloane Street. I still think a house in the country would have been better.

The French have dispersed another Spanish army near Salamanca.[18] It is, therefore, I believe, thought proper or prudent that the British army should now retire to Portugal. We shall not remain quiet long.

I have scarcely been a night in the same place lately, and found it impossible to write to you when with the Spanish army.

Believe me, your most affectionate brother,

J. Colborne

---

18. Battle of Alba de Tormes, 26th November.

Chapter 10

Campaign of 1810

The 2nd Battalion of the 66th Regiment, which Colborne now commanded, formed part of the 2nd (Hill's) Division of Wellington's army.

On 18th December Lord Wellington informed Sir Rowland Hill of his arrangements for the defence of Portugal. 'I shall form two principal corps, both consisting of British and Portuguese troops, the largest of which will be to the northward, and I shall command it myself, and the latter will be for the present upon the Tagus, and hereafter it may be moved forward into Alemtejo.' The command of the latter corps he now gave to Hill. Accordingly, Hill's division quitted Spain for Portugal.

To The Rev. T. Bargus, Barkway

Abrantes
3rd February, 1810

Dear Mrs. Bargus,

I had the pleasure of receiving your letter soon after my return from La Mancha.

It is not impossible but that we may be compelled to abandon this country in the spring or summer; however, of that we shall be better able to judge in a few weeks.

I do not wish to have Roscius disposed of yet. He may be useful to me should any accident bring me to England with my regiment.

I now command the regiment, and am much pleased with the officers of it. The corps has suffered considerably during the campaign by sickness and battle. The senior lieutenant-colonels are on the staff as brigadier-generals, which will probably be the cause of my going to India when we get out of Portugal.

The French entered Seville on 1st February, and are on the march to Cadiz. We have sent four regiments to that garrison. We shall not be attacked here till April in my opinion.

I am not sorry to find myself once more with a British army. My poor friends the Spaniards are really to be pitied; the nation has been lost by an infamous government. With the battle of Ocaña every hope ended. The general-in-chief was a weak and silly man, without a military idea. It was a most distressing scene.

Most sincerely yours,

J. C.

On 12th February, in consequence of the French having approached Badajos, Hill was directed to move forward to Portalegre in order to protect the sick in Elvas till they could be removed to Lisbon. He had with him his own British division, two brigades of Portuguese infantry, one brigade of British cavalry, the 4th Regiment of Portuguese cavalry, and one brigade of German and two of Portuguese artillery. He was instructed to cooperate with certain Spanish troops then supposed to have crossed the Tagus, and to prevent the French, if possible, from attempting any serious operation against Badajos. However, they had retreated on his approach.[1]

To Miss Alethea Bargus

Portalegre
24th February, 1810

My Dear Alethea,

We have once more passed to the south of the Tagus.

---

1. Sidney's *Life of Lord Hill* (1845).

The French, under Marshal Mortier, have appeared before Badajos, which movement has alarmed us a little, as our hospitals are not yet removed from Elvas. Joseph Bonaparte and Victor entered Seville on the 1st inst. Part of their force has proceeded towards Cadiz. I think they will not be able to take it. Venegas, the governor, is a very honourable man, and a great friend to us. The enemy is threatening in several points north and south, but I do not think he will attempt anything serious for several weeks. You must send us out reinforcements immediately.

I like my battalion very much. It is in very good order, but I wish it was stronger.

Some of the regiments are still very sickly. This is very extraordinary, as we are now in a most delightful climate. Your brother never enjoyed ruder health, and except having been desperately in love (which he attributes to remaining three weeks in the same place), has met with nothing since his last letter to ruffle his temper. However, it has been the cause of his making considerable progress in the Portuguese language. You see you have fully my confidence and all my secrets.

Your most affectionate brother,
J. C.

Portalegre
21st March, 1810

My Dear Alethea,

The French have made no considerable movement on this side of the Tagus lately. We are still in our old position. The enemy's force is increasing to the north. Napoleon is expected at Salamanca, Marshal Ney is before Ciudad Rodrigo with 25,000 men. In my humble opinion we shall not be attacked until May. The Spaniards are still my favourites; had they but a tolerable government they would become the finest people in Europe. Their character in England is quite mistaken; they are in general abused by the British army without reason. The inhabitants of Badajos are determined to defend themselves. The place is weak, and must fall unless the people follow the example of Saragossa and Gerona.² In that case, there is no calculating how long the besiegers may be kept at work.

The army under Romana and Odonnel immediately in our front still puts on a good countenance, and skirmishes with French detachments frequently, in spite of disasters and the black appearance of their country's cause. The poor fellows have been driven about by the enemy from province to province, exposed to the summer's heat and winter's cold, without provisions, without clothing, and scarcely knowing what money is. Do you think a British army would cling together under such unfavourable circumstances?³ The fact is, we are a most boastive nation, and have disgusted the Spaniards wherever we have mixed with them. However, you must not believe all I say, as I am called a madman by many, and even by my friends, an enthusiast.

I think in a few weeks I shall be able to judge what prospect there may be of our army being successful.

Your most affectionate brother,

J. C.

Colborne's statement, that some of his friends called him an enthusiast, is perhaps explained by the following story told by him in his later years; after speaking of General Cameron, afterwards Sir Alan Cameron, whom he had known in Holland and Sweden, he went on to say:

---

2. Saragossa surrendered to the French on 21st February, 1809, after a siege of two months, Gerona on 10th December, 1809, after a siege of six months.
3. Colborne, who had seen more of the Spaniards than most English officers in the Peninsula, was always their warm defender. He wrote in an article years later: 'The privations and misery endured by a large mass of the people of Spain from their patriotism and hatred to their oppressors, were seldom equalled. With a brave, hardy, active, abstemious, peasantry, fond of glory, it may appear extraordinary that the struggle of the Spaniards was prolonged for six years without any decided success, but the central *junta* and the presumption and obstinacy of most of the men placed at the head of the armies rendered their perseverance and courage useless.'

I met him some years after in Spain. It was the worst time he could have seen the army, when it was retreating into Portugal. He had been riding on some way with me, asking me about everything, and I had been giving him a rather good account of the Spaniards. He then rode some way in front, and turning round, called back to me before all the soldiers, 'Colborne, *you know you always were a d—d enthusiast!*'

He was a rough old Goth. When he shook hands with you he gave you such a squeeze that it made you squeal again. There is a story that he once fought a duel with a cousin of his in a cave, and cut him in half. Some people said that he once threw his wife overboard in a passion and then jumped in and saved her. However, I believe she was in a fever, and threw herself in. He was in Holland with a Highland regiment which he had raised himself, and when the Duke of York told him that they were going to draft his regiment, the 79th, into another, he said in broad Scotch, 'That's more than your Royal Highness's royal father could do; for they are all Camerons!'[4]

Colborne had not long had the command of the 2nd Battalion 66th before he found himself commanding the brigade of which the 66th formed a part. It consisted, besides, of the 3rd Buffs (1st Battalion), 31st Huntingdonshire (2nd Battalion) and 48th Northamptonshire Regiments.

In consequence of Reynier's threatening to cross the Tagus, General Hill wrote, on July 13th, that he should, in consequence, incline to his left, and hold everything prepared to cross at Villa Velha if he found him (Reynier) serious in crossing the river. Accordingly, on the 15th, Hill set off to Alpalhao to be ready to act on either side of the Tagus.[5] As will be seen from Colborne's next letter, Reynier crossed as anticipated, upon which Hill crossed also.

---

4. Cameron raised a regiment called the 79th or Cameron Highlanders in 1794. This was drafted into the 42nd in 1797, after which Cameron raised a second regiment under the same name which served in Holland in 1799. The above story is also told by Colonel W. K. Stuart, Reminiscences of a Soldier, II.
5. Sidney's Life of Lord Hill.

To Miss Fanny Bargus

Camp near Atalaya
25th July, 1810

My Dear Fanny,

We are on the march, encamping every night. Be it known to you, I am now a very great man, and if I continue so, a few days (or weeks) more, my situation must either prove advantageous to me or much the reverse. I command a very fine brigade, by accident, and we most probably shall be engaged in a short time. At present we are watching General Reynier's march, who crossed the Tagus from Spanish Estremadura, which naturally led General Hill's division to cross also, and advance in a parallel line to defend that part of the frontier of Portugal between the Tagus and Lord Wellington's right. On the 23rd inst. General R. Craufurd's Division was severely engaged in front of the Coa, and having to contend with very superior numbers, was obliged to retire behind that river. His loss amounts to 250 and 23 officers.

This climate is very changeable, as well as that of Sloane Street. The first three marches several men died on the road from the excessive heat, but these last two nights we have been made rather uncomfortable by incessant rains and cold, sharp winds. The officers do not suffer much from these changes, as they have tents, but the men have no kind of shelter from rain.

One year since I have seen you! Time seems to have taken huge strides; and the events of the first part of 1809 are so fresh in my memory that the intermediate occurrences are forgotten. It is thus we get old without perceiving the advance of Time, and but for our grey hairs might dispute his claim.

Most affectionately yours,
J. Colborne

To Miss Alethea Bargus

Camp near Atalaya
28th July

My Dear Alethea,

We have now a short halt, and as one does not know when there will be another, I will acquaint you with our proceedings.

I thank you for your letters, and if you knew the pleasure I experience at seeing your hand you would write every post. Blots I always admired, as I think I once told you; they are certain indications of sincerity and first thoughts. Therefore, recollect, the more, the better.

I am now generally on my horse the whole day, but nothing shall prevent me from sending you a few lines.

General Reynier, who commanded a corps of French to the south of the Tagus, suddenly passed to the north side, which obliged us to follow his example, and we are now not far distant from him, but doubtful by what route he intends to enter Portugal. General Robert Craufurd was attacked on the 23rd inst. Two regiments bore the principal attack, 43rd and 95th Regiments. They behaved very well, and drove back the enemy three times. General Craufurd's position being too far advanced, he retired behind the Coa in the night.

I am so fortunate (or unfortunate) as to command a brigade at present. Such a thing will probably not come in my way again for many years. Thus, if we are to be engaged, it would be better, perhaps, for me that the attack should take place immediately. Not that I am so selfish or unfeeling as to wish the experiment tried without an object, or on my own account. The less fighting we have now, the more effectually we shall be able to oppose the enemy if forced to act on the defensive.

Let me hear from you constantly, my dear Alethea, and believe me,

Your affectionate brother,

J. C.

From the beginning of August, Hill occupied a strong position at Sarzedas, near Castello Branco, with Reynier in his front at Zarza la Mayor. Colborne was warned to be on his guard, as the French might attack him any day. So he had the troops out daily to practise them in different manoeuvres, that they might never be taken unawares. At night he used to patrol, and he was always on the *qui vive*; so much so, that a colonel in his brigade, not liking the system, and thinking it would be worse when the enemy did come, made his appearance one day with his head tied up on the score of illness, and, to the amusement of his officers, got leave to go home.

Wellington, meanwhile, was watching Massena, who was prosecuting the siege of Almeida, and it was expected that, when Almeida had fallen, Massena would try to redeem his promise of invading Portugal and driving the English into the sea, and that Reynier would be required to join him. By the beginning of September Almeida was destroyed by the blowing up of its magazine, and consequently surrendered, and on the 12th Hill perceived that Reynier was marching northwards, and wrote that he was himself prepared to cross the Zezere. On the 20th, by Wellington's orders, Hill was at Espinhal, and on the 21st at Foz d'Aronce. Lord Wellington, falling back, took his stand on the Sierra Busaco, prepared, from that stronghold, to defy Massena, the 'spoilt child of victory,' with Reynier and Ney and nearly 70,000 of Napoleon's conquering troops. Colborne said, in later years:

The battle of Busaco was gained solely in consequence of Hill's precise attention to Wellington's orders, for which he was always remarkable, so much so, that the Duke once remarked to me, 'The best of Hill is that I always know where to find him.'

On this occasion he had desired Hill, if he saw the French making a move, immediately to march and join him, with other directions how to proceed should such and such things occur. General Stewart remarked to me, 'A very pleasant situation Hill's is. He has been given the choice of acting in eleven different situations.'

I was standing with Sir Rowland on the roof of a house, when we saw the Portuguese outposts driven in, and at once concluded that Reynier had crossed the Tagus. Sir Rowland gave orders for the army to march that very day, and for five days we and Reynier were marching in parallel columns about 50 miles apart. If we had not reached Busaco in time, Wellington's position would have been untenable, and he could not have fought the battle.

> On the 26th September Hill moved across the Mondego and led his troops up the steep mountain of Busaco, and quickly disposed them on the right of Wellington's army. At the foot of the position were 25,000 Portuguese about the same number as the troops of Wellington and Hill behind them. At dawn on the 27th the attack began. Massena sent his troops up the heights and, ignorant of the presence of Hill's and Leith's forces, tried to turn Wellington's right. To the surprise of the French, the forces under these officers suddenly emerged from their previous concealment and halted at the spot whence the brave 74th had just driven back a column of the enemy.' But the French made no second venture, and Hill's division, though it had rendered essential service, was not engaged.[6]

To Miss Alethea Bargus

Camp near St. Miguel
29th September, 1810

My Dear Alethea,

On the 27th inst the French attacked our line on the heights of Busaco early in the morning. It was a fine sight. I

---

6. Sidney's *Life of Lord Hill.*

say sight, for our division was not engaged. The enemy was permitted to ascend almost to the top of the hill where our line was posted, but was driven back in every part with great loss. Massena commanded; his killed and wounded amount to 3,000. This action has very much changed the appearance of affairs in Portugal. The Portuguese troops have established their character with the exception of one regiment of Militia. They behaved in a most gallant manner, and full as well as the British. We expected to be attacked again on the 28th, but we now find the enemy quitted his position on the night after the action, and is supposed to have moved to our left, or towards Oporto.

I still command the brigade, but I am afraid a senior officer will arrive before we are engaged.

Most affectionately yours,

J. C.

The supposition mentioned by Colborne, that Massena had moved towards Oporto, caused Wellington to withdraw from the Sierra de Busaco, while General Hill, crossing the Mondego, marched on San Miguel, where he endeavoured to watch the French movements. Thence he marched by Santarem to Alhandra, four leagues from Lisbon, which he reached on 8th October. The retreat of the British forces before Massena's advance caused indescribable misery to the inhabitants of the country now abandoned. They were all ordered, on pain of death, to leave their houses, and destroy all the property they could not transport. The appalling scenes which marked this flight of a whole people remained in the memory of all soldiers who witnessed them. When Sir Harry Smith, in February, 1848, met the Boers of Natal trekking over the Drakensberg with Pretorius, he stated in his despatch to the Colonial Secretary that he had seen nothing to resemble it except at the time of Massena's invasion of Portugal.

This retreat proved the rare foresight of the British

commander, who silently, since the preceding winter, had been constructing in front of Lisbon the impregnable lines of Torres Vedras from the Tagus to the sea. Within those lines the British army stood secure, waiting for the moment when Massena, foiled of his aim, should be forced, by want of provisions, to withdraw his host. Colborne, in an article written in later years, spoke in glowing terms of the generalship shown by Lord Wellington in 1810:

Between the months of February and August, 1810, the affairs of the Peninsula appeared almost hopeless. Andalusia had quietly submitted. The last large army of the Spaniards had been dispersed. Seville was occupied; the Isla de Leon menaced by a considerable corps. A few moveable columns maintained easily the communications of the French with Madrid. Several corps of Spaniards were actually in the service of the intrusive king. Massena had taken Ciudad Rodrigo, was besieging Almeida, and preparing to march on Lisbon through Beira with an army of about 70,000. Lord Wellington manoeuvred in Beira and in the Alemtejo with an army of about 50,000 English and Portuguese. He had to contend against a Ministry frightened at the risk of exposing a British army, and while he, unmoved by their fears, was carrying into execution one of the most scientific campaigns of those days, the British Ministers were thinking of preparations for embarking the troops, and, we believe, did send out an engineer officer to make a report as to the facilities of embarking. The responsibility of repelling the invasion rested on the shoulders of Lord Wellington. He had also to contend against another faction in the Portuguese Government that imagined he was withdrawing. As soon as it became known that his intention was to retire ultimately on Lisbon, the Bishop of Oporto drew up a strong remonstrance, in which he threatened that the Portuguese troops should be withdrawn from Lord Wellington's command if he did not defend the frontier. And it is a curious fact that this violent remonstrance arrived at Rio Janeiro in the same month that Lord Wellington's despatches were received by King John, telling of the retreat of Massena from the lines. If the correspondence of Lord Wellington, Lord Hill, and the detached generals with the Ministry is ever published, those are the documents by which Lord Wellington's genius and foresight will be judged. We believe that there never was an invading army so ably managed, or whose movements appeared to be made more subordinate to the inferior force opposed to it, than that of Massena by the British commander.

During the late autumn of 1810 Colborne was stationed just outside the lines, at their right extremity, where he occupied the town of Alhandra, on the bank of the Tagus, and the advanced posts near Villa Franca. It was a post of the most arduous responsibility and labour, but for that reason it had been committed to him. General Beresford, on joining the army, had said to Wellington, 'I recommend you to employ Colborne; he is equal to anything.'

For weeks the picquets were attacked every day, and Colborne never took off his spurs. The first time he did so, through sleeping near the Tagus, he caught the ague. At nine o'clock he would take a hasty breakfast, that being the hour at which there was least likelihood of an attack. He scarcely ever had a time of greater excitement and more work, but he was happy, though officers and men constantly prophesied that he would suffer for it afterwards. Now it was that his eye became so practised that he astonished his friends by the distance at which he could discern objects. Colborne told the following stories of this time. The first illustrates the relations of French and English to one another during the war:

At Alhandra some of my brigade were drinking in a winehouse with some French soldiers. They took one of them prisoner, and brought him to me. I said, however, 'This will never do, to take a man prisoner when you were quite friendly with him before, in the wine-house.' So I sent him back to General Reynier's Division under charge of an officer of my regiment. The officer told me that when he was delivered up to the French general, the latter gave him playfully two or three slaps with his glove, saying, 'You silly fellow, to allow yourself to be taken prisoner in that manner.'

Officers at that time were encouraged to enter the Portuguese service. A step in advance of their present rank was held out as an inducement, and in the Portuguese service they often rose very rapidly. Ashworth entered the Portuguese service as a captain, and very soon had the command of a brigade. This brigade was attached to our army, and soon came to serve with General Hill's division, to which Ashworth's own regiment was attached, so that, being a brigadier-general, he had to post the picquets and give orders to his former commanding officer, who was very angry, saying, 'What, do you really suppose I am going to receive orders from you, who were one of my captains a few months ago?'

'Oh,' said Ashworth, 'I've nothing to do with that; you must arrange that with General Hill. These are my orders.'

To Miss Alethea Bargus

Alhandra
9th November, 1810

My Dear Alethea,

It gives me great pleasure to see your handwriting some four or five months after the date of your letters. They find their way at last, as you observe, after a long march. I wish you would write always by the Packet, by which means I should have the pleasure of receiving your letters in six or seven days from Sloane Street, now we are so near Lisbon. By the last post we had the London papers of the 27th October at the army on the 5th of November.

I really have been very actively employed since my arrival in this part of Portugal, and am not often off my horse, as I command a post outside the lines the town of Alhandra, where part of my brigade is stationed, and which it is destined to defend. The unfortunate inhabitants have all left their houses, and their furniture, poor people, is converted into barriers, &c. How should you like to see your piano, writing tables, chairs and trunks heaped together at the south end of Sloane Street to impede the enemy's march?

I have never seen so much distress and misery experienced by the mass of the people as in the late flight of the inhabitants towards the capital. Not a person remained at his home, whole towns and villages decamped, taking with them only what a cart could convey, and leaving the rest of their property to be pillaged by the armies of friends and enemies. We have been marching constantly since June, so you must make some allowance for my irregular correspondence.

The French, instead of entering Portugal with 100,000 men, and sending a force by the Alemtejo, have had the folly to undertake the difficult task of marching to Lisbon with about 60,000, persuaded that we were to fight a battle and embark. With this idea Massena followed us close, but on viewing our position on a chain of high hills that run from the Tagus to the sea, about five leagues from Lisbon, he halted, and has now remained opposite to us a month, without undertaking anything of importance. Various are the opinions about his future operations and whether he will be obliged to retire for want of provisions.

I am inclined to think that he will endeavour to maintain himself until his reinforcements arrive, or that he will not fall back farther than the River Zezere, a formidable obstacle in the winter to an enemy invading or pursued. But I see no difficulty he will find in retiring, should he be allowed to establish a bridge of boats, about which he is supposed to be now employed.

We have a very large force, but so composed that we could not well venture from our heights to attack Portuguese, Spaniards, English, Germans, &c., militia, volunteers and *ordinanzos*. With this medley we shall remain, I suppose, in our forts and works which cover the hills, and leave the rest to Fortune and Massena's evil genius.

Your most affectionate brother.

J. C.

P. S. Remember, my letters are sacred, and must not be repeated.

CHAPTER 11

Campaign of 1811

A week after this letter was written, on 16th November, Massena retired to Santarem, and a day later Hill's Division crossed the Tagus by a pontoon bridge, and followed the enemy to Chamusca, where Colborne's Brigade took up its quarters till the following spring, Colborne having charge of the posts on the Tagus, at its confluence with the Zezere. Hill falling ill, the command of the division was held during December by Sir William Stewart, Marshal Beresford being appointed to relieve him about 1st January, 1811.

Just before the retreat of the French, when we were on one side of the Tagus and they on the other, the most amusing conversations used to be held between groups of officers of the two armies. There was a Captain Campbell, of the 42nd, who was a funny fellow, and used to make all sorts of jokes about their retreat, and end up by telling them that they had been out all night trying to get provisions. They used to ask us all sorts of questions. I had had a bridge put up across a rivulet near, which looked very pretty, and they asked what it was for.

'Cest pour une modele,' Campbell said.

They asked, 'Who is that officer always riding about?'

'Why, he is commanding the brigade.'

'What regiment does he belong to?'

'The colonel of the 66th.'

'That is very odd; *our* 66th is here. You have it opposite to you.'

The bridge I had just had made. A rivulet came through our encampment, and I had some companies on one side and some on the other. It happened that there was a tree growing just in the middle of the stream; so I had four trees cut down and cut through the middle, and they were then placed so as to rest on the tree in the stream. They formed a perfect arch, and looked very pretty. When Marshal Beresford came round I invited him to ride over with his staff. He was afraid to go at first. However, I showed him the way, and he was so pleased that when he went back he desired all the officers along the line to make a bridge in their divisions. Soon after, when I rode down, to my great amusement, I found them all very busy trying to fix a tree in the middle of the stream, not knowing that I had found one growing there.

Napier writes:[1]

. . . . Beresford erected batteries opposite the mouth of the Zezere. But against the advice of the engineers, he placed them at too great distance from the river, and in other respects unsuitable, and offering nothing threatening to the enemy; for the French craft dropped down frequently towards Santarem without hindrance until Colonel Colborne, of the 66th Regiment, moored a guard-boat close to the mouth of the Zezere, disposing fires in such a manner on the banks of the Tagus that nothing could pass without being observed.

The following account is compiled from the accounts of the affair given by Napier, by Burgoyne (Wrottesley's *Life of Sir J. Burgoyne*), and by Cannon, *Hist. Record of 13th Dragoons*.

On the 6th March Massena quitted Santarem, and retreated up the valley of the Mondego towards

---

1. Napier, Book XI, chap, x.

Ciudad Rodrigo, the chief part of the 2nd Division, under Sir William Stewart, following him up as far as Thomar, and annoying his rear. From Thomar the division was ordered to return to the left bank of the Tagus to relieve Badajos, which was hard pressed.

However, on 13th March Badajos had fallen, and Campo Mayor was being besieged by Mortier. Beresford's instructions were now to relieve Campo Mayor and to besiege Olivença and Badajos. Campo Mayor surrendered on 21st March, but the Marshal, being within two marches of it, judged that he might surprise the besieging corps, and with this view, put his troops in motion on the 23rd. In the morning of the 25th his advanced guard of cavalry, supported by a detachment of infantry under Colonel Colborne, came suddenly upon Campo Mayor, just as Latour Maubourg (who had been left by Mortier to dismantle the works) was marching out in confusion with 880 cavalry, three battalions of infantry, some horse artillery, and the battering train of 13 guns.

The allies pursued him. Colonel Colborne was on the right, and at a considerable distance from the enemy, but Colonel Head, with the 13th Light Dragoons, was on the left, close to them, and supported by Colonel Otway with two squadrons of the 7th Portuguese. The French halted with their infantry in square and their cavalry formed in their front and rear. Colonel Head was directed to attack with the two squadrons of the 13th, amounting to 203 officers and soldiers, and he led them forward with the most distinguished gallantry.

A regiment of French hussars advanced to meet the 13th. Several men were overthrown by the shock. The combatants pierced through on both sides, and facing about, charged each other again with the most heroic bravery. After a sharp sword-conflict the hussars who had not been cut down fled. A French squadron, formed on the enemy's right, wheeled inward and attacked the British left, but the 13th overthrew them after a short contest. The French continued their flight. The 13th followed, undeterred by the fire of the French infantry. They galloped forward, cut down the French gunners, and, believing the other brigades would easily dispose of the French troops thus passed, they continued the pursuit.

For some time the French Dragoons resisted, but their formation soon became so completely broken that they surrendered as soon as they were overtaken. The pursuit was continued at a rapid rate, the object being to gain the front and capture the whole, as well as the enormous quantity of baggage on the road. But the 13th were not aware of what was taking place in their rear. The French infantry remained formed in square, with the British heavy cavalry in their front.

The heavies were ordered to advance, and then suddenly halted, as Marshal Beresford, who was himself with the main body of infantry in the rear, had been informed that the 13th had been cut off, and the loss of one regiment appeared a serious disaster. He said he would wait for the infantry, though the 66th and some light infantry were up, and the great body of the infantry were not two miles behind.

The French infantry, thus finding themselves unmolested, retired steadily, recovered their artillery, and effected their retreat. Meanwhile the 13th and some Portuguese squadrons commanded by Colonel Otway, who formed as a support during the attack, were pursuing the French troopers at a rapid pace.

On arriving at the bridge of Badajos they were fired upon by the guns of that fortress. The regiment then halted, and retired to secure the prisoners and captured artillery and baggage. Some of the French drivers, refusing to surrender, were sabred, and the mules were mounted by men of the 13th. The retreat was continued several miles, the men in high spirits at their wonderful success. At length they were met by the retiring French infantry and by all the beaten cavalry which could find refuge with it. For a few exhausted dragoons to have engaged that body of troops would have been madness, and the 13th were forced to abandon their captures and make a detour to the right to join the army.

Colborne told the story himself in this fashion:

From my position I could plainly see the French evacuate the town, and I saw an admirable operation of the 13th Light Dragoons, who passed through the French cavalry and dispersed them, and if they had been supported by the heavy cavalry, a most excellent *coup de main* would have been achieved, and the whole French force might have been made prisoners. But just at the moment General Lumley, who commanded the heavy cavalry, to my great mortification, sent me a message by his aide-de-camp that the infantry must halt, as it was useless in face of the superior strength of the enemy to continue the engagement. 'The whole of the 13th,' it was added, 'are taken.'

I told the aide-de-camp that I had seen the contrary with my own eyes, and I should do no such thing. The aide-de-camp said, 'Shall I take the general this message?'

To which I replied, 'Yes, he thinks the 13th are taken, but there they are.'

However, through this error, the heavy cavalry were halted, and the whole operation failed. I was so indignant that I expressed myself very warmly and General Stewart demanded an explanation, thinking my remarks applied to him. I would not retract, but would only say, 'Whose ever fault it was, a most brilliant *coup de main* has failed.'

General Stewart, who till then had been one of my kindest friends, and who was a most amiable man, only said, 'Well, then, in future, Colonel Colborne, I shall only address you in the most official manner.' Thenceforth he always addressed me as 'Dear Sir,' instead of 'Dear Colonel.'[2]

On the way home I heard a French soldier, one of the few prisoners we had taken, offer a ring to one of our men who was guarding him, in order to secure his good offices. It was very absurd to see the man's wish to accept it, contending with his fear that it was rather a shabby thing to do. 'Ah, now, I don't like to take it from you. I dare say it was your sweetheart gave it you.'

At the same time, he took it.

> Napier thinks that after thus recovering Campo Mayor, Beresford, by marching on Merida, might have brought about the fall of Badajos. He neglected this opportunity, and put his fatigued troops into quarters round Elvas.

To Miss Alethea Bargus

Elvas
30th March, 1811

My Dear Alethea,

You may be assured that when I am seriously ill I shall let you know in due time. I had an intermittent fever in December and January, but with the aid of a powerful ally called bark, I made a hard battle with the enemy, and fairly fought off my illness by being my own physician.

The brigade I command was posted opposite the mouth of the Tagus, where the French had collected 60 or 70 boats. It was a very interesting part until Massena retreated. As I was much occupied there, it most probably was the

---

2. Sir Harry Smith writes in his Autobiography: 'I have often heard Colonel Colborne (Lord Seaton) affirm that if he were asked to name the bravest man he had ever seen (and no one was a better judge) he should name Sir William Stewart.'

cause of my recovery. We only followed the French as far as Tomar, and then returned to the south of the Tagus, under the command of Marshal Beresford. The army under Soult and Mortier having taken Badajos (13th March) and Campo Mayor (21st March), we proceeded immediately towards the latter place with 20,000 men. The French, who did not expect us, were nearly surprised in Campo Mayor, and we had a grand chase after them for two leagues. Their force amounted to 900 cavalry and about 1,000 infantry. I had not the smallest doubt but that we should have taken them all, but to our great mortification they reached Badajos owing to a glaring error on our part.

We are now about to cross the Guadiana, and if things be tolerably managed a great change may be produced in the affairs of Spain. My friend General Graham has gained great credit in the affair near Cadiz,[3] although the result of the action was of no importance.

What a narrow escape I have had of making £20,000 in a few hours! I allude to General Abercrombie's expedition.[4] Had I gone with him I should have been at least £20,000 richer. I think I could have disposed of that sum admirably, but, as we have all the honour here, and cannot look into futurity, I bear my loss with my usual philosophy.

It will now be a long time before I return to England; therefore I mean to dispose of my poor Calabrian,[5] or shall I give him to Mrs. Bunbury? I have a great idea of offering him to that lady, as she seemed very fond of him in Sicily. I shall take your advice on that subject. Tell me in your next what I shall do with him.

There is another lieutenant-colonel appointed to the 66th. He has applied to come out to this country, but I un-

---

3. Battle of Barrosa, 5th March.
4. General Sir John Abercromby, Commander in Chief at Bombay, had just effected the conquest of Mauritius.
5. Apparently Antonio, Colborne's servant, had been left in England.

derstand he has been refused. This secures me from the East Indies for some time.

Your most affectionate brother,

J. C.

Beresford halted at Elvas till he could procure the means of crossing the Guadiana at Jerumenha. On the 7th April all his troops had crossed. On the 11th Beresford took post at Albuhera, after leaving Cole to take Olivença, which surrendered on the 15th. The whole army was then concentrated about Zafra, ready to undertake the siege of Badajos, which was invested on 5th May. Beresford's headquarters were now at Almendralejo. On 2nd May, as Napier writes:

Colonel John Colborne was detached with a brigade of the 2nd Division, two Spanish guns, and two squadrons of cavalry to curb the French inroads, and to raise the confidence of the people.[6] Colborne, a man of singular talent for war, by rapid marches and sudden changes of direction, in concert with Villamur, created great confusion amongst the enemy's parties. He intercepted several convoys, and obliged the French troops to quit Fuente Ovejuna, La Granja, Azuaga, and most of the other frontier towns, and he imposed upon Latour Maubourg with so much address that the latter, imagining a great force was at hand, abandoned Guadalcanal also, and fell back to Constantino.

Having cleared the country on that side Colborne attempted to surprise the fortified post of Benalcazar, and by a hardy attempt was like to have carried it; for, riding on to the drawbridge with a few officers, in the grey of the morning, he summoned the commandant to surrender, as the only means of saving himself from the Spanish army which was close at

---

6. In the instructions given to Colborne on 29th April by Colonel D'Urban, it is stated: 'The object of this movement is to check the inroads of the enemy's parties of pillage, to give confidence to the people of Estremadura, and to cover the collection of our own supplies, while it will announce in Andalusia the neighbourhood of a British force by showing troops upon the frontier.'

hand and would give no quarter. The French officer, amazed at the appearance of the party, was yet too resolute to yield, and Colborne, quick to perceive the attempt had failed, galloped off under a few straggling shots. After this, taking to the mountains, he rejoined the army without any loss.[7]

He had marched 250 miles in 11 days.[8] The following letter was written early in the course of these operations:

To Colonel D'Urban

Bivouac near Magilla

Dear Sir,

We marched from Llera yesterday evening in consequence of having heard that the enemy had made a requisition for bread and forage at Magilla, and we arrived in time to secure a part of the provisions which had been ordered for him. The magistrates seem very glad to see us, and I think we shall have no difficulty in procuring provisions.

I find the enemy has about 3,000 infantry at Guadalcanal, 300 cavalry at Azuaga, and 200 infantry at Fuente Ovejuna; the remainder of his force is at Cazalla and Constantino, amounting in the whole (including the troops, at Guadalcanal, &c.) to about 5,000, 800 of which is cavalry. I intend moving to Granja this evening. Should I deviate from the original route by marching from Granja towards Fuente Ovejuna (the direct road to Cordova), it is very probable the enemy will retire from Guadalcanal to Cazalla. I shall be guided by the intelligence I receive at Granja, and will inform you if I make any change in your route. It appears the French have been reinforced from Cordova with about 1,000 infantry since they retired from Badajos.

Your faithful servant,
J. Colborne
Lt-Colonel

---

7 Napier, Bk. XII., chap. vi.
8. Groves, The 66th Regiment.

On his return to the army on 14th May, Colborne found it in a new situation. In consequence of the news that Soult had marched from Seville and effected a junction with Latour Maubourg, Beresford had raised the siege of Badajos, and was preparing to receive battle on the heights of Albuhera.

Beresford's force consisted of about 32,000 men, of whom only 7,000 were British. Colborne's brigade was posted on the left of the line near the village of Albuhera, the Spanish and Portuguese held the right.

Soult arrived on the evening of 15th May, and perceiving that Beresford had neglected to occupy a wooded range of hills on the right of his position, posted 15,000 men and 30 guns there. Of the presence of this force Beresford remained completely ignorant. The French advanced on the position on the morning of the 16th, Godinot making a feint of attacking the village, while Soult led a heavy column of infantry supported by artillery against the Spaniards on the right. He soon drove them from the heights and began to deploy his force along the position.

Colborne's brigade was hurried up to check this movement, and had almost succeeded in driving the French infantry back, when a strong force of Polish lancers and chasseurs, which had got round the right of the line unperceived, charged the brigade in rear and threw it into confusion. 'Our men,' wrote Colonel Clarke of the 66th, 'now ran into groups of six or eight to do as best they could. The officers snatched up muskets and joined them, determined to sell their lives dearly. Quarter was not asked, and rarely given.'

In this melee Colborne's brigade suffered dreadfully, the Buffs, 48th and 66th being nearly annihilated. At length Brigadier Lumley, seeing the desperate state of affairs from the plain below, sent four squadrons of heavy cavalry against the lancers, and at the same time the 29th Foot, Hoghton's Brigade and some artillery came up to the assistance of their well-nigh vanquished comrades.

The fight was now continued with redoubled fury and awful carnage. Marshal Beresford, in spite of all his efforts, could not get the Spaniards to advance, the ammunition began to fail, and another French column was established in advance upon the right flank. Beresford saw nothing for it but to give the order for retreat. But at this critical moment Colonel Henry Hardinge, entirely on his own responsibility, rode off to the 4th Division, which had just come up from Badajos, and induced its leader, Lowry Cole, to advance, supported by Colonel Abercromby with the 3rd Brigade of the 2nd Division.

Cole mounted the hill, drove off the lancers, recaptured the guns and dashed up to the right of Hoghton's Brigade, just as Abercromby passed to the front on its left. The appearance of this 'astonishing infantry' turned the fortune of the day, and the mighty mass of Frenchmen, in Napier's words:

> .... went headlong down the steep. Eighteen hundred unwounded men, the remnant of 6,000 unconquerable British soldiers, stood triumphant on the fatal hill.[9]

After the battle of Albuhera the 3rd, 29th, 31st, 48th, 57th and 66th Regiments were so reduced in numbers that they were formed into a Provisional Battalion.[10]

To the Rev. Duke Yonge

18th May, 1811

My Dear Duke,

Since April the brigade I commanded has been in continual movement. During the siege of Badajos I was sent into the Sierra Morena as a moveable column to attract the enemy's attention, and we performed a march of about 260 miles

---

[9] Harry Smith, writing to Colborne from the Cape in 1832, speaks of 'Those glorious days, so nobly kept alive in the gigantic language of our old comrade, Bill Napier, 'stood triumphant on the fatal hill."

[10] The above account of Albuhera is condensed from Groves, *The 66th Regiment*.

in a very short time. Marshal Soult was collecting his force at Seville, and on the 15th his advanced guard arrived at St. Martha, three leagues from our position. Marshal Beresford was obliged to retire from his lines before Badajos and concentrate his force. The Spaniards, under Blake and Balesteros, joined our army on the night of the 15th, and we occupied a position near Albuera. Soult began his attack at 8 a.m., and having menaced the village of Albuera, I was ordered into it, but as soon as I had marched there, the enemy commenced his attack on the right, and was in the act of turning it. Our brigade was then ordered to occupy the ground where the Spaniards should have been, and we were brought up under very disadvantageous circumstances, and obliged to deploy under the enemy's fire. The regiments were ordered to charge before the deployment was complete, and without support; in the act of charging two very heavy columns, a regiment of Polish cavalry passed by our right, which was unprotected, and having gained our rear, the three right-hand regiments were almost destroyed. The Spaniards on our left behaved very well, but, as we had not any support, the few who were not killed or wounded were taken prisoners. The 4th Division came up and drove the enemy off, supported by the 2nd and 3rd brigades of the division. Soult retreated about 2 p.m. Our loss has been immense, nearly 6,000, the greater part British. The enemy retreated to Almendralejo last night, and I believe we are to pursue him immediately. This has been a most unfortunate affair for me, although I had nothing to do with the arrangement, but merely obeyed the orders of General Stewart. Yet, it being my first trial, and having had so considerable a command, it is truly unfortunate for your brother. I did not receive any injury personally, although in the hands of the Poles some minutes. Poor Colonel Duckworth was killed leading on the 48th; he received three shots at the same time. His horse was wounded. Pray communicate this sad intelligence to Mrs. Duckworth. I was very intimate with him. The poor fellow had been long sighing to revisit his home. You can easily conceive what a stroke this has been on me, and yet if Bonaparte had been in my place nothing could have saved the three battalions. The enemy had 4,000 cavalry and 20,000 infantry.

Yours sincerely,
J. Colborne

Colborne's conduct at Albuhera received the following commendation from his superior officer:

To H. E. Marshal Sir W. Beresford

17th May

The conduct of the 1st Brigade, under the command of Lieutenant-Colonel Colborne, was very gallant. Although the loss in prisoners and in colours has fallen on that part of the division, you are probably aware, Sir, that the 1st Brigade was suddenly attacked in flank and rear by a body of the enemy's cavalry, while it was engaged in the almost desperate effort of charging the whole attacking force of the enemy. The form of the hill up which that brigade was so ably led to the charge by its commander, and the obscurity occasioned by the smoke of musquetry and a heavy squall of rain prevented the enemy's cavalry from being either seen or sufficiently early resisted.

The colours of the 2nd Battalion of the 48th and 66th Regiments were unfortunately lost on this occasion, but they were not so lost until the officers who bore them were killed. . . .

W. Stewart
Major-General

CHAPTER 12

Ciudad Rodrigo

Meanwhile, on the 18th July Colborne had left the 66th Regiment and become lieutenant-colonel of the 52nd. It was no slight acknowledgment of his military qualities that he was thus appointed to a regiment which had been trained to light infantry service by Sir John Moore, and now, with the 2nd Battalion 95th Regiment (Rifles) and one regiment of Portuguese Caçadores, formed part of the 2nd Brigade of Craufurd's famous Light Division.

That the appointment was specially gratifying to Colborne is shown by the following letter of Sir H. Torrens, dated Horse Guards, 6th August, 1811:

> I have derived great satisfaction .... to find that I had anticipated your wishes by having submitted your name to the Commander-in-Chief for an exchange into the 52nd. I thought I could not be far wrong in judging of your anxiety to get the command of a corps in which your much-lamented friend and general took such pride, and the discipline and distinguished character of which he so permanently established by his peculiar zeal and military talents.

On the 5th May preceding the 52nd had taken part in the battle of Fuentes de Onoro. In connection with this battle Colborne told the following story:

Colonel Mainwaring, of the 51st, was placed in a position in which he thought he was sure to be surrounded by the French. So he called his officers and said, 'We are sure of being taken or killed; therefore, we'll burn the colours.' Accordingly, they brought the colours and burnt them with all funeral pomp and buried the ashes, or kept them, I believe. It so happened that the French never came near them. Lord Wellington was exceedingly angry when he heard of it, as he knew well enough where he had placed the regiment. So he ordered Mainwaring under arrest and tried him by court-martial.

An old colonel, who undertook his defence, said, 'I believe it was something to do with religious principles!'

'Oh,' said Lord Wellington, 'if it was a matter of religious principles, I have nothing more to do with it. You may take him out of arrest; but send him to Lisbon.'

So he went to Lisbon, and was never allowed to command his regiment again; he was sent home.

The 2nd Brigade of the Light Division was commanded in the summer of 1811 by Major-General Drummond, and after his death in the autumn, by Major-General Vandeleur. With these generals, as major of brigade, was Harry Smith, a born soldier like Colborne himself, and one who quickly recognized in Colborne a leader after his own heart. And though in temperament the two were widely different, Smith ardent, effusive and romantic, Colborne somewhat self-restrained and reserved, a mutual attachment grew up between them which lasted so long as both lived.

At the moment when Colborne was appointed to the Light Division, of which he was to be one of the prime heroes, it was beginning a long march northwards from Monte Reguengo, near Campo Mayor, to the banks of the Agueda. After being cantoned for five weeks at Saugo, on 26th September the 52nd joined Wellington's army at Guinaldo.

Hence the army retired without a battle, the Light Division forming the rearguard. After some harassing marches, the army went into cantonments on 1st October.

During part of the autumn Colborne had been obliged to be in England owing to a severe attack of ague. According to the diary of Miss Yonge, his future wife, he arrived in England about 26th August. He went down from London on 16th September to his brother-in-law's house at Antony, where Miss Yonge was staying. On the 7th October the party at Antony moved to Puslinch, and on the 10th Colborne left for Falmouth to return to the Peninsula. From this time Miss Yonge corresponded with him, and there is no doubt that he had asked her to be his wife. He sailed on 27th October, and reached Lisbon on the 13th November.

The 52nd were at Zamora from the 17th October to the 14th December, when they changed their quarters to Las Agallios, where the men were employed till the 5th or 6th January in making fascines and gabions for the siege of Ciudad Rodrigo.

Before any progress, however, could be made with the siege, it was necessary to capture the outlying fort of San Francisco. This operation was entrusted to Lieutenant-Colonel Colborne, and the judgment and skill he showed in effecting it more than justified the selection. It is referred to by Colborne himself as showing that 'success in assaults can only be expected from high discipline and order, and not from bayonets and forlorn hopes without a fire on the defences.' He gave the following account of it in a letter to Captain Moorsom[1], dated Dublin, 26th April, 1859.

The Light Division marched from El Bodon, or near it, early on the 8th and reached the ground in front of the Upper Teson about noon. The detachments intended for the assault of the redoubt were not volunteers; they were com-

---
1. To be used in Moorsom's History of the 52nd Regiment. Communicated to me by Lieutenant-Colonel Mockler-Ferryman.

panies commanded by the senior captains of each battalion; two from the 43rd, four from the 52nd Regiment, two from the 95th, and one from each of the Portuguese battalions.[2] Four companies were selected from the advanced guard to occupy the crest of the glacis and open fire, while the party with the ladders, in charge of Captain Thompson, of the Engineers, in the rear of these companies could be brought up and be assisted in placing the ladders for the assault. In the rear of the whole the companies destined for the actual escalade followed.

In this order we started and advanced, after a caution had been given by me in respect to *silence*, and each captain had been instructed *precisely* where he was to post his company and how he was to proceed on arriving near the redoubt. An officer of the 95th and two sergeants had been stationed before dark on the brow of the hill to mark the angle of the redoubt covering the steeple of the church in Ciudad Rodrigo. When we reached the point marked by the officer of the 95th, I dismounted and again called out the four captains of the advanced guard and ordered the front company to occupy the front face and the 2nd the right, &c.

Captain Mulcaster, of the Engineers, suggested that it would be better to *wait* for the light ladders which were coming up. I, however, thought that no time should be lost, and proceeded with the *very heavy* ladders which had been made during the day.

When about fifty yards from the redoubt I gave the word 'double-quick.' This movement and the rattling of canteens

---

2. Sir Harry Smith writes in his Autobiography: When the detachments of the Light Division brigades were parading, my brigade was to furnish 400 men. I understood four companies, and when Colonel Colborne was counting them he said, 'There are not the complement of men.' I said, 'I am sorry if I have mistaken.' 'Oh, never mind, run and bring another company.' I mention this to show what a cool, noble fellow he is. Many an officer would have stormed like fury. He only thought of storming Fort San Francisco, which he carried in a glorious manner.

alarmed the garrison; but the defenders had only time to fire one round from their guns before each company had taken its post on the crest of the glacis and opened fire. All this was effected without the least confusion, and not a man was seen in the redoubt after the fire had commenced.

The party with the ladders soon arrived and placed them in the ditch against the palisades, so that they were ready when Captain Mein, of the 52nd, came up with the escalading companies. They got into the ditch by descending on the ladders and then placing them against the *fraises*. The only fire from which the assailants suffered was from shells and grenades thrown over from the rampart.

During these proceedings Gurwood, of the 52nd, came from the gorge and mentioned that a company could get in by the gorge with ladders. I desired him to take any he could find. Thompson, of the Engineers, had no opportunity of being of use; the whole arrangements were executed by the exertions of captains of companies, and the order preserved by them. We entered the redoubt by the ladders safely; no resistance or opposition was made.

The company at the gorge had tossed open the gate, or it had been opened by some of the defenders endeavouring to escape. Captain Mein, I believe, was wounded from a shot from one of our own companies as he was mounting on the rampart. Most of the defenders had fled to the guard-house. Not one man was killed or wounded after we entered the redoubt.[3]

The garrison of Ciudad Rodrigo opened a heavy fire on the redoubt immediately we had taken possession of it. The

---

3. Wellington stated in his despatch: 'Two captains and forty-seven men were made prisoners: the remainder of the garrison being put to the sword in the storm.' The latter statement Colborne always warmly repudiated. 'I think a great many escaped before we entered, but all who were there took refuge under the guns, and were taken prisoners.' When the fort was taken, Colborne says that his orderly-sergeant MacCurrie said, in tones of deep feeling, 'Thank God, that's over.'

force under my command was collected outside and marched down to the rivulet at the bottom of the glacis of the Place and covered the working parties opening the first parallel till moonlight. Had the redoubt not been taken, five days would have been required to attack it regularly. The governor had been in the redoubt half an hour before we attacked it. The investment, in fact, had been completed some days before the 8th by the guerrilla cavalry. The Light Division returned to El Bodon about 12 on the 9th, relieved by another division.

Moorsom thus comments on the story of this brilliant achievement:

> The remarkable success of this assault was probably due to the following points: the clear conception and explanation of the plan of attack, so that each individual in charge knew what he had to do; the high discipline and order in which the plan was carried out under the eye of the officer commanding the party; and the care taken to cover the redoubt with a sheet of fire while the escalade was being made, rather than trusting to the rush of a few bayonets against many defenders.[4]

A reported conversation of Colborne's gives a few additional details:

It was pitch dark that night, and the firing went on so long that the rest of the army thought we should not take the fort, and were very anxious about it. We were firing into the fort from the glacis across the ditch, but our men could not be seen. The only danger was of our firing on each other. The firing was so steady and continuous that I could not see any sign of the enemy on the ramparts, though I could see into the fort most distinctly.

Colborne thus reported on his achievement:

---

4. Moorsom's Historical Record of the 52nd Regiment.

To Major-General Craufurd
Commanding Light Division

El Bodon
9th January, 1812

Sir,

I have the honour to report to you the proceedings of the detachment of the Light Division ordered to attack an advanced work before Ciudad Rodrigo. The four companies conducted by Major Gibbs approached it so rapidly that the enemy had but little time to annoy them by his fire. Captain Crampton, of the 95th Regiment, first formed up his company on the crest of the glacis, and was followed by the divisions under the command of Captain Merry, of the 52nd, and Captain Travers and Lieutenant McNamara, of the 95th, who silenced the enemy's fire whilst Captain Duffey, of the 43rd Regiment, and Captain Mein, of the 52nd, with their companies, and Lieutenant Woodgate, of the 52nd, who had charge of the ladders, leaped into the ditch and escaladed the work. Two officers and 47 rank and file of the enemy were made prisoners by the activity of Major Gibbs, who moved round to the gate and prevented them from making their escape. I beg leave to mention that the intrepidity and exertions of Captain Mein and Lieutenant Woodgate could not be exceeded, both of whom were wounded, the latter severely. Lieutenant Bankesley, of the 95th, I am sorry to add, has also received a very severe wound.

I have the honour to be, Sir, your most obedient humble servant,

J. Colborne
Lt-Colonel, 52nd Light Infantry

> Colborne received great praise for the skill with which he captured the redoubt of San Francisco. Wellington wrote: 'I cannot sufficiently applaud the conduct of Lieutenant-Colonel Colborne and of the detachment under his command upon this occasion,' and George Napier writes:

The colonel formed his party and gave his orders so explicitly, and so clearly made every officer understand what he was to do, that no mistake could possibly be made. The consequence was that in twenty minutes from the time he moved to the attack the fort was stormed and carried. The watchword of 'England and St. George' was heard shouted loud and strong and re-echoed by the division which was under arms.[5]

As Colborne told the tale afterwards:

Lord Wellington, Colonel Barnard, of the 95th, and General Craufurd were most anxiously awaiting the event. When they heard the cheer, Barnard, unable to restrain his emotion, threw himself on the ground in the vehemence of his delight so that General Craufurd, who was at a little distance and did not see who it was, exclaimed, 'What's that drunken man doing?' Craufurd was a man who seldom expressed approval, but on this occasion he said, 'Colonel Colborne seems to be a steady officer.'

As soon as the fort fell I despatched a soldier to Lord Wellington, who had been looking on all the time. This soldier ran up to him in great excitement and said, 'I've taken the fort, Sir.'

Wellington replied, 'Oh, you've taken the fort, have you? Well, I'm glad to hear it.' and got up and rode away.

After such great anxiety it was most delightful to go and wrap myself in my cloak, and I seldom remember having had such a sound and delightful sleep.

The siege of Ciudad Rodrigo was now busily prosecuted, and on the 19th January, two breaches being reported practicable, the assault was made. The forlorn hope was led by Lieutenant Gurwood, 52nd, with 25 volunteers; the storming party which followed by Major George Napier, 52nd.

---

5. *Early Life of Sir George Napier.*

Colborne himself headed his regiment in the assault. The ascent was extremely sharp and contracted, and when two-thirds of the lesser breach had been reached the struggle became so violent in the narrowest part that the men paused, and every musket in the crowd was snapped under the instinct of self-defence, though not one was loaded. Colonel Colborne, however, pressed on with his 52nd, and though wounded in the shoulder by a musket ball, led the men on. Napier, though struck down by grape-shot, called to the troops to trust to their bayonets. The officers thereupon sprang to the front and the ascent was won.

The assault was successful at the cost of many valuable lives, including that of the brilliant leader of the Light Division, General Robert Craufurd, while among those severely wounded were Colborne and George Napier. An officer of the 52nd, writing home two days after the assault, expressed the feelings which these misfortunes had called forth:

> We have, as a division, sustained a very heavy loss in General Craufurd, who is not expected to recover from his wounds; but, as a regiment, a much more severe one, though we heartily trust it is only temporary, in Colonel Colborne, who, though he has only commanded us a few months, has gained the hearts of every officer and soldier in the regiment.[6]

Colborne was thus mentioned in Lord Wellington's despatch:

> I have already reported my sense of the conduct of Major-General Craufurd and of Lieutenant-Colonel Colborne and of the troops of the Light Division in the storming of the redoubt of St. Francisco on the evening of the 8th instant. The conduct of these troops was equally distinguished through-

---

6. Letter of Captain J. F. Ewart given in the *43rd and 52nd Light Infantry Chronicle*, 1893.

out the siege, and in the storm nothing could withstand the gallantry with which these brave officers and troops advanced and accomplished the difficult operation allotted to them, notwithstanding all their leaders had fallen.

Colborne referred in conversation to the storming of Ciudad Rodrigo as follows:

When Lord Wellington summoned Ciudad Rodrigo he said, *'J'ai l'honneur de vous sommer.'* They said afterwards it was useless his having summoned them, because Napoleon's orders forbade them to surrender until they had been attacked three times. Before the storming the fire was kept up till the last ten minutes till after dark. I recollect hearing Robert Craufurd's voice squeaking out, 'Move on, will you, 95th? Or we will get some who will.' The Rifles had made a sort of stop. Craufurd was wounded soon after and died the next morning. I remember he sent to ask after me.

Craufurd was a fine fellow, though very stern and tyrannical, but after all, that was the way he got his division into such fine order. He was the terror of all Commissaries; I really believe he was nearly the death of one. He always got provisions however; that was something. A Commissary told me that Craufurd once desired him to keep a journal after the manner of a log-book, that he might see how and where he spent every half-hour of his time! He was the first man who introduced a proper manner of marching. 'Sit down in it, Sir, sit down in it,' he used to call out if he saw a soldier stepping across a puddle. That was the way he got them to march so beautifully. Although he was so tyrannical, once on his return to the division after a period of absence the soldiers cheered him, which said a good deal for him. He took some church plate once, however. The people said they would not give him any provisions; so he said, 'Very well, then, I'll take the church plate'; which he did.

I always think of a remark made to Barclay (lieutenant-colonel of the 52nd) by Beckwith, who commanded another brigade in the Light Division. We were near Talavera, and provisions were often very scarce. Craufurd, who commanded the Light Division, was the most unpopular fellow that ever was, but he was very clever, and he always managed to get his dinner supplied when no one else could get one. One day Craufurd sent Barclay a bottle of very good cherry brandy a great luxury in those days when water was far more common than brandy. So as Barclay was drawing the cork before us all, Beckwith said, 'What, Barclay, do you drink anything from such a fellow as that?' So Barclay filled his glass, and as he was tossing it off, said, 'Don't I, indeed? Here's damnation to him!'

There was a great drop into the town after we got into the breach. There was one place I thought I could have got in at. I wanted very much to have tried with the 52nd. I used to examine it every morning with my spy-glass. I dare say I should have got a proper good Ticking if I had, for I heard afterwards there was no way of getting down.

> Colonel Colborne received an awful wound, but he never quitted his regiment until the city was perfectly ours and his regiment all collected.[7]
>
> Some idea of Colborne's sufferings from this time onwards, and of his bitter disappointment at the check to his career caused by his wound may be gathered from his own account, as reported by his daughters:

The worst wound I ever had I received at Ciudad Rodrigo. A bullet from the walls hit my right shoulder and passed some way down my arm. This was about 20 minutes, I suppose, after the attack had begun. I was knocked down by the wound at the moment, but I was able to go into the town. I had another wound in my leg at the same time, but the first was so bad that I did not think of that. I was taken the next

---

7. Harry Smith in his *Autobiography*.

day to a convent, and three weeks after I was carried on 20 men's shoulders to Coimbra, in Portugal. That journey in the open air was perhaps a good thing for me, though it took a week and gave me a great deal of pain at the time. I always had an appetite and could eat. The surgeon said, 'I think you must do well, you always have such an appetite.' A part of the gold wire of my epaulette was carried into the wound, and for long after, whenever I moved, this wire gave me the greatest torture. I could not lie on my side on the left shoulder, as it hurt the other to be raised, and it was dreadful pain to lie on my back, the bones in my back being quite sore. They were obliged to raise my bed off the ground on one side to give me ease.

The day after the wound a surgeon came and cut the wound across and across, probing for the ball. When the ball was taken out, 15 months after, it did not hurt me so much. I was so accustomed to be probed in every direction, it did not seem much. In spite of the probing they could not find the ball, and then inflammation came on and the arm swelled, and they could do nothing.

Lord Wellington's surgeon came down to see me and told me that I should have a stiff arm. A great many of them wanted to take it out of its socket. One saved me. He said, 'He has been knocked about enough. Let him take his chance.'

I recollect a physician coming to see me at Coimbra and saying, 'Now I will tell you one thing. These surgeons know nothing of medicine; they are only surgeons, so you must not mind them. They as nearly as possible killed me. I had a wound, and fortunately recovered from delirium in time to see all the stuff they were going to give me to drink. So I threw it all away or they would have killed me.' (He told me all this with the door shut.) 'But if you don't mind them, but attend to what *I* tell you, you will recover. First take a raw egg every day about one o'clock, beat up with one teaspoonful of brandy, and nine, mind, nine, of water; that's to strengthen you and give you an appetite. Then never take anything acid.

These surgeons would give you acids, but vinegar has some relation to the bone and would hurt it.' He gave me many more directions and the reasons for them.

I stayed several months in Coimbra,[8] and by the end of that time all the bits of wire were taken out. In June I went home.[9] (He arrived in England June 4th.) I was obliged to go; I was fit for nothing. I had nowhere to stay and I wanted a change of air. I was so nervous that I used to be obliged to say, 'Give me a glass of wine, I am going to cry.' I could not help crying continually. Once I felt it coming on as I was being carried across a stream in my journey and a good many soldiers were looking on, but I was so ashamed of their seeing me and thinking I was crying because I was hurt, that that, I think, prevented me. How delightful it is to hear a voice that you know! I recollect so well when I was lying sick and in such pain hearing the voice of a very old friend of mine Pierrepont 'Well, Colborne, so here you are, you poor old fellow!' He was killed soon after.

---

8. During these months Badajos was stormed (6th April). Of this assault Colborne told the following story: Sir Andrew Barnard, who commanded the division, left particular orders with Colonel Elder, commanding a regiment of Portuguese Caçadores, to remain in reserve, as, knowing his impetuous character and eagerness to be foremost, he feared he might advance too soon. He himself advanced with the rest of his division to the trenches. Here the greatest confusion prevailed, owing to their being too much crowded, but very soon Colonel Elder, hearing the firing, came dashing into the trenches, adding still more to the confusion. When Barnard saw him he exclaimed loudly against his impetuosity. 'Ah, Colonel Elder, Colonel Elder, for your own glory you would throw away the whole British army.'
9. From Coimbra to Lisbon (where he was obliged to remain some time longer before he was fit to sail) he travelled with his fellow-sufferer George Napier, who thus writes: About three weeks from the loss of my arm I commenced my journey towards Lisbon. In a few days I arrived at Coimbra, where I found my friend Colonel Colborne in bed, suffering dreadful pain from his wound. Here we stayed some time till Colborne was able to travel by easy stages to Lisbon. When we arrived there he was so ill and weak that it was impossible he could undergo the fatigue of the voyage.' Napier therefore embarked alone. *Early Military Life of Sir G. T. Napier.*

The following letters were received by Colonel Colborne's family after his wound. Those from Colborne himself were now written with the left hand.

To Mrs. Duke Yonge

Coimbra

My Dear Delia,

I am sorry to tell you that my wound has turned out badly the bone is fractured very high up, and in this state I was moved 30 leagues in a wagon on a very bad road.

Remember me to Duke and Delia and little Jack.

Believe me, your affectionate brother,
J. Colborne

To Rev. Duke Yonge

Coimbra
23rd February, 1812

My Dear Duke,

I arrived at this place on the 20th inst. My wound has turned out very badly. One ball has not yet been extracted, nor have I had one hour's natural sleep since the night I was wounded. I do not write this as a complaint, as soldiers must be prepared for pain, but as an excuse for not writing. I have now to look forward to a stiff joint....

Yours sincerely,
J. Colborne

To the Reverend Duke of Young

Cuimbra,
20th March, 1812

Sir,

I have thain the liberty of wrighting thouse few lines to you to informe you that my marster the Colonl was wounded one the 19 of Jany, at the sege of Rotherrick, and I should a wrote to a let you noed before, but I did expect he ould abeen in England before this time, but owing to take such a long march before he was able, caused him to remain a Cuimbra, but I am happy to say he is duing well at present: his wound was very dangerish, and the ball cannot be found, but I hope you will not make yourself any ways uneasey about it, for he is duing very well: when the Colonl was wounded I should a wrote the next day, but Lord Willinton sent Lord March to the Colonl, and the Colonl wrote a few lines in is bed, and I was so trobled that I did not no what to doe. I am happy to informe you the Colonl has a good apptite, and walks about: and I hope be the blessing of God, he will be. soon able to oundertake is jouney to England: and likewise I have the happness to informe you, that Lord Wellington has sent the best surgon to him can be found in the country, to atuend him and no outher: the surgon expect the ball will be out every day, and then he will be able for his duty in six mounths again: the genneral docter will riot alow him to be moved one any a count, tell such time he is able for any thing and the bone is perfectley sound; the bone has been nitten three weeks.

Sir, I hope you will give my best respects to all the famuley, and I hope the have all well. I wrote to John Blackworth the second day after I landed in Lisborne, but I reseved no answer: my best respects to all my felow servants, and very happy to informe how well my marster is douing. I should be very happy to hear from you all. Sir, I remains your most humble,

Antoney de Bane

The writer of the above letter was no doubt the Calabrian servant Antonio, of whom we have heard before. He seems to have been despatched to Lisbon just before his master's disablement.

To Miss Alethea Bargus

Coimbra
23rd March

My Dear Alethea,

Your brother is still in bed, after being wounded more than six weeks. I was moved too soon, and now it is found that the bone is fractured close to the joint. When I shall be fit to join, God knows.

Believe me, your most affectionate brother,
J. Colborne

Though Colborne was able to return to England in June, for ten months after receiving his wound he lay on his back, and the ball was not extracted until April, 1813. The following letter gives this happy news:

To Miss Fanny Bargus

Antony
25th April

My Dear Fanny,

You may now congratulate me on having lost a companion with whose company I have long been oppressed.

I went to the Military Hospital at Plymouth on Saturday, determined to submit to any operation that might facilitate the extracting the ball. After much pain and many trials the black gentleman was pulled out by the forceps without an incision. I look forward to my recovery now with delight, and hope I may bid adieu to pain and mutilation.... Your most affectionate,
J. Colborne

> Sir Harry Smith writes:
>
> The pain Colborne suffered in the extraction of the ball was more even than his iron heart could

bear. He used to lay his watch on the table and allow the surgeons five minutes' exertions at a time, and they were three or four days before they wrenched the bone from its ossified bed. . . . Of course the shoulder joint was anchylosed, but he had free use of the arm below the elbow.

Colborne said in conversation:

It was my right shoulder. Do you not see the difference? I can move this arm quite round, and I can only do so with this one. The head of the bone was carried away; you see this shoulder is round and perfect and this one is falling away.

I was away from the army a year and six months, which was a great mortification to me. I dare say I should have got some wound somewhere else, but it was a terrible spoke in my wheel.

That he had not been quite forgotten, however, during his absence from the seat of war is shown by the following communication from Lord Wellington, received at this time:

> Freneda
> 15th March, 1813
> H.R.H. the Prince Regent of Portugal has been pleased to appoint you a Knight of the Order of the Tower and the Sword.

But the gratification which such news brought was quickly drowned in a deeper joy.

Since October, 1811, Colborne had been engaged to Miss Elizabeth Yonge, of Puslinch. On the 25th March, 1813, his half-sister, Alethea Bargus, had been married in London by her guardian, Dr. Goddard, to Miss Yonge's brother, the Reverend John Yonge; and now that he had recovered from his wound Colborne saw the fulfilment of his own hopes. From his wife's diary we learn that on 2nd June he joined her at Flaxley, near Gloucester, the residence of her connection, Mr. Crawley, and on the 21st, the day of the battle of Vittoria, they were there married. They stayed in London till 6th July, went to Puslinch on the 8th, and to Antony on the 10th, and parted on the 12th. 'Colonel Colborne,' writes his wife on that day, 'sailed in the *Sparrowhawk* for St. Andero. I returned to Puslinch.'

CHAPTER 13

Campaign of 1813

In July, 1813, I went out again. I embarked quietly at Plymouth in a small corvette by permission of the admiral, and we ran up the Bay of Biscay in three days. The siege of San Sebastian was going on, but I knew nothing of it, and did not know where the army was. I thought I should have to go to Corunna, and from there make a long inland journey. However, as we got near the coast of Spain the captain thought he perceived guns and firing around San Sebastian, and when we got glasses to assist our sight he proved to have been correct. So I was landed close at hand and walked a mile and a half to General Graham's tent. Then I called on Lord Wellington. He said he was glad to see me again, but I looked rather thin and pale. Then I went to dine with Sir George Murray, who said, 'Well, you had better join your regiment directly; you have been given the position on that hill to protect the army. Soult has been collecting his army, and he could attack us from there.' I went up to a very high point to see the first attack on San Sebastian (25th July). So in about four days from leaving England I found myself in active service again.

At the moment when Colborne resumed the command of the 52nd (20th July) the Light Division was commanded by Baron Alten, and its 2nd Brigade, consisting of the 52nd, the 2nd Battalion 95th Rifles and a regiment of Portuguese Caçadores, by Major-General

Skerrett. The regiment was posted at Lesaca. The assault made on San Sebastian on 25th July having been unsuccessful, the siege was still prosecuted, as was that of Pamplona simultaneously.

Meanwhile Soult, at the head of the French army, made an effort to penetrate the pass of Roncesvalles, relieve Pamplona, and if he succeeded, San Sebastian also. Wellington was obliged to send a great part of his army to cover Pamplona and temporarily suspend the siege of San Sebastian, and the Light Division was kept moving between the two places. When Soult had been repulsed at the battles of the Pyrenees, 27th and 28th July, the Light Division was pushed forward. Soult fell back behind the line of the Bidassoa and the Light Division countermarched, and arriving on 1st August at Sumbilla, reoccupied Vera on the 2nd. The siege of San Sebastian was now vigorously resumed. Colborne said:

One morning during the siege of San Sebastian, Colonel Upton, of the Guards, was waiting with some friends in his tent for breakfast, when his servant rushed in, exclaiming, 'The French are marching on the Guards!'

'And a pretty good thrashing they'll get; bring breakfast,' Upton replied, and coolly ate his breakfast before he would go to his regiment.

On the 9th San Sebastian surrendered, and Pamplona followed on 29th October.

In the early morning of 1st September the French, owing to Skerrett's want of precaution, crossed the bridge of Vera in spite of the valiant resistance offered by Captain Cadoux, 95th, and his company of Riflemen. Colborne said:

I remember one night I was sitting on a camp stool with another officer, Mein, who was asleep. I was nodding myself when we heard the French huzza. It was about three o'clock in the morning, and they had just succeeded, to my great mortification, in crossing the bridge owing to the Rifles being surprised. Mein started up with a leap of several yards, drew his sword, and rushed off half awake, though we had heard nothing but the huzza. We were obliged to send three or four men after him, and it was five minutes before he came back.

Major-General Skerrett having had to go home on sick leave, Colonel Colborne now came into temporary command of the 2nd Brigade of the Light Division, to whose officers the substitution of Colborne for Skerrett gave the greatest satisfaction. Sir Harry Smith writes in his *Autobiography*:

> Our brigade was now commanded by Colonel Colborne, in whom we all had the most implicit confidence. I looked up to him as a man whose regard I hoped to deserve, and by whose knowledge and experience I desired to profit.[1] He had more knowledge of ground, better understood the posting of picquets, consequently required fewer men on duty (he always strengthened every post by throwing obstacles trees, stones, carts, &c. on the road, to prevent a rush at night), knew better what the enemy were going to do, and more quickly anticipated his design than any officer; with that coolness and animation under fire, no matter how hot, which marks a good huntsman when he finds his fox in his best country.
>
> The French were now erecting works upon a position by nature strong as one could well devise for the purpose of defending the Pass of Vera, and every day Colonel Colborne and I took rides to look at them, with the pleasant reflection that, the stronger the works were, the greater the difficulty we should have in turning them out an achievement we well knew in store for us.

---

1. In a letter written from the Cape on 2nd March, 1832, Harry Smith called him 'the master in the art of outposts, under whom I learned more in six months than in all the rest of my shooting put together.'

The attack on the fortified position of Vera took place on 7th October. On the evening before Colborne had performed a very adventurous feat in order to examine the dispositions of the French. It was necessary to send a letter to the French posts, and he offered to carry it himself.

The sentry at the first post challenged me, but I disregarded this and rode some way down the lines, holding out with the letter my handkerchief as a flag of truce, and I had time to look round well and ascertain all I wanted before a French officer appeared. Having delivered my message, as you may imagine, I set spurs to my horse and soon reached our lines, where all the 52nd officers were eagerly awaiting the result of my adventure. Before I quitted the French lines I heard the officer upbraiding the sentry for his stupidity in allowing an English officer to pass.

Colborne gives the following account of the great attack on Vera:

At Vera there were two fortresses on an immensely steep hill, one above the other. Below the lower one the hill divided into three tongues. I arranged that the Rifles and Caçadores should go first up the hills on the right and left as skirmishers, and the 52nd, which was to attack, up the hill in the centre. I managed the attack in this manner. I did not allow the picquets to be relieved in the usual manner at daybreak, but ordered them to march on and the columns to support them, so that they were actually in the town of Vera before the French had any suspicion that an attack was intended.

The Rifles being the first to attack the fort, the French mistook them for Portuguese Caçadores, and rushing out of the redoubt drove them back, so they all came tumbling on the 52nd. The French were excessively astonished when they saw the red-coats behind the Rifles. The adjutant of the 52nd was surprised to find we were so near the fort.

'Why, Sir, we are close to the fort.'

'To be sure we are,' I said, 'and now we must charge.' I then led the 52nd on to a most successful charge, to the admiration of Lord Wellington and others who were watching from another hill.

At this moment Sir James Kempt, who was leading the 1st Brigade of the Light Division to a simultaneous attack on the right of the town of Vera, a mile or two off, sent to General Alten to know if the 52nd could not render him some assistance. 'Colonel Colborne give him some assistance!' he said. 'If he could see the hill Colborne's Brigade is on, he'd see that Colborne has quite enough to do himself.'

The French, thrown into confusion by this tremendous charge, retreated to the next fort. Colonel —— now came up with the reserve and said rather sneeringly, 'They're all talking of your charge, as they call it.'

'Why, you can't have seen it,' said I. '*Call it* a charge, indeed. It was a most wonderful charge.'

By a second charge as fine as the first the French were driven from the second fort in great confusion.

After this, leaving my column, I rode on alone with the present Sir Harry Smith into France. I was separated from the column a great distance, when to my dismay I saw a body of 400 French passing along a ravine below me. The only way was to put a good face on the matter. So I went up to them, desiring them to surrender. The officer, thinking, of course, the column was behind me, surrendered his sword, saying theatrically, '*Je vous rends cette épée qui a bien fait son devoir!*' The 400 followed his example. In inward trepidation I despatched Harry Smith to bring up the column as quick as possible while I kept the French officer in play, and it fortunately arrived before the French had discovered their error. I desired my servant MacCurrie[2] to take the officers' swords to the camp.

---

2. According to Sir Harry Smith's account, corroborated by Moorsom, the following story should be told of Lieutenant Cargill, 52nd.

On his way he met Lord Wellington, 'Where did you get all those swords from?' said he to MacCurrie.

'Colonel Colborne has just taken them from 400 prisoners he made as we were going into France.'

'And how do you know you were so near France?'

'Because I saw all the men were coming back with pigs they had caught,' he answered, not considering the scrape he would have got me in had it been true, for allowing my men to plunder.[3] However, it was quite false; not one of the men had even seen a pig.

In the meantime, Sir Lowry Cole, who was behind with his division in reserve, sent to ask how much further I intended to go, 'for I don't intend to go any further.'

'Oh, I have gone quite far enough,' said I.

That evening I overheard one of the 52nd soldiers propose a toast, 'The colonel's health, and d—n the man who gets a shot into him.'

> Sir Harry Smith tells in greater detail the story of Colborne's capture of the 400 French in the ravine, and concludes, 'I never witnessed such presence of mind as Colborne evinced on this occasion.'[4]
>
> He also tells of a kind effort made by Colborne to procure him his majority after the action, and the mortification Colborne felt when his request was first granted and then found impracticable, considering the claims of senior officers.
>
> Colborne's conduct in connection with the capture of the heights of Vera was thus mentioned by Lord Wellington:

---

3. Colborne used to tell another story which turns on Wellington's prohibition of plundering. 'I remember once in Spain, just after an order against plundering had been given out, Lord Wellington met a soldier with a quantity of honey which he had just taken; so he called out 'Hello, where did you get that, Sir?' The fellow, not knowing at all who he was, answered 'Oh, just over there; there are plenty more hives,' thinking he wanted to get some himself.'

4. *Autobiography of Sir H. Smith.*

Colonel Colborne, of the 52nd Regiment, who commanded Major-General Skerrett's Brigade in the absence of the major-general on account of his health, attacked the enemy's right in a camp which they had strongly entrenched. The 52nd Regiment, under the command of Major Mayne (Mein), charged in a most gallant style and carried the entrenchment with the bayonet. The 1st and 3rd Caçadores and the 2nd Battalion 95th Regiment, as well as the 52nd Regiment, distinguished themselves in this attack. Major-General Kempt's Brigade attacked by the Puerto, where the opposition was not so severe; and Major-General Charles Alten has reported his sense of the judgment displayed, both by the major-general and by Colonel Colborne, in these attacks.[5]

The Light Division in a few days was pushed forward to a position facing the hill called La Petite Rhune. The enemy's position extended from St. Jean de Luz on his right to Nivelle on his left, his centre La Petite Rhune and the heights beyond it. Sir Harry Smith writes:

> The enemy, not considering this ground strong enough, turned to it with a vigour I have rarely witnessed to fortify it by every means art could devise. Every day before the position was attacked, Colonel Colborne and I went to look at their progress. Lord Wellington himself would come to our outpost and continue walking there a long time. One day he stayed unusually long, he turns to Colborne, 'These fellows think themselves invulnerable, but I will beat them out, and with great ease.'
>
> 'That we shall beat them,' says Colborne, 'when your lordship attacks, I have doubt, but for the ease ———,'

---

5. *Despatches*, XI.

'Ah, Colborne, with your local knowledge only, you are perfectly right. It appears difficult, but the enemy have not men to man the works and lines they occupy.' (Lord Wellington then composed and dictated to Sir George Murray the plan of attack for the whole army.) 'Now, Alten, if during the night previous to the attack the Light Division could be formed on this very ground so as to rush at La Petite Rhune just as day dawned, it would be of vast importance and save great loss, and by thus precipitating yourselves on the right of the works of La Petite Rhune you would certainly carry them.' This Petite Rhune was well occupied both by men and works, and a tough affair was in prospect.

General Alten says, 'I "dink" I can, my lord.'

Kempt says, 'My brigade has a road. There can be no difficulty, my lord.'

Colborne says, 'For me there is no road, but Smith and I both know every bush and every stone. We have studied what we have daily expected, and in the darkest night we can lead the brigade to this very spot. Depend on me, my lord.'

As we started for our position before the great, the important day (Battle of Nivelle, 10th November), the night was very dark. We had no road and positively nothing to guide us but knowing the bushes and stones over a mountain ridge. Colborne stayed near the brigade and sent me on from spot to spot, which we both knew, when he would come up to me and satisfy himself that I was right. I then went on again. In this manner we crept up to our advanced picquet within a hundred and fifty yards of the enemy. We afterwards found Kempt's brigade close to our right, equally successfully posted.

Colborne said himself:

By taking my brigade the way I did, I saved them an immense five hours' march. Sir J. Kempt's brigade, who had toiled round by the regular road, were thoroughly fatigued and worn out. However, I had a desperate fright on the road. An aide-de-camp came suddenly galloping up in the darkness, 'Captain So-and-so is leading his company right into the French line.'

It was the case. This officer had unfortunately mistaken the way the troops in front were marching, and in a few minutes more would have gone straight into the French position. It had been a very hazardous proceeding on my part, and its success depended on the utmost caution my short way lay so near the French camp. I galloped immediately in great alarm to the straying captain and succeeded in putting him on the right track.

Harry Smith tells of another alarming incident which occurred as they were resting before the attack.

About an hour before daylight, by some accident, a soldier's musket went off. It was a most anxious moment, for we thought the enemy had discovered us, and if they had not, such shots might be repeated, and they would; but most fortunately all was still. I never saw Colborne so excited as he was for the moment.

At daybreak the signal was given to attack. Colborne had arranged that in his column the attack should be made by the 52nd, supported by the Caçadores. Colonel Snodgrass, who commanded the latter regiment, came to him and said, 'I wish, Sir, you would alter your dispositions, for if the 52nd were to give way, I think the Caçadores will give way, too; but if they lead the attack, with the 52nd behind, it will be of no consequence if they give way or not.'

'Oh, no,' said Colborne, 'it is too late to alter my arrangements, and make yourself quite easy; the 52nd will not give way.'

At the appointed moment the 52nd hastened straight down the slope in its front, but as soon as it had crossed the rocky watercourse at the bottom brought up its right shoulders and pushed rapidly on in a line nearly parallel to the watercourse on its left and to the French works about 500 yards off on its right. The enemy either, in the darkness of the mountain shadows, did not see, or perceiving, had not the presence of mind to check this bold flank movement of Colonel Colborne's own devising. The 52nd gained the line of the extreme flank of the French works, brought up its left shoulders, scrambled up the rocky slope and stood in rear of the enemy's right on the plateau of the Petite Rhune.[6]

At this point a scene of extraordinary magnificence burst upon the view. The sun was just springing in full glory above the horizon and lighting up the boundless plains of the south of France. The Pyrenees stretched away to the eastward in an abrupt series of enormous sloping walls, and the long lines of white wreathing smoke near their bases showed the simultaneous advance of the whole allied army. In the foreground to the right the 1st Brigade of the Light Division had done its work, and was rapidly pouring over the entrenchments. The French defenders of the last of their Pyrenean summits were rushing into the huge round punchbowl which is bounded by the eastern and western spurs of La Petite Rhune. After some attempt at pursuit the 52nd collected on the right rear of the now abandoned French redoubts. The line of the French main position, commencing upon a comparatively low range

---

6. Sir Harry Smith writes: As soon as the 2nd Battalion 95th, succeeded in putting back the enemy, Colonel Colborne, at the head of the 52nd, with an eye like a hawk's, saw the moment had arrived, and he gave the word 'Forward.' One rush put us in possession of the redoubt . . . on the edge of the ravine.' *Autobiography.*

of hills, was in front of the regiment, with an intervening rocky watercourse, which it would seem was deemed impassable by our enemies. The 52nd moved by threes to the small open ravine and wood in their front under a smart fire of artillery from the ridge which was next to be assailed. In front of this wood the watercourse was crossed by a small and narrow stone bridge, on the opposite side of which was a road running close and parallel to the watercourse with a sheltered bank towards the enemy. The officers and men of the 52nd crept by twos and threes to the edge of the wood and then dashing over a hundred yards of open ground passed the bridge and formed behind the bank, which was not more than eighty yards from the enemy's entrenchments. The signal was then given, the rough line sprang up the bank, and the enemy gave way with so much precipitation as to abandon, almost without firing a shot, the works on the right of the advanced ridge, no doubt under the apprehension that their retreat would be cut off if they remained to defend them.[7]

So far, two great successes had been obtained with little loss. But the 52nd had worse to undergo. On the most prominent summit of the ridge, 800 yards further (the enemy's main position), a star-redoubt still held out unsupported.

Major Charles Beckwith, Acting-Quartermaster-General of the Light Division, now rode up to Colonel Colborne with what was taken by him to be an order to attack this last fort with the 52nd. It was afterwards stated that no such order had been issued. Colonel Colborne accepted the task as practicable, believing that, as the French seemed to be retiring, the holders of the redoubt would not defend it. On the contrary, they stood firm. The 52nd

---

7. Colonel Gawler, quoted by Moorsom.

suffered so fearfully as they moved up the slopes to attack, that they recoiled and took shelter in a little ravine. After letting them take breath for a while Colonel Colborne could not refrain from a second attempt. It was once more a failure. But again Colborne's cool audacity saved the situation. Colborne said:

There was I, on the top of this hill heading the 52nd, and exposed to a most murderous fire, the balls and shells falling like hailstones. I saw Harry Smith fall with his horse on him, and thought he was killed. My aide-de-camp, Captain Fane, dismounted and entreated me to do the same. 'Pray get off, Sir, pray get off.'

I was never in such peril in my whole life, but thinking the boldest plan was the best, I waved my handkerchief and called out loudly to the French leader on the other side of the wall, 'What nonsense this is, attempting to hold out! You see you are surrounded on every side. There are the Spaniards on the left; you had better surrender at once!' (Frenchmen had a horror of falling into the hands of Spaniards.)

The French officer thought I was addressing his men and inciting them to surrender, which would have been very improper, and I ought not to have spoken so loud, but the danger was imminent and the moment critical that the French should surrender was our only chance of escape. The French officer exclaimed, '*Vous parlez à mes hommes, je prévois un désastre,*' meaning that I and my regiment would be destroyed. However, I replied, 'That is all nonsense; you must surrender.'

On this, the Frenchman appeared to hesitate, and finally asked me into the fort to arrange matters. There, with his pen in his hand, he pretended to be thinking of terms, but on my again repeating that it was nonsense, he surrendered at once with his regiment, the 88th.

The 52nd stood formed in a double line and gave the brave Frenchmen the satisfaction of marching out with all the honours of war. Colborne continued:

Next morning the returns from the 52nd were 200 killed and wounded. 'How is that possible?' I said to the adjutant. 'I see here before me the very men returned as wounded.'

However, on examination the numbers turned out to be correct, but a hundred men who had only flesh wounds had refused to go to the rear, and had gone to their duty as usual.

Chapter 14

Into France—1814

The day after the battle of Nivelle the 2nd Brigade encamped near Arbonne, and on the 19th November went into quarters in the village. On the 24th it was moved to the chateau of Casteleur, near Arcangues. On the 10th December the enemy drove back the picquets, occupied the range of hills at Casteleur, and made a most desperate attack on the Light Division's post at Arcangues. 'This was nearer a surprise,' writes Sir Harry Smith, 'than anything we had ever experienced.' But Colborne, as usual, was prepared. He gave this account of the manner in which he perceived the coming attack:

As I was standing, in the grey of the morning, by a picquet about a mile or more from the main body, looking at the opposite hill, I thought I saw flashes of fire-arms, and said to Harry Smith, 'Those must be some men discharging their pieces.'

Then, to my surprise, I thought I perceived a large body of French advancing at some distance. We looked through our glasses and soon discovered it was the whole French army in movement. While I was considering what was to be done, Smith impatiently exclaimed, 'Come, something must be done; what are you going to do?' for he was always in a state of uneasiness about any sudden attack, on account of his wife, who followed the army.

I merely replied, 'I must think a little, first,' and in a few minutes gave directions about bringing up the 52nd, &c. As I sat on horseback by the side of a house, reflecting on what dispositions to make, I had my cap shot through.

The officers standing near remarked, 'What a narrow escape!' The French continued these attacks for two days. At last, as I was patrolling in great anxiety, I thought I heard sounds indicating a retreat. I saw a shadow thrown backwards on a wall near a French watch-fire, and I heard a French officer say, '*Retirez-vous à gauche de l'ennemi.*' And after watching carefully for some time, I found, to my delight, that they were really gone.

On the 13th December Soult was repulsed by General Hill at St. Pierre, near Bayonne. With regard to this engagement Colborne remarked:

Wellington committed a great error. Hill's Division was quite isolated. Soult passed the bridge and attacked it with his whole army, yet such was the goodness of the British troops, he was repulsed. Soult said himself afterwards, 'Well, if one division of your troops can stand against seventy or eighty thousand of ours, there's no more to be said; but it is an error.'

Another French officer said to me, 'Were not those troops of ours fine men? Yet your little hump-backed soldiers repulsed them.' Soult's were extremely fine men.

Lord Wellington had ridden up towards the end of the action, and saw it out. Hill, of course, wrote a despatch giving an account of the affair, and sent it to Lord Wellington, expecting to see it published in the *Gazette*. Much to his disappointment, however, Wellington only used it to compile his own despatch, in which he made very little mention of Hill's affair.

When the enemy retired towards Bayonne the 2nd Brigade Light Division returned to its quarters about Casteleur. Here it stayed till the 4th January, 1814. From the 8th January to the 16th February it was in cantonments at Sala. On 25th February, after some days' marching, the Light Division arrived close to Orthes. Colborne said:

On the day before the battle of Orthes, I remember seeing Lord Wellington in a little white cloak, sitting on a stone, writing. Charles Beckwith, who was standing near me, said, 'Do you see that old White Friar sitting there? I wonder how many men he is marking off to be sent into the next world.'

A part of the army was on one side of the river and a part on the other, and I suppose he was writing his orders to them.

The night before the battle Napier and I took up our quarters in a mill, a nice clean place. The miller's wife was a great talker, and made almost as much noise as her mill, and both she and her husband were delighted to have us there, thinking we should protect their house.

> At daybreak on the 27th the Light Division, weakened by the temporary absence of the 43rd and 1st Battalion 95th, crossed the Gave de Pau. The 1st Battalion 95th had been transferred a month before to the 2nd Brigade and the 2nd Battalion to the 1st Brigade, and the 2nd Brigade (52nd Regiment, 1st Battalion 95th and Caçadores) was now commanded by Colonel Barnard. Colborne, who had hitherto commanded it during the illness of Major-General Skerrett, now returned to the command of the 52nd. Sir Harry Smith writes:
>
>> We saw the enemy very strongly posted both as regards the elevation and the nature of the ground, which was intersected by large banks and ditches, while the fences of the fields were most admirably calculated for vigorous defence.
>
> The 3rd, 4th and 7th Divisions having crossed the river on the preceding day, the Light Division now formed up on the left of the army. The 4th and 7th Divisions attacked the enemy's right, the 3rd and 6th attacked the centre of the position, and the 2nd Brigade Light Division was in reserve on a spur of the main ridge of St. Boes. The 1st Brigade Light Division were some miles in the rear near St. Jean de Luz.

The attack on the right did not succeed, and Cole's leading regiments, after partially gaining the village of St. Boes, were again driven back. Neither was the centre making any progress, and a portion of the 3rd Division had been repulsed down the hill when the 2nd Brigade Light Division, which up to this point had been little engaged, was ordered to attack the left flank of the heights occupied by the enemy's right. The 95th remained on the knoll in support, the Portuguese Caçadores had been thrown out to the left and had been driven back, when the 52nd Regiment, under Colborne, rode along in column of threes to the front. Here Colborne must tell his own tale.

Sir James Kempt and I were standing together, he near his brigade, I with the 52nd. General Alten came riding over and said, 'Now, Colborne, you go on and attack,' much to the mortification of Sir James, who had not been employed once during the day.

He exclaimed, 'And I, General? Am not I to go on?' and then aside to me, 'Confound the old fellow! God forgive me!'

Lord Wellington was standing dismounted on a knoll with Lord Fitzroy Somerset. When I rode below him he called out, 'Hello, Colborne, ride on and see if artillery can pass there.' (The marsh was generally impassable.)

I rode on, and galloped back as fast as I could and said, 'Yes, anything can pass.'

'Well then, make haste, take your regiment on and deploy into the plain. I leave it to your disposition.'

So we continued to move in column from the Roman Camp up the road to St. Boes till we arrived at the ridge, where we met Sir Lowry Cole coming back with his division and anxiously looking out for support. He was much excited and said, 'Well, Colborne, what's to be done? Here we are, all coming back as fast as we can.'

I was rather provoked, and said, 'Have patience, and we shall see what's to be done.'

At that moment a cannon-ball fell close to me, and my poor little nag started and reared at a fine rate, being hit all over the body by the stones which had been thrown up.

Then I saw Picton's Division scattering to the left. The adjutant came up and asked, 'What are we to do?'

I said, 'Deploy into the low ground as fast as you can.'

They did it beautifully. When all the rest were in confusion the 52nd marched down as evenly and regularly as if on parade, accelerating their march as they approached the hill occupied by the right of General Foy's Division. The French were keeping up a heavy fire, but fortunately the balls all passed over our heads. I rode to the top of the hill and waved my cap, and though the men were over their knees in the marsh they trotted up in the finest order. As soon as they got to the top of the hill I ordered them to halt and open fire. I remember my major, George Napier, coming up to me about ten minutes later with a face of great concern, and saying, 'Poor March is wounded!'

'Well,' I said, 'I can't help it. Have him carried off.'

We were soon supported by the other divisions and the French were dispersed. Lord Fitzroy Somerset, who came with an order from Lord Wellington that we should not on any account advance further, and remain in line, rode up to me at the top of the hill and said, 'Well, I think we shall do it now.'

The French soon began to retreat, and we moved on to the position which had been occupied by Foy. Lord Wellington and his staff were riding behind and saw it all. He said in his despatch, 'This attack led by the 52nd Regiment dislodged the enemy from the heights and gave us the victory.' He could not help saying that.

> At the time when Colborne was ordered to advance with the 52nd for no other corps of the Light Division was engaged except the 1st Caçadores, which had just previously been repulsed 'the moment,' as Napier says, 'was most dangerous.' Soult, according to the story, had slapped

his thigh, exclaiming, 'At last I have him.' Cole and Picton had alike failed. Colborne was left to give his own orders the words to deploy, to advance, to halt and fire came from him alone. To him, 'with the active assistance of George Napier and Winterbottom,' to him and the 52nd, 'soldiers,' as W. Napier says, 'who had never yet met their match in the field,' the victory of Orthes was mainly due. Colborne's attack carried the ridge, and in his own words:

.... arrested the offensive movement of the French by uniting the operations of the 4th and 3rd Divisions, both of which had been checked or repulsed at the time the 52nd opened fire.

The narrow pass behind St. Boes was opened, and Wellington, seizing the critical moment, thrust the 4th and 7th Divisions, Vivian's cavalry and two battalions of artillery through, and spread a front beyond. The victory was thus secured.[1]

After the battle of Orthes the 52nd was in cantonments at Barcelona from the 9th to the 19th March. On the 20th it attacked the enemy near Tarbes. During the night of the 21st the enemy retired upon Toulouse.

On the morning of the 10th April the Light Division crossed the Garonne by a pontoon bridge near Ausonne and the whole army moved forward to the attack. The Light Division approached Toulouse by the Montauban road and subsequently moved to its left to the support of Lieutenant-General Freyre's Spanish corps, which was destined to attack the heights of La Pugade. The Spaniards, having failed in their attacks, fell back in the greatest disorder, but by a forward movement of the 2nd Brigade, Light Division, under Colonel Barnard, the French were checked in their pursuit and the

---

1. Napier, Bk. XXIV., ch. iii.

communication over the River Ers was preserved. In the course of the afternoon Cole's and Clinton's Divisions attacked the redoubts of La Pugade on the Calvinet side, while the 52nd and 95th advanced on the opposite side. After a very determined resistance the enemy abandoned all his works about 5 p.m., and the allied army formed upon the heights overlooking the town.[2]

Colborne thus commented on the battle of Toulouse:

I remember getting up very early at about 4 in the morning to see the men come over the river on a bridge of boats. It had just before been carried away. There were two French soldiers on the other side, and one rode away and the other stayed to see us.

When the battle began the Spaniards were sent up a hill to attack the French who were at the top. It was a most difficult thing. I should have been sorry to have had to do it with two Light Divisions, and I remember standing at the bottom, looking at them with wonder and trembling, and then seeing them come running down as hard as they could. The French drove every man away. I had a little wound then, a three-cornered piece out of my left arm, but I ran as hard as I could to the 52nd. All the officers, seeing the Spaniards flying, were calling out, 'Stop them! Stop them! Don't let them go!' but I called out, 'Yes, yes, let them go and clear our fronts.'

So they ran on, and our van was left clear.

The next day I was riding near the place when Lord Wellington and his staff passed, and he called out to me, 'Well, Colborne, did you ever see anything like that? Was that like the rout at Oçana?'

So I said, 'Oh, I don't know; they ran to the bridge, I believe.'

'To the bridge, indeed! To the Pyrenees! I dare say they are all back in Spain by this time.'

---

2. Moorsom.

They were not like the Caçadores; they were badly disciplined, and they never ought to have been set to do such a difficult thing. I remember a Frenchman saying to me afterwards, 'I was watching the battle from the roof of a house, and when I saw the Spaniards run I would have given all I was worth to have seen one red-coat on the crest of the hill.' The French people were very anxious then to have the war over.

When the Spaniards came back Lord Wellington said to Pakenham, 'There I am, with nothing between me and the enemy!'

Pakenham said, 'Well, I suppose you'll order up the Light Division now.'

He replied, 'I'll be hanged if I do.'

It was the worst arranged battle that could be, nothing but mistakes.

> Colborne, giving this account at his dinner table, showed the various positions with wineglasses:

There was Toulouse, and this is the hill in front which the French had fortified, and Hill's Division was over there and had nothing to do with it; and Picton's made a false attack there, which turned out a real one, and he lost 1,500 men; and then Marshal Beresford had to come round there and across the river, all down the French lines, with the French firing at him, so that he lost a great many men, to resume the attack on the extreme left which the Spaniards had abandoned. So two isolated attacks were made. It was a most extraordinary battle. I think the Duke almost deserved to have been beaten.

At Toulouse, too, the 52nd and I did great work, but I must not brag of my doings, or I shall be like Sir H—— D——, who told someone here that 'he had been greatly distinguished both in the field and in the Cabinet.' and the person to whom he said so went and told everyone else and they all laughed at him finely.

After the battle was over, at about 6 o'clock in the evening,

I was on the hill with the 52nd, standing on the glacis we had taken. There was a redoubt opposite, and I had no idea there was a man there, I thought they had all evacuated it long before, when suddenly *bang* went a gun just opposite, scattering grape-shot all around us. One of the 52nd officers was standing by me, but fortunately none of us was hurt. I then saw that the redoubt was full of soldiers. That, I think, was the last gun fired in the war. Then the French retired into the town, and next morning marched out of it, and we entered, and soon after heard of Napoleon's abdication and the proclamation of peace.

The great war, thanks to the tenacity of the Duke of Wellington, was brought to a glorious conclusion. What Colborne thought of his great commander is seen in the following words written about 1826:

They who have observed the Duke of Wellington, and are acquainted with the difficulties he encountered in Portugal and Spain; who are persuaded of this fact, that he, with a small army under his immediate control, was the chief cause of detaining in Spain and employing during five years from 100,000 to 200,000 French troops, will pronounce that his reputation, high as it is, has not reached near its proper level. When his resource, firmness, economical management of his troops, the information that guided his operations, his foresight in nicely calculating on the presumption of the French commanders, his splendid combinations . . . . shall be demonstrated, as well as the gigantic genius and strength he displayed in throwing off that dead weight on military operations, the shackles of the *Corps Diplomatique,* Europe will not refuse him that celebrity which is his due, and which political intrigues alone could deprive him of.

On the 22nd April the 52nd went into cantonments at Castel Sarrasin. Sir Harry Smith tells of the obligation he was under at this time to Colonel Colborne, who exerted himself to get him appointed to the expedition going under Major-General Ross to America, and how Colborne rode with him in one day to Toulouse and back to get the matter arranged.

Daylight saw me and dear Colborne full gallop thirty-four miles to breakfast. We were back again at Castel Sarrasin by four in the afternoon, after a little canter of sixty-eight miles, not regarded as any act of prowess, but just a ride. In those days, there were men.

On the 3rd of June the Light Division set out for Bordeaux, where it arrived on the 14th. On the way (11th June) the two regiments of Portuguese Caçadores, which had been associated with it for nearly four years, took their departure for home. Colborne said:

We had a very affecting scene when, after the war was over, we parted company with the Caçadores. The brigade was drawn up in two columns and they marched through. We were really very sorry to part.

On the 4th June Colborne was made brevet-colonel and aide-de-camp to the Prince Regent, receiving at the same time the Peninsular gold cross and three clasps. The 52nd embarked at Pauillac on the 17th June and landed at Plymouth on the 27th. On the same day Colborne joined his wife at Puslinch. From there they paid a visit to Antony, and on the 20th July left Puslinch for London, where, on the 25th, Colonel Colborne received the appointment of military secretary to the Prince of Orange, then commander of the British forces in the Netherlands, and looked upon for the moment as the destined husband of Princess Charlotte of Wales. In this capacity Colborne had the practical direction of the force in the Netherlands until Napoleon's return from Elba.

Colborne proceeded to Brussels on 7th August, unaccompanied by his wife, but returned to Devonshire to fetch her at the end of November. On the 4th December they witnessed the 'gay wedding' of Lord Fitzroy Somerset to Lady Emily Wellesley, and soon after were disturbed by a report that the 52nd was to go to America, in which case, Colborne informed the Prince of Orange, he would accompany his regiment. This prospect was dispelled, however, by the course of events.

On the 2nd January, after the reconstitution of the Order of the Bath, Colonel Colborne became a K.C.B.

In spite of this succession of honours, however, he seems not to have been fully satisfied with the treatment he received. Late in his life, when Mr. Leeke remarked to him, 'I suppose you, Sir, have not passed through your military career without meeting with your mortifications and trials?' he replied, 'No, indeed! In 1814, at the close of the Peninsular War, when they made me a K.C.B., King's aide-de-camp and a full colonel, I was exceedingly annoyed and vexed at their putting two junior lieutenant-colonels over my head in the list of colonels.

On my remonstrating on the unfairness of this proceeding, they made the excuse that these men were thus favoured because they had brought home despatches. If I had not been a poor man if I could have afforded it, I would have thrown my commission in their faces. In after years they offered to place me before these men, but I then refused it.'[3]

Colborne had many stories of the Prince of Orange:

The Prince went out to Portugal as a volunteer, and that was where he first knew the Duke. He had been at Oxford for some time, and he brought out with him two tutors, one of them a Mr. Johnson. The Duke could not bear Mr. Johnson because he once asked the Duke a mathematical question. The Duke was talking about musk rats, saying they left a taste in bottles of wine. So Johnson said, 'But, Sir, I don't

---

3. Leeke, II.

understand how the rats, being so much larger, can possibly get into the necks of the bottles.'

The Duke said, 'Oh, I don't know how they get in, but I know they do it.'

I ventured once at Brussels to give my opinion to the Prince of Orange, and he was rather offended at my differing from him and turned round and said, 'How do you mean, my good sir?' It was the only time I think he ever spoke sharply to me. However, a few days later he came to me and said, 'I should just like to look at that memorandum you made the other day.'

The King of Holland once complained to the Prince of his mixing so much with English officers. He replied, 'Why, you had me brought up among the English and educated like the English, and you can't expect me now to cut all my old friends.'[4]

Another time the King said in the presence of the Court, 'Why, you will never be fit to be the King of your own country. You can't even speak your own language. Do you think, if I were to die tomorrow, you would be fit to succeed me?'

The Prince said, 'Yes, I do.' He came to me in high spirits afterwards, saying, 'I think I have astonished them all.'

He was very fond of the Belgians and of being at Brussels: they are a much more lively people than the Dutch.

Next door to us lived Sir Robert Godden. He was a very good sort of fellow, but had very cold manners. He had an attache named St. George who once came into my room and said indignantly, 'Is it possible I can live with Sir Robert after this?

He called me today and said, 'Lord —— is coming to dine with me, and I must request you will not open your mouth, for we shall be talking of things you know nothing at all about!' I believe St. George did leave him soon after on account of that very speech!

---

[4]. Lady Sarah Napier writes in December, 1814, of the Prince of Orange: 'The eldest son .... will ruin himself in Belgium by his devotion to the English.' *Life and Letters of Lady Sarah Lennox.*

The Duke of Wellington proposed to the King of Holland a line of fortifications along his frontier, but the King said, 'My idea is to have a fortified town at each end, and then if the enemy enter we can soon drive him out, but how am I to defend so many fortifications?'

The Duke said, 'Oh, we'll always send you over 50,000 pensioners.'

'Oh, no. If the enemy were once to get into those fortified towns we should never get them out again; we are better without them.' And I partly agreed with him.

I was very much amused at a conversation that took place in my presence between the Prince of Orange and Mr. Stuart. It was just as Bonaparte had returned from Elba, but before war was declared. At my suggestion, half-a-dozen officers had been sent in different directions to give intelligence of his advance, and a courier had been stopped and searched and his despatches taken from under his saddle. The Prince had the despatches and sent for Mr. Stuart, the British Ambassador, who, when he came, said, 'You should not have taken them; war has not been declared. It might be a very serious thing.'

'Oh, then,' said the Prince, 'we will send them back again directly without opening them.'

'No,' said Mr. Stuart, 'that's no use. You had better open them now you have them, for if you were to swear you had not opened them after having had them half an hour in your possession, no one in Europe would believe you.'

However, they were of no consequence, merely Bonaparte's notifications to the Danish and other courts that he had been once more called to power by the voice of the French nation, &c.

The Prince married a sister of the King of Prussia. It was said that the marriage was arranged by the Duchess of Oldenburg. I was sorry when I heard of it, as I knew there was no chance then of his being all but King of England. I believe he has been very unhappy since he lost Belgium.

When Bonaparte came back from Elba the Duke of Wellington, then ambassador in Paris, was at Vienna. He was then appointed Commander-in-chief (the Prince of Orange not being fit to command an army), and came down from Vienna to Brussels. I had gone back to my regiment just before.

The Government at home had written to me, begging me to prevent the Prince from engaging in any affair of his own before the combined operations. He could not imagine why, but he found out that Clinton and others had been writing about it. I remember that old Sir Hudson Lowe, who was a great fidget, was very much afraid of something of this sort. The Prince had taken the army before Enghien, and Lowe came to me, saying, 'I really think he is trying to bring on a battle before the Duke arrives!'

Chapter 15

Waterloo

The 52nd Regiment had received orders to sail for America, and had twice put to sea and been frustrated by contrary winds when the news of Napoleon's escape from Elba and the renewal of the war caused its hasty recall. The regiment sailed from Plymouth on 27th March, 1815 and reached Brussels on 4th April.

William Leeke, who joined the 52nd as an ensign on 11th May, tells us that he found it at Lessines. A few days later Sir John Colborne, after sending his wife home from Brussels, joined, and took command of the regiment. Having mentioned that Colborne advised him to provide himself with a horse, Leeke adds:

> Sir John Colborne always strongly advocated the importance of infantry officers, when on active service, having riding-horses, and used to say that if, from insufficiency of income they found it difficult to manage this, still they should stint themselves in wine and in everything else in order to keep a horse, if possible. As mounted officers they were more useful under very many circumstances; they were less tired at the end of a day's march and more ready for any duty which might be required of them; they could be more effective in bringing up stragglers on a long and weary march; some of them might be usefully employed when extra staff-

officers were required. I think on the long march of upwards of 50 miles from Quevres-au-camp to Waterloo all but two of the officers of the 52nd were mounted.[1]

The 52nd now formed part of Adam's Brigade of Clinton's Division. This division was cantoned in June about Quevres-au-camp. It must have been late on the 15th June when, as Colborne told the tale:

.... orders suddenly came for us to move in consequence of Napoleon's advance. Night was coming on, and I observed, 'I'll undertake to say, from my experience, that if you march tonight, considering the circumstances—a strange road, darkness, the expectation of coming in contact with the enemy—you won't go two miles.' And so it turned out. Our division did not march till morning, and before we had gone three miles we came up with stragglers and regiments halted, and passed several divisions in great confusion.

The 52nd halted at midnight near Braine-le-Comte in torrents of rain. At 2 a.m. on the 17th the regiment again fell in and reached Nivelles about 7. After remaining there about four hours it moved off slowly, in company with other troops, towards Waterloo, the pace being due to the weariness produced by the previous marching and the fact that, by Colborne's order, each man carried 120 rounds of ball cartridge, 60 rounds of it in the knapsack; a precaution of which the wisdom was seen in the battle. Leeke writes:

> About midway between Nivelles and Hougomont the 52nd halted for rather more than two hours. I heard Sir John Colborne asking if any of the officers could lend him the cape of a boat cloak as he wished to lie down for a couple of hours and get some sleep. I had a very large boat cloak with a cape and hood to it. I unhooked the cape and hood and

---
1. *Lord Seaton's Regiment at Waterloo*, I.

handed them to him. He wore them over his uniform during the whole of the Battle of Waterloo.[2]

At about half past seven p.m. Adam's Brigade, consisting of the 52nd and 71st regiments, the 2nd Battalion and part of the 3rd Battalion 95th Regiment, was posted on the high ground immediately to the eastward of Merbe Braine, its particular place in the position in which the Duke of Wellington intended to fight next day. Here it passed the night. Colborne writes of this night:

I recollect after the long march I was so tired that I threw myself on the ground in my cloak and was sound asleep almost directly. I just heard someone say, 'Let him sleep! Let him sleep!' I suppose they had been going to wake me about some trifle or other.

But according to a story told by Lord Albemarle, Colborne did not spend the whole night thus in the open. Lord Albemarle tells how he himself (then Ensign Keppel), in the pouring rain of the night of the 17th, wearied out with marching, threw himself on the bare hillside and slept soundly till 2 o'clock, when his servant woke him and led him to a cottage in the hamlet of Merbe Braine.

> Here fragments of chairs, tables, window-frames and doors were heaped into the chimney-place. Around the fire so made were three men seated on chairs and drying their clothes. Not a word was spoken, but room was made for me. I followed their example. At daybreak my fellow-occupants of the hut resumed their uniforms. With the appearance of one of them I was particularly struck a fine, soldier-like man, considerably over six feet in height. This was Colonel Sir John Colborne.[3]

---

2. *Lord Seaton's Regiment at Waterloo*, I.
3. *Fifty Years of My Life (3rd Ed.)*. My attention was kindly drawn to the above story by Field-Marshal Lord Wolseley, who informed me that he had often heard it from Lord Albemarle's lips.

At twenty past eleven on the 18th the ball was opened. The 52nd were now formed in open column on the ground of the bivouac. In common with the rest of Clinton's Division and the Brunswick contingent, they were at first kept in reserve in second line nearly on the right of the British army. The farm of Hougomont in front of the extreme right of the British position was occupied by part of Byng's Brigade of Guards and some Nassau troops, and the ridge from thence half-way to the Charleroi Road (the centre of the position) by the rest of Cooke's 1st British Division of Guards, *viz.*, Maitland's Brigade and some companies of Byng's Brigade. As to the battlefield, Colborne said afterwards in conversation:

Some days before the battle of Waterloo, the 14th, I think, the Duke of Wellington was on the field, and fixed on that place as the one on which the battle, he thought, could be fought. He was asked if any entrenchments should be cast up. He said, 'No, of course not; that would show them where we mean to fight.' At the time, many were of opinion that we should march into France.

I remember hearing old Picton say just before the battle, 'I never saw a worse position taken up by any army. I have just galloped from left to right.' He went on to talk of the expected *Gazette* in very high spirits. 'Some friends of mine,' he said, 'asked me to write to them, but I said, "Won't the Gazette do for you?"' He was killed a few hours after.

It is convenient to insert here one or two more stories which Colborne told late in life in connection with the battle or with some of its heroes.

Captain Whinyates[4] took great pride in his 2nd Rocket Troop, but just before the battle of Waterloo the Duke thought it would be more advantageous to do away with it

---

4. Colonel Whinyates tells me that the Duke eventually let the Troop take 800 rockets into action with six 6-pr. guns, and the rockets were used with good effect.

and use the horses for guns. Sir George Wood told me that he remonstrated with the Duke, and said, 'It will break the young man's heart, Sir, if you do that.'

The Duke answered pettishly, 'Confound his heart.' However, a fortnight after he said to Sir G. Wood, 'Well, how is the young man's heart?'

'He bears it remarkably well,' answered Sir G. Wood.

'Then tell him,' said the Duke, 'that it shall not be the worse for him.'

Lord Anglesey was a capital officer. I have had several opportunities of admiring his sagacity and coolness. I remember once before a battle his coming down with the greatest coolness, twisting his moustache, and saying, 'The enemy appear small, but I think there are more behind.' And another time, 'Our lads are ready for the charge, but I think they had better march forward first,' all with the greatest *sang-froid* imaginable. There could be no comparison between him and Murat, because Murat had always far more troops under his command.

Old Alava was highly amused once at Brussels at hearing a discussion between Lord Anglesey and Vivian about their dress. Vivian came to consult his master about what dress he should wear at a levee, and they were talking about it just like ladies. 'Oh, we must put on our yellow boots and pelisses.'

Old Alava came away laughing, 'Well, I never should have supposed that those two fellows had anything in their heads.'

I recollect poor Sir John Moore getting into a scrape once for saying, when asked if the hussars were to wear their pelisses, 'Oh, yes, and their muffs, too.'

> The concluding hours of the battle of Waterloo were the most glorious in Colborne's life. All that he had learnt hitherto, his quickness of eye, his rapidity of judgment, his instant resource, his daring acceptance of responsibility, now contributed their part to defeat Napoleon's last mighty effort, and wrest, for England and her allies, the

hard-fought victory. We may leave for a moment any discussion of the part played in the last scene of Waterloo by other troops. If all that they claim be conceded to them, Colborne's glory is hardly the less.

We will therefore give an account of the part played by Colborne in the battle, based on accounts furnished by himself,[5] and by Captain W. C. Yonge, of the 52nd,[6] and by Mr. Leeke, of the 52nd,[7] who were both connected with him by marriage.

The 52nd moved from its original position near Merbe Braine soon after 3 o'clock, or four hours after the action commenced, and advanced with the other regiments of the brigade to the right centre of the front line. Here the brigade formed squares, taking the place of the Brunswick Light Infantry Battalions, which, in close columns, repeatedly charged by cavalry and pierced through by showers of cannon shot, had suffered severely.

At the moment of the arrival of the brigade nothing could be more disastrous than the appearance of this part of the position, the ground so thickly strewed with these poor mangled Brunswickers and the long line of British guns, as far as the eye could reach, every one of them silenced, overpowered by the number and greater weight of metal of the French artillery, the gun carriages, many of them, cut to pieces by the shot, and the gunners either killed or driven to seek the shelter of the squares from the cavalry, who careered among them unmolested. Between the great attacks the fight still smouldered about the wood and orchard of Hougomont, and, apparently for the support of the troops engaged there, after a halt of about half an hour on the summit of the ridge, the brigade, advancing down the slope of the hill, took post in the plain to the left of the enclosures, the 71st in

---

5. See Appendix 2.
6. *Memoir of Lord Section's Services*, privately printed, 1853.
7. *Lord Seaton's Regiment at Waterloo*, 1866.

battalion square next the wood, the 52nd in squares of wings to their left, and the 95th in echelon further to the left and rear.

Here the brigade remained for an hour or two. Two of the enemy's guns were on a high bank or ridge in front of the 52nd at about 200 yards' distance, though only to be seen by the mounted officers, and these guns and a howitzer fired constantly on the squares. The right and front faces of the 52nd meanwhile opened a fire obliquely on some French Cuirassiers who were making a movement towards the rear of Hougomont, towards the 71st, behind which regiment the remainder of Clinton's Division was posted. These Cuirassiers continually menaced the 52nd. Leeke says that when they attempted to charge it came as a relief, because at those times the French cannonading stopped.

While the regiment was in squares and being cannonaded an incident occurred which we can give in Colborne's own words:

A shell came close to a corner of a column of the 52nd, followed by a ball which passed exactly over the whole column, who instantly bobbed their heads.[8] In the excitement of the moment, more to encourage the men than anything else, I called out, 'For shame! For shame! That must be the 2nd Battalion, I am sure.' (They were recruits.) In an instant every man's head went as straight as an arrow.[9] But a report got about that I had addressed myself particularly to a young man named Scott, an officer who had just joined; and at Paris I was

---

8. Capt. Yonge, in hearing the story, interpolated at this point, 'Perhaps you did not see the cause of the men's ducking their heads. A sergeant had a ball pass between his legs, cutting a piece out of each of them, and he cried out pretty loud. That had an effect on some who had never been in action before.'
9. One who had heard Lord Seaton tell the story gives the conclusion thus: 'Then ———' he would say and the narration was completed by the drawing up of his noble head into its grandest military bearing. *Christian Remembrancer*, October, 1867.

asked the question by some officers. I assured them there was no foundation for the report. I had observed young Scott behaving particularly well and charging up the hill, seemingly in remarkably good spirits. I said, indeed, that I was sorry I had made the remark at all. This young Scott afterwards left the army and went to Cambridge, where he wrote a very pretty prize poem entitled *The Battle of Waterloo*.

However, my exhortation to the men had its effect. Soon afterwards Charles Beckwith came riding over to me and said, 'Well, I hope now you *are* satisfied.' There was a galling fire pouring down on us and the other regiments were rather quaking and the 52nd were standing as firm as possible. Beckwith said, 'What do you think I've just heard Lord Uxbridge say? "I've charged at the head of every cavalry regiment, and they all want spurs."' Beckwith was in the Quartermaster-General's department. On his way back, poor fellow, he lost his leg by a cannon-ball about three-quarters of an hour, I suppose, before the battle was over.

The Duke of Wellington now sent orders to Sir John Colborne by Colonel Hervey to withdraw the regiment up the hill. Colborne desired Colonel Hervey to tell the Duke, if the order had been given from the vicinity of the enemy's guns, that the 52nd was protected by the ground in front. Colonel Hervey promised to convey this message.

However, half an hour later, seeing the Nassau Regiment running in disorder out of the wood of Hougomont, and supposing that Hougomont would be abandoned and the flank of the 52nd exposed, Colborne began to retire the regiment through Colonel Gold's guns to the cross-road on the ridge. The 71st fell back at the same time.

As the regiment was retiring, under a murderous cannonade, with Colborne riding in its rear, a colonel of the French Cuirassiers galloped out of the French ranks, shouting repeatedly, *'Vive le Roi!'* and riding up to Sir John, said, *'Ce coquin Napoleon est là avec les Gardes. Voilà l'attaque qui se fait.'*

Colborne looked through his glass at the spot indicated by the officer and, it is said, saw Napoleon for the only time in his life. He was in his greatcoat, with his hands behind his back, walking backwards and forwards in front of the position while dense French columns were in full march on the plateau of La Haye Sainte, near the farm.

Meanwhile the 52nd had been halted on the summit of the hill. Colonel Gold's guns in front of them on the cross-road were silent; there was scarcely any firing except in the rear of La Haye Sainte and on our left centre.

Sir John Colborne's anxious attention was given to a column rapidly advancing, in agreement with the warning of the French colonel, to a point somewhat to the left of the 52nd. He could see no preparations to resist the attack and was alarmed lest the British line should be pierced. The only remedy appeared to be to attack the column in the flank.

Accordingly without any orders from his superior officer he took upon himself the bold measure of advancing the 52nd and wheeling its whole line on its left as a pivot, as if it had been a single company, so as to bring it nearly at right angles to its previous formation and facing directly on the line of march of the attacking columns. Leeke says:

> As we passed over .... the crest, we plainly saw about 300 or 400 yards from us in the direction of La Belle Alliance. . . . two long columns . . . . of about equal length advancing . . . . in the direction of Maitland's Brigade of Guards, stationed on our left. The whole number . . . . appeared to us to amount to about 10,000 men.[10] There was a

---

10. Colborne puts the number at 6,000 or 7,000.

small interval of apparently not more than twenty paces between the first and second column; from the left centre of our line we did not at any time see through this interval.[11]

The 52nd having been thus placed in two lines nearly parallel with the moving columns of the Imperial Guard, Colborne ordered a strong company to skirmish in front. At this moment Sir Frederick Adam, commanding the brigade, rode up and inquired what Colborne intended to do. He replied, 'To make that column feel our fire.' Adam approved, ordered Colborne to move on, and rode off to the 71st to order that regiment to follow. The Duke at the same moment had sent Colonel Percy to order the 52nd to advance, but his order had been anticipated by Colborne.

The company of skirmishers having been ordered to advance without any support except from the battalion and to fire into the French column at any distance, the 52nd formed in two lines of half companies after giving three cheers, followed, passing along the front of Maitland's Brigade of Guards, who were stationary and not firing. Four companies of the 2nd Battalion 95th were on the left of the 52nd, the 71st and the rest of the division a little behind. As soon as the French column felt the fire of the skirmishing party a considerable part of it halted, and, facing to their left towards the 52nd, opened a very sharp fire on the skirmishers and on the battalion.

The 52nd advanced till they found themselves pro-

---

11. Colborne used to say, however, 'We could see daylight between them.' According to the important memorandum by General Petit in the Morrison Collection, London, the main attack was made by the following troops of the Old Guard, in squares of battalions in Echelon, the right battalion leading 1st Battalion 3rd Grenadiers, 4th Grenadiers, 4th Chasseurs, 1st Battalion 3rd Chasseurs, 2nd Battalion 3rd Chasseurs (total about 3,675 men). He says that the 2nd Battalions 2nd Grenadiers and 2nd Chasseurs (total about 1,250 men) were despatched after the main column, but apparently not as part of the same attack.

tected by the hill from the fire of the Imperial Guard. The two right-hand companies having been thrown into some disorder, Colborne called a halt to rectify the line. He then ordered the bugles to sound the advance and the whole line charged.

The Imperial Guard, without waiting for the charge, broke, and rushing in confusion obliquely to the rear, involved in their disorder the other troops in *echelon*[12] to their right, suffering immense loss from the running fire of the 52nd at point-blank distance. The 71st, too, opened fire on the retreating multitude, which to these regiments standing on the higher ground showed, as it crowded the valley towards La Haye Sainte without a vestige of ranks remaining, like the vast wreck of a great army. Never was disorganisation more sudden or complete.

Wellington, seeing it, ordered the general advance of the whole line, which, with the arrival of the Prussians, effected the victory. But we return to the story of Adam's Brigade.

The two regiments and the four companies of the 95th, bringing up their left shoulders still in line, followed the routed Guard at double-quick.

Suddenly a body of British cavalry, the 23rd Light Dragoons, was seen approaching the left company of the 52nd at full gallop. They were at first mistaken for French and fired upon, but being recognized, they were allowed to pass through. Colborne's horse was wounded and the mistake led to a brief halt, during which the Duke of Wellington came up and said, 'Go on, go on!'[13]

---

12. So Captain Yonge, meaning 'in echelon to their right and rear.' But according to Mr. Ropes the front column was to the right.
13. I follow Siborne and Leeke in putting this incursion of the 23rd Dragoons after the rout of the French column. Colborne, who is followed by Yonge, seems sometimes to put it before: apparently not considering that any rout of the complete character described by Yonge took place till the last body of French were dispersed.

After becoming disengaged from the cavalry the 52nd found that some guns on the right towards La Belle Alliance were firing grape into the front of the regiment and making some gaps in the line. Sir John Colborne was on foot. Both he and Colonel Rowan had had their horses shot, and though they had jumped on the horses of an abandoned French gun and called out to be 'cut out,' they had had, after all, to dismount and follow the regiment in its rapid advance unmounted. Seeing the effect of the guns, Colborne shouted, 'Where are those guns? They are destroying the regiment.'

Lieutenant Gawler told him their position and was directed to take the right section and drive them in. He did so, afterwards halting for the regiment, which had now brought its left shoulder rather more forward, to come up.

Colborne and Colonel Rowan soon found plenty of horses with empty saddles and were once more mounted.

Near the Charleroi road three squares of the Guard[14] remained formed and fired on the 52nd and 71st, but as soon as these regiments began to ascend the hill the squares ceased firing, faced to the rear as if by word of command, and were soon out of sight—to which movement some cannon shot passing from the rear over the heads of the two regiments, and giving them the first intimation of the approach of the Prussians, was doubtless, as it is said, an additional inducement.

At 500 or 600 yards beyond La Haye Sainte the 52nd came out on the Charleroi road, having in their rapid advance left behind a confused mass of guns, tumbrels and several hundreds of the enemy who became prisoners.

Sir John ordered the 52nd to 'pass the road,' and having passed to form line and wheel to the right. The 52nd then moved on in line, keeping their right on the road, and pass-

---

14. According to Houssaye, these consisted of the 2nd Battalions of the 1st Chasseurs, 2nd Grenadiers and 2nd Chasseurs. Petit seems to put only two battalions here, the 2nd Battalions of the 1st Chasseurs and 3rd Grenadiers.

ing La Belle Alliance, were joined by skirmishers belonging to Bülow's corps of Prussians, which shortly after that came obliquely from the left. No part of Sir H. Clinton's Division but the 52nd crossed the Charleroi road, the rest having struck to the right towards Rossomme. At nightfall the 52nd halted and were shortly afterwards passed by Bülow's Corps in column, going in pursuit of the routed army.

Colborne's first care next morning was to send back a strong party of the 52nd to remove the wounded of the regiment, an attention which was not bestowed on those of the army generally, a large portion of them remaining on the field the second day after the battle.

Captain Yonge thus comments on the story which has been told:

> The action which has been related is for several reasons worthy of particular notice. First the wheeling of a battalion in line, though under such circumstances the only practicable mode of changing front, was altogether unprecedented; just one of those promptings of inspiration that mark the mind of a great general. Executed amid a continual roar of artillery that rendered words of command inaudible, trusting chiefly to the further companies that they would be guided by the touch to their inward flank, it could hardly have been ventured at all but for the previous precaution of the commanding officer, who, when the order was given by the Duke that all the regiments in the centre should form four deep, rather than loosen his files by that formation, had preferred to double his line by placing one wing closed up in rear of the other; another instance to show how the knowledge of details and constant attention to them are essential in order to enable an officer to apply his men to the best purpose. Second. That owing to the skill with which the movement was made, seizing the very acme of time, never, per-

haps, was more signal service done by a body of troops so disproportionate in number to the force attacked; that force being composed of the elite of the enemy's army, the most veteran troops in Europe. A line on the flank of a column exhibits in the highest degree the triumph of skill over numbers. The column has only the alternative of flight or destruction. Third. That this adventurous movement was undertaken, upon his sole responsibility, by the commanding officer of a single battalion, and that from the first onset of the 52nd, that regiment and the 71st proceeded to the close of the day without receiving orders from any general officer, whether of brigade or division, the 71st conforming to the movements of the 52nd. Fourth. That the successful charge and immediate pursuit of the broken column carried Adam's Brigade far ahead of the rest of the army, constituting them, as it were, an advanced guard to the main body of the British army.

And Captain Yonge's insistence on the importance of Colborne's bold movement is echoed by General Sir James Shaw-Kennedy, in spite of his adopting Siborne's theory of the two attacks of the Imperial Guard:

> It is perhaps impossible to point out in history any other instance in which so small a force as that with which Colborne acted at Waterloo had so powerful an influence on the result of a great battle in which the numbers engaged on each side were so large. The discipline of the 52nd Regiment was at all times admirable; and Colborne caused the movements on this occasion to be made with a precision which ensured coolness, gave security against all attack, and rendered both the firing and the advance in line of the battalion of the most formidable character.[15]

---

15. *Notes on the Battle of Waterloo* (1865).

And in a private letter, dated Bath, 15th May, 1864, the same eminent writer speaks still more strongly:

> If you wish to know the two most brilliant events of Lord Seaton's life, you must become fully acquainted with how he conducted the 52nd Regiment at the battle of Orthes, and how he commanded and led the regiment in his most brilliant and successful attack on the French Guards at Waterloo. Having read a good deal of military history, I don't think that I impose upon myself a formidable task when I say that no man can point out to me any instance, either in ancient or modern history, of a single battalion so influencing the result of a great general action as the result of the Battle of Waterloo was influenced by the attack of the 52nd Regiment on the Imperial Guard, of which it defeated first four battalions,[16] and afterwards three other battalions; and Colborne did almost all this from his own impulse and on his own responsibility. Napier was a witness of what was done at Orthes; *I* of what took place at Waterloo.

Colonel Gawler, who took part in the movement, writes:

> The flank attack on the Moyenne Garde was really a most important and hazardous measure, and to the enemy most destructive in its consequences. In itself, abstractedly, it was a more brilliant thing than either the storming of the Pass of Vera or the turning of the crisis at Orthes, for both of which Sir John Colborne and the 52nd Regiment obtained especial credit. I was engaged in all, and speak as an eye-witness.[17]

---

16. The writer follows Siborne, who maintains that the leading column of the Imperial Guard was defeated by Maitland's Guards and that Colborne's movement was directed against a second column consisting of four battalions.
17. Unpublished letter to Captain Siborne, May 15th, 1843.

Colonel Gawler was the means of publishing[18] an interesting French testimony to the effect of Colborne's movement contained in a letter addressed to him by Colonel Brotherton on 2nd August, 1833. Colonel Brotherton states that having met a French officer who had been with the Imperial Guard in the attack he had himself adverted to the singular coincidence of the Imperial Guard encountering our British Guards at such a crisis.

Upon which the French officer observed, without seeming in the least to detract from the merit of the troops which the column had to encounter in its front, who, he said, showed *'très bonne contenance,'* that I was wrong .... in supposing the attack was solely repulsed by the troops opposed to it in front; 'for,' added he, *'nous fûmes principalement repoussés par une attaque de flanc très vive qui nous ecrasa.'*

We may add the testimony of a young Engineer officer, contained in a letter written two days after the battle.

> An attack was made by the Imperial Guards and reserve. For some time the combatants were enveloped in the smoke, and the event of the day was in suspense. The column, however, was taken in flank and broken. Assailed on all sides it became a flight.[19]

Chesney,[20] while giving the Guards a great part of the credit of repulsing the Imperial Guard, continues:

> Enough remains for that famous regiment, already high in the roll of history, whose splendid flank attack and steady pursuit, with the final overthrow of the intact battalions which it met at the foot of the hill, prove that neither Colborne nor his men were over-praised in the glowing pages of the Peninsular War. The Dutch have assigned much of the credit here to Chasse's Division, which oppor-

---

18. *United Service Journal*, 1833.
19. *Letters of an Officer of the Corps of Royal Engineers* (John Sperling), 1872.
20. *Waterloo Lectures*.

tunely reinforced the line about the time of the assault, but the proof is undeniable from the testimony of numerous eye-witnesses, that Colborne, keeping steadily in advance of the rest of the Anglo-allied infantry, defeated the only battalions left unbroken of the Guard.[21]

It was long before the achievement of Adam's Brigade obtained recognition.

The Duke of Wellington's despatch of 19th June said nothing as to the manner in which Napoleon's last attack was defeated. Nothing could be vaguer than its language:

> About seven in the evening ... the enemy made a desperate effort with cavalry and infantry, supported by the fire of artillery, to force our left centre, near the farm of La Haye Sainte, which, after a severe contest, was defeated; and having observed that the troops retired from this attack in great confusion ... I ... advanced the whole line of infantry, supported by the cavalry and artillery. The attack succeeded ... the enemy fled.

Unfortunately, when he came to praise his troops, the Duke used words which were capable of misinterpretation:

> The division of Guards, under Lieutenant-General Cooke, Major-General Maitland and Major-General Byng, set an example which was followed by all.

These words apparently refer to the fact that the first French attack of the day on Hougomont was repelled by the Guards, and do not mean that the British Guards defeated the Imperial Guards at the close of the action Cooke having then left the field.

Yet though Colborne was too much engaged to know

---

21. The two battalions of the 1st Grenadiers, according to Petit, were still standing.

anything about it at the time the 3rd Battalion of Maitland's Brigade of Guards were undoubtedly engaged, either with the head of the column which Colborne assailed in the flank, with some column in echelon with it to its right, according to Mr. Ropes' theory, or with a body of massed skirmishers, according to Mr. Leeke's. And from this basis of fact, or a misunderstanding of the Duke's words, it was quickly accepted that the attack of the Imperial Guard had been repelled by the British Guards, and by them alone.

Lord Bathurst, Foreign Minister and Minister of War, speaking on the battle in the House of Lords on June 23rd, used these words:

> Towards the close of the day Bonaparte himself, at the head of his Guards, made a desperate charge upon the British Guards, and the British Guards instantly overthrew the French.[22]

No word of Colborne's wheeling movement, of the flank fire, of the triumphant charge for 800 yards of Adam's Brigade! And the *Gazette* of 29th July contained the announcement:

> His Royal Highness has been pleased to approve of the 1st Regiment of Foot Guards being made a regiment of Grenadiers, and styled the 1st, or Grenadier, Regiment of Foot Guards, in commemoration of their having defeated the Grenadiers of the French Imperial Guard upon this memorable occasion.

Colborne, who believed, rightly or wrongly, that he had had a main hand in deciding the battle, on reading the Duke's despatch and this announcement at Paris, saw, with bitterness, that he had been ignored and the praise which should have come to him and to the 52nd was given to others. Till that time, he says, he had heard nothing of the charge of the Guards.

---

22. *Times*, 24th June, 1815.

Even under his sense of wrong, he uttered no complaint. His attitude is well seen in a story told to Lady Montgomery-Moore by Sir Charles Rowan. When the officers of the 52nd were once discussing the battle at Paris, and blaming the Duke, Sir John, overhearing them, said quietly and emphatically, 'For shame, gentlemen! One would think you forgot that the 52nd had ever been in battle before!' From that day the matter was never mentioned; it became a point of honour to take it as the Colonel did.

For many years Colborne refrained from reading accounts of the battle of Waterloo. He was a busy man, and he says they roused many painful recollections. Perhaps on this account he paid too little attention to the claim of the Guards to have repulsed a column of the Imperial Guard. The memoranda he eventually wrote on the part played by himself and his regiment in the battle (or rather, by his regiment, for he scrupulously kept himself in the background) were inspired by the publication, or intended publication, of three works by other men: Gawler's *Crisis and Close of the Action at Waterloo*, Siborne's *Waterloo*, and Moorsom's *History of the 52nd Regiment*.[23]

But the strong belief he held throughout that the 52nd, 'by stopping the progress of that column, made the great charge of the day,' throws into brighter relief the proud self-repression with which he refused to claim that credit for himself which he believed he deserved, and the generosity with which he ever excused the defects in the Duke's despatch, deprecated the attaching of importance to the impressions of subordinate officers, and eulogized the Duke's generalship alike at Waterloo as in the Peninsula. This was the tone of all Colborne's references to Waterloo:

Never did any commander gain a victory more by his per-

---

23. See these Memoranda, Appendix 2.

sonal exertions and by his prompt presence at points where the efforts of the enemy had nearly succeeded.... Despatches are written in haste, and it is impossible for a general to do justice to his army.... Every officer being intent on some particular object, with a distinct part to perform, his eye is confined to a small angle.

Miss Charlotte Yonge writes of him:

> I heard him myself only excusing the Duke by saying nobody knew how difficult it is to write a despatch after a battle, and that the Duke was distressed by the sufferings of his wounded staff-officer in the house and room with him. Moreover, that there had been a messenger sent after himself, who had failed to find him as he was looking after his wounded, or probably there would have been no such omission. That entire absence of self-assertion has always seemed to me one of the most striking signs of a really great nature I ever saw.... Indeed, I always remember him and Mr. Keble as the two most humble men I ever knew.[24]

The following letter to Miss Fanny Bargus was written by Colborne immediately after the battle. Its reference to the part played by the 52nd is disappointingly meagre. No doubt Colborne described the battle more fully to his wife, but his letters to her are not preserved, having been burnt, as is said, at the time of the rebellion in Canada.

To Miss Fanny Bargus

Nivelles
19th June, 1815

My Dear Fanny,

You will be anxious to hear of us after the most severe conflict I have ever witnessed, and I think it will be the most

---

24. *Monthly Packet*, 1888, Christmas Number.

important in the result. William Leeke is very well. Our infantry behaved nobly, and the 52nd as usual.

I have only time to write you these few lines. You will be surprised at the *Gazette*; we have lost some of our most valuable officers. My kind regards to your mother and Maria.

Your affectionate brother,

J. Colborne

Chapter 16

March to Paris

Sir F. Adam having been wounded at Waterloo, Colborne now commanded the brigade.

On 19th June the 52nd marched from Maison du Roi to Nivelles, where they enjoyed a wash for the first time for three days on the 20th to Binche on the 21st they entered France and marched to Bavay, on the 22nd to Le Cateau Cambresis, where they remained till the 25th.

Leeke tells us that at this time his boots were very dilapidated, and Colborne, noticing it, made him a present of a new pair of his own. Marching by Joucour, Lauchy, Roye, Clermont, they reached La Chapelle on the 30th, where Colborne and other officers were quartered in the Chateau of Marshal Moncey and for the first time for a fortnight undressed and slept in a bed.

On the 1st July they first saw Paris, and once more met some French soldiers, some skirmishers having been sent out from St. Denis. Colborne sent down a party of the 71st, who drove them off. On the 2nd the 52nd were alone at Argenteuil on the Seine.

On the 3rd July the French, under Davoust, twice attacked the Prussians, but were beaten and pursued almost to the walls of Paris.

On the same day a Convention was signed, and in the afternoon the 52nd crossed the Seine and proceeded to the bridge of Neuilly, which Sir John

Colborne had received orders to cross, but from which the French refused to retire. The two front companies of the 52nd were advanced a short distance in front of the column with fixed bayonets. Sir John coolly took out his watch and allowed five minutes to the French commander in which to give up the bridge or have it stormed; in two or three minutes it was given up. The village of Neuilly was occupied, and the 52nd passed the night in the walled graveyard.[1]

Colborne gives the following account of this occurrence:

I had been ordered to take a brigade across the bridge of Neuilly and put them on the other side towards the Bois de Boulogne. Some staff officers, Rowan and others, were standing on the bridge. A French officer on the other side said we should not pass and the staff officers supported him, but I said I should see to that, and went on the bridge, while the column continued to advance. The French officer now began calling out, 'Stop the column; you cannot and you shall not pass!'

I really began to have some doubts whether he was not going to blow up the bridge. However, I went on, and the column after me. It was rather a rash thing, but I was determined to go over, as I had my orders to post my brigade on that side. So while the French officer went on vociferating, *'Vous ne passerez pas!'* I marched them across and right through the embrasure. On the other side we found a troop of dragoons. Very fine-looking fellows they were, but all rather drunk. Their officer also came up in a tremendous rage and asked, *'Qu'allez-vous faire? Allez-vous à Paris ce soir?'* and all his dragoons began galloping round us and covering us with dust. However, I marched my men straight on, and

---

1. Moorsom.

posted them and ordered them to lie down, and there we stayed all night, with our sentries and those of the French close together.

Then I rode a little further to see the town. I met an old Frenchman, who said to me, 'You had better not go any further, there is a whole body of dragoons round the corner, *ils sont si enragés.*' So, on hearing that, I galloped back as fast as I could. The soldiers were partly in a sort of garden with a wall round it. I remember Charley Rowan saying to me next morning, 'Well, I never spent such a night and did not think of closing my eyes the whole time.'

I do not know how it was. I suppose the French officer had his orders to keep the bridge and I had mine to cross it. He could not have defended it with his small force, but a little way from us there must have been 80,000 men. They were under Davoust, I think. Napoleon was then on his way to Cherbourg, I suppose.

On the 4th July the French army quitted Paris. The 52nd proceeded to the Bois de Boulogne, where they stayed till the 7th, when General Adam's Brigade (the 52nd, 71st, 2nd and 3rd Battalions 95th) had the honour of entering Paris. They were the only troops which occupied the city; the rest of the army remained in the Bois de Boulogne. The brigade was encamped in the Champs Elysees, the 52nd being to the left of the road leading towards the Seine. Two companies and the quarter-guard of the 52nd were close to the garden wall of the Duke of Wellington's house and to the Place Louis Quinze, now the Place de la Concorde, the remainder 100 yards further away.

General Sir Alexander Montgomery-Moore writes that Lord Seaton pointed out to him in Paris in 1857 the spot where his tent stood,[2] and said the Duke of Wellington came and stood on the little dwarf wall and called out,

---

2. He had also a billet in the town. See Leeke.

'Here, Colborne, here are two things for you,' handing him the orders of Maria Theresa of Austria and St. George of Russia.[3] Colborne once remarked:

I took them, saying, 'They do not give me the least pleasure,' but an old colonel who was sitting by me said, 'Colborne, it is my belief you care for them just as much as other people.'

When I went to thank Sir George Murray for the orders the latter said, 'Well, I am glad you are pleased, for Colonel Lygon has just been here to return the Cross of the Second Class of the Order of St. Vladimir, as he says it would be degrading to the commanding officer of the Life Guards to wear what every officer of the Russian army is entitled to after two years.'

When the Duke heard of this, all he said was, 'Won't Colonel Lygon accept it? Well then, give it to Colonel Somebody-else, who will.'

Adam's Brigade remained in the Champs Elysees till the 2nd November. Colborne said:

I had the superintendence of the British camp, which extended from the Place de la Concorde to the Tuileries, immediately under the Duke of Wellington's quarters. I took the greatest pains to have it kept neat and clean, and succeeded so well that the Duke once took some officers to look at it, and leaning over the wall that divided it off from his house, said, 'This is the sweetest camp I have ever known, and I have known a good many.'

---

3. His appointment to the 4th Class of the Order of St. George is dated Paris, 19th August, 1815, that as Knight of the Order of Maria Theresa, Paris, 2nd August, 1815. The statutes of the latter order (whose centenary on 18th June, 1857, Colborne, then Lord Seaton, attended at Vienna) are interesting: *All officers of all ranks may be admitted into this order for bravery in action only. It is an order of valour, and neither birth, rank, meritorious or long service, or even wounds are of themselves sufficient qualification. The candidate must describe the action, and prove his part in it, when the Chapter may recommend the Sovereign to appoint him to any class of the order which he may deserve: an ensign might by bravery become at once a Grand Cross of the Order.*

At Paris I used sometimes to have 30 men or so marched out early in the day for about 10 miles as a punishment, but I do not think now that it is a good thing to do.

Mr. Leeke writes:

> Sir John Colborne took the 52nd several times to the Champ-de-Mars which, was a very extensive and good exercising ground. There we first practised the half-face movement in column, which I think was taken up from the Prussians, and was afterwards found to be a most useful movement. One day we came across the Emperor of Russia and his staff in the Champ-de-Mars, and Sir John very neatly threw the regiment into close column just as the Emperor was arriving in front of the flank company and saluted him with covered arms. As the Emperor was merely riding across the Champ-de-Mars, and as we were only there for drill, the salute with carried arms in close column was the only available method of showing him any attention.

Mr. Leeke also tells a story of a 52nd soldier being condemned to be shot for insubordination towards an officer of another regiment:

> I saw an interview between the Duke and Sir John Colborne, which I had reason to believe was connected with this man's execution. The Duke had come into our camp from his garden door, and as Colborne almost immediately joined him I fancy the interview had been arranged before. The Duke, who generally appeared to be a person of a very quiet demeanour, seemed on this occasion to speak with some considerable earnestness, and Colborne, who was most anxious, as we all were, that the man's life should be spared, was equally energetic. The conversation did not last more than seven or eight minutes, and I did not learn the result until the or-

der for the execution appeared in orders. Next day, when all was ready for the execution, an aide-de-camp, the bearer of a reprieve, rode into the square. I think it was an order from the Duke granting the man a pardon, and stating that it was partly in consideration of the high character of the regiment to which he belonged that the Duke was induced to take this course.[4]

The following stories told by Colborne relate to this time:

Hardinge was attached to Blucher on the march to Paris, and has frequently told me that Blucher used to say every night, 'Well, I shall be sure to get Bonaparte somewhere when we get to Paris; if so, I shall take him directly to Vincennes and shoot him in the very place he shot d'Enghien.'

Blucher gave Hardinge Louis XVIII's own copy of the *Memoirs of Madame de la Rochejacquelein*, which Napoleon had taken with him to read on the campaign, and which had been found in his carriage.

Once at dinner at Paris the Duke was giving a description of the battle of Waterloo, when Sir F. Adam asked him across the table, 'Pray, what would your Grace have done if the French Guards had not been dispersed?'

'Oh,' said the Duke, 'I should have retired to the Bois de Soignies and given battle again the next morning.'

'But if you could not have done that?' said Adam, pressing him.

'It never could have been so bad as that, you know,' said the Duke hastily, and got up and called for coffee, rather ruffled, I think, at the question being put.

'When the Venetian horses were taken down from the Arc du Carrousel I dressed in plain clothes and went into the Place du Carrousel to hear what the people said. They did not

---

4. Leeke, *I*.

seem to mind it at all. They said, *'Ma foi, ils ont beaucoup voyagé'* and that sort of thing, but not as if they were angry; and when the Griffin was taken, they said they were glad to say good-bye to that *'grande tête laide'*. Six or seven thousand of our soldiers were parading about as there had been some fear of a disturbance, but it all passed off very quietly. It was the Austrians who were taking the things away, but as we were the only troops then in Paris we got all the odium, though we were the only people who were to gain nothing.

I remember hearing a Frenchman say that he had been to the Louvre every day of the year when all the pictures and statuary were there, just to look at two or three at a time.

It was said that the Duke wished to intercede for Ney with Louis XVIII., but the King guessed his intention and talked to him the whole evening so as to leave him no opportunity. A Royalist said to me, 'If Ney is not executed it will be impossible for us to remain in Paris.'

The following story is told of Ney's treason in 1814. It had been announced that Ney would inspect his troops one morning. When he rode to where they were drawn up, he raised his hat and cried, *'Vive l'Empereur!'*

His aide-decamp said, 'You mistake. You mean *"Vive le Roi"*.'

'No mistake, Sir,' he replied, *'Vive l'Empereur!'*

On one occasion the Duke de Chartres had been fired at, the ball passing through his carriage, and the assailant was condemned to die. The Duke, when pressed to save the man's life, said to me, 'I will never intercede for an assassin.'

It seems only a short time since old Lowe came proudly into my tent at Paris and showing me the letter which gave him the offer of going to St. Helena. He said then that he was quite determined not to accept it, but they afterwards made it, 1,200 a year, and he thought it was too good a thing for a poor man to refuse.

Sir Hudson Lowe always hesitated in his replies, a thing

the Duke of Wellington could not endure. On one occasion the Duke said, 'Where does that road lead to, Sir Hudson?' Sir Hudson began drawing his plans from his pocket before answering. The Duke, putting his hand to his mouth, turned round to an officer with him, saying, 'D—d old fool!'

Another officer, General ——, knew the Duke's ways so well that, whether he was sure of a thing or not, he always answered directly. For instance, if the Duke asked, 'How many rounds of ammunition have we?' he answered immediately, 'Four hundred and twenty.' On a friend remonstrating, 'How could you say that, when you could not possibly know?' he would answer, 'Oh, I knew it must be thereabouts, and if I am wrong I can tell him afterwards.'

On 2nd November the brigade, now once more commanded by Sir F. Adam, moved from Paris to Versailles, and in the middle of December to St. Germain. Sir John Colborne now obtained a long leave of absence.

After an extended tour of Europe with his wife and family Colborne once again left his Devon home on the 18th May, 1818, in order to rejoin his regiment in France. It was the last year of the occupation, and Colonel Colborne resumed the command of the 52nd at St. Omer.

Leeke tells that Sir John's establishment of horses being incomplete, he bought a horse off Leeke, which, the first day he appeared on parade, bolted and carried him to his quarters a mile and a half away, Sir John having an imperfect command of a horse owing to the results of the wound in his right shoulder received at Ciudad Rodrigo.

In the middle of August the 52nd marched to Valenciennes. On the 23rd October the army was reviewed by the Emperor of Russia, the King of Prussia, &c., and a month later was withdrawn from France. Mr. Leeke quotes from Colonel Hall an account of the surrender of Valenciennes to its natural possessors:

The authorities wished to embody some of the National Guards to receive over the place, but Colborne would allow no Frenchman in arms until we had quitted it. The regiment marched out and halted on the glacis, leaving the main guard in the Grande Place. When the citadel had been given over to the civil authorities the town was also formally surrendered.

The 52nd Regiment embarked at Calais on the 28th November and landed at Ramsgate next day. Colborne went on to do singular service for his country in a variety of military and civil posts, but it is always for his bravery, his command of strategy and tactics and his distinguished career in the Napoleonics wars for which his country will ever be grateful to him.

Appendices

Appendix 1
Colborne on Sir John Moore's Campaign in Spain

LETTER TO COLONEL WILLIAM NAPIER
CONTAINING A DIARY OF THE CAMPAIGN

16th March, 1827

My Dear Napier,

I am afraid you pester yourself too much with divisions and the details of their operations. Look at the first volume of the *Précis Militaire*. What an advantage an author has who disencumbers himself of all the stuff that is only fit to enter the journal of a writer who intends his work for a few English book-clubs.

I entreat you to look over again attentively the last memoranda I gave you at Brook Farm, I mean the march from Lisbon to Corunna. *I* think I have mentioned in them every occurrence fully as much as the operations of those months deserve, and I hope you will only dwell particularly on the following points. These I trust will appear as prominent as you may judge consistent with your work, *viz.*:

1. That when Sir John Moore decided on the march of the first brigades to Salamanca he expected that Sir D. Baird would have arrived early in October in the neighbourhood of Salamanca; that he could not have anticipated the delay occasioned by the folly of the *junta* of Corunna. That as it was

more probable that the army would incline towards Madrid than to any other point, he was right, in the doubt about the practicability of the roads, to march his artillery by the Badajos road, as he could easily move all his infantry (including the Corunna Division, had it arrived at the time he had good reason for supposing it must assemble in Castile) to the right to Avila, or to a more forward position.

2. That if his force had been collected at Salamanca early in October, he positively could not have assisted the Spaniards, and that if he had moved towards Madrid he probably would have been so entangled with the Spaniards that the case must have turned out as hopeless as it did afterwards, and the movements of the French would have been more concentrated. All this ought to be explained, because Jones places great importance on the prolonged march of the artillery, and Southey says that Madrid would have been saved if Sir John Moore had remained in its neighbourhood with his division.

3. That the only operation he undertook was the one to serve the cause. For if he had moved into Portugal the country was unprepared to make any defence, and no general could have acted with tolerable security without some point to which he could retire on.

4. That having been thrown on Gallicia, the best thing that he could do was to draw the French after him, and to get out of an exhausted country by embarkation.

I believe I was present at every affair and skirmish from Benevente to Corunna, but there was scarcely anything that occurred, except the cavalry skirmish at Benevente, that deserves notice. The affair at Lugo was a mere two hours' skirmish or reconnaissance.

I think the dates of the march of the divisions from Sahagun that I have given you are correct. I cannot give you the march of each division. In my memoranda that I gave to you at Cobham you will find the movements of the principal columns correctly stated. On referring to my little journal I perceive that headquarters left Sahagun on the 25th and marched to Mayorga. Our first skirmish on the advance to Sahagun, with the exception of Stewart's little affair at Rueda, was on the 21st of December. The following is a copy from my journal.[1]

21st. Marched to Sahagun, five leagues from Valderas. Lord Paget reached Melgar de Abajo with the 10th and 15th Dragoons at 2 this morning. On our arrival at Sahagun we found that the French cavalry amounting to 600 or 700 had come out of Sahagun at daylight and were attacked by the 15th Dragoons under Lord Paget, who defeated them and took two lieutenant-colonels, 11 officers and 144 men. I went down with the adjutant of the regiment and other officers to the ground where the affair took place. Lord Paget appeared to have gained a decided advantage in charging at the time he did and forcing the enemy to receive his charge on the best ground.

25th. Marched from Sahagun to Mayorga.

26th. Marched from Mayorga through Fuentes to Benevente; arrived there in the evening. A small party of the enemy's cavalry had approached the bridge and carried off some of the commissariat cattle.

27th. The general received a report from Lord Paget that the enemy's cavalry, having entered Mayorga, were followed by part of the 10th Dragoons, who charged them and took 70 prisoners. The 18th Dragoons fell in with another party and took 20 prisoners. The enemy's cavalry patrolled as far as the bridge of Castro Gonzalo about 6 p.m.

---

1. The copy contains particulars not given in the original journal, which is preserved at Beechwood.

28th. Generals Hope and Fraser retired with their divisions towards Astorga. The 18th Dragoons attacked a French patrol near Villa Pando, which was afterwards the cause of an alarm.

29th. The reserve marched this morning. Four squadrons of the enemy crossed at the ford and attacked the picquets, which, on being reinforced, repulsed the enemy. Sir J. marched early in the morning. I remained till 8 or later. As I was packing up my papers my servant informed me that the French had forded the river. I rode down towards the river at full speed; met several dismounted troopers and some French officers prisoners. The picquets appeared to me retiring in good order, the troop of the German Hussars had reinforced the picquets and charged the leading French squadrons. The French cavalry, formed in four squadrons, were advancing steadily towards Benevente. Our picquets were retiring and forming up frequently in front of the leading French squadron. Some of the troops of the 10th Hussars were beginning to assemble about 400 yards in rear of the picquets.

At this moment Lord Paget rode up. 'You see there are not many of them. I wish to draw them on till the 10th are ready, but I don't know what they may have on the other side. Our lads, the picquets, are up to a charge.' By this time the 10th were assembled, and the French were a few hundred yards from them, rather to their right. Lord Paget wheeled the 10th into line, gave the word, 'Charge!' I rather think that the French wheeled about at the very moment the word *charge* was given. They galloped at full speed in tolerable order towards the river, and passing over better ground than the 10th did, gained some paces on them. Those of the enemy that were badly mounted were taken, but the main body appeared to me not to be overtaken in their flight. The French passed the river in a dense column and formed up for a few minutes on the other side. Two guns had arrived on the ground at this period, and fired, I believe, about two rounds, which sent them up the opposite bank. Lefebvre was taken, being badly mounted. A German officer told me that he took him, and that Lefebvre defended himself, but I did not give credit to his assertion. Jansen was the German officer's name.

1st January. Marched from Astorga in the evening. I rode out to the cavalry picquets and had heard a few shots in front. Arrived at Combarros, halted a few hours. Marched about midnight on receiving Lord Paget's report that the enemy were in force. At Nurenas the general wrote to Corunna and Lugo that it was his intention that the army should retire on Betanzos.

2nd. Arrived at Bembybre as Sir David Baird's Corps was marching out of it. The enemy's patrols were seen by ours during the night.

3rd. Marched to Villa Franca. The enemy's cavalry entered Bembybre about 1 p.m., to the number of 600. I remained in front of Bembybre till I saw their advanced guard. The patrol of the 15th retired before them. The reserve halted between Bembybre and Cacabelos to protect the stragglers.

4th. The enemy's cavalry appeared in great force on the heights above Cacabelos about 2 o'clock. Sir J. Moore was in Villa Franca. I rode out to the advanced picquet of our cavalry. I found the reserve under arms. The 52nd and 20th Regiments were posted on the right and left of the road leading to Villa Franca, behind the bridge of Cacabelos. The 95th were posted in front of the village with the river behind them, under a hill, so that the approach of the enemy could not be discovered by them. Many staff officers of cavalry were on the road behind the cavalry picquet The enemy appeared to have about a squadron on the road, and their vedettes were advanced close to ours. In this situation we remained about an hour. Suddenly I observed our picquet retiring rapidly, and all the staff and cavalry officers with them. We all met on the bridge together. The passage became blocked up by the 95th pressing towards the same point. This halt was for a very short space, but the enemy's cavalry were approaching at a brisk gallop behind us. Some of the 95th got into the houses and, I believe, these were taken. I rode up the hill towards Villa Franca. The 52nd and 20th had been withdrawn by order of Sir J. Moore to the summit of the hill. Advanced picquets were stationed below and fired on the French cavalry that passed the bridge. The enemy retired immediately.

On my arrival on our position I found Sir J. Moore there with two battalions and two guns. The guns had fired as the enemy passed the bridge. The 95th were posted in vineyards to the right of the road, nearer to the river than the other battalions. We all took out our glasses and observed large masses of cavalry deploying on the height in front of Cacabelos. I think I said, or some officer said, that there were 20 squadrons. We had a dispute whether there were infantry or not. About half an hour before dark the enemy made a show of passing the river in front of the 95th and did push on their skirmishers. The 95th commenced a tremendous fire, which I thought was unnecessary, which continued till after dark. Sir J. Moore ordered the 76th and all that were in Villa Franca to march. He desired me to go to Ross and to desire that the 20th might remain on the road in front of Villa Franca till about 10 o'clock. I found all quiet and no appearance of the enemy. Sir John Moore marched about half past 9 and arrived at Herrerias early in the morning, where we halted a few hours. It was from this place that Sir J. wrote to Baird, Hope and Fraser and Broderick that the army would halt at Lugo and assemble there. These despatches were forwarded by Captain Napier to Baird and sent on by him by a dragoon, who lost them.

5th. Arrived at Nogales. Letters were despatched again to the generals in the rear and the commissary-general to push on provisions for Lugo.

6th. The reserve marched from Nogales. The vedettes of the enemy appeared about 8 o'clock on the high mountain above

Nogales. Here, at a short distance from the town, a mine was sprung to render the road impassable. I remained to see the explosion, but it failed, and made a very trifling obstacle.

The enemy's cavalry moved on steadily, and did not appear in any great force till the evening, about 2 o'clock. Our column halted on the road about this time while the money in the bullock car was thrown over. I think I observed about three squadrons near us, and where we halted, they showed no disposition to press us. Towards the evening we halted again on some advantageous ground with two pieces of artillery ready to fire. The enemy remained at some distance and retired a little to their left to shelter their advanced guard. About 5 or 6 o'clock we retired quickly down the hill in front of Sobrado or Constantina and passed the rivulet or river before the enemy could discover that we were in full retreat. They came on at a brisk trot when we were in position and the picquets posted at the bridge skirmished with their advanced guard. A few shots were fired at them from our guns on the position. I observed that the cavalry filed off to occupy the different villages on their side of the river—no appearance of an intention to attack.

I went down after dark, or as soon as the firing had ceased, and visited the bridge, which was blocked up with carts. The reserve cooked and halted till after midnight.

We marched about an hour after midnight and arrived at Lugo early on the 7th.

(Thus says my journal, but I see Jones[2] asserts that we marched from Villa Franca to Lugo in 43 hours, which must be a mistake. Noble's[3] book is full of lies and blunders; his dates, however, agree with mine. He confuses the position of Constantina, three leagues or more from Lugo, with our position in front of Lugo. But I rather think I have occasioned the

---

2. Sir J. T. Jones in his *Account of the War* (1818).
3. Le Noble, the anonymous author of the *Campagne des Français en Galice et Portugal*, 1809. For this identification I am indebted to the kindness of Mr. C. W. C. Oman, Fellow of All Souls'.

misstatement of Jones, who copied from James Moore. Perhaps you can ascertain this from George Napier. My journal is correct as to the number of hours, but perhaps I have made some mistake in the day we marched from Villa Franca. For I see that the general order about the ill-conduct of the troops is dated Headquarters, Lugo, the 6th.)

7th. On the 7th the enemy opened a fire from two or three field pieces on our right and continued firing the greater part of the day. Towards the evening Soult pushed on two or three battalions to our position, near the centre. The enemy having shown in some force, Sir John Moore was on the position, making his arrangements. The 51st and the 76th Regiments, who were opposite the skirmishers of the enemy, gave way, and many of them retired, or rather, ran back in confusion. Sir J. Moore rode up to Crauford, I think, or some colonel or general, and desired him to send out skirmishers. The battalions, or the 500 or 600 men of the enemy, were immediately checked.

Sir J. Moore desired me to place Baird's Divisions on the left, which had received orders to march from their quarters. I rode to the left and met the head of the column. On my return I found everything quiet. Sir J. Moore imagined that this reconnaissance was preparatory to an attack in the morning. He gave orders for the different divisions to be under arms early on the 8th.

8th. The enemy on the 8th made no appearance that indicated an attack. The corps commenced their retreat from Lugo in the evening. Lord William Bentinck's Division and some of Baird's Corps did not get into the high road until 1 or 2 o'clock in the morning of the 9th.

9th. The army halted at Valmonde or Valmeda continued the retreat on the night of the 9th. There was more confusion on this night than on any other, from the circumstances which have been mentioned already, *viz*., from the permission given by Baird to halt on the road during a storm, and from the men being allowed to shelter themselves under the hedges adjoining the road, so that when orders were given to resume the march many regiments did not muster 100 men. The stragglers amounted to, perhaps, 1,500.

10th. These were pressed hard by the French cavalry the greater part of the day. We had a small rearguard of cavalry, but I should think not more than a squadron. Grant, of the 15th, I know was present, and attempted to form up a body of stragglers that checked the enemy. But there was no affair of cavalry between Lugo and Betanzos. Sir E. Paget halted about two miles from Betanzos and continued in that position, I believe, the whole night. The main body of cavalry had marched on to Corunna.

11th. On the 11th January the army marched from Betanzos. The 28th Regiment halted at the end of the town while the engineer was superintending the completion of a mine to destroy the bridge. The French cavalry advanced at a brisk trot through the streets at this moment. One company of the 28th opened a fire and they immediately retired. The column on this day retired without being molested. The Guards and Fane's Brigade marched into Corunna, Hope's Division remained at El Burgo. The bridge over the Mero was destroyed on the 12th. The other divisions were quartered in villages between El Burgo and Corunna.

12th. On the 12th Sir J. Moore examined El Burgo and rode over the heights of Portoso, but he imagined that he could not occupy this position as he could not cover the St. Iago road, and on account of the great distance between Portoso and Corunna.

13th. Beckwith retired from the Mero on the 13th, but was ordered to reoccupy El Burgo. The bridges over the Mero were destroyed. An officer of Engineers lost his life in mining the bridge near Cambri.

14th. The advanced guard of the enemy passed the Mero on the 14th.

15th. On the 15th he took possession of the heights. The transports from Vigo were in sight on the evening of the 14th.

16th. On the 16th, soon after Sir J. Moore arrived on the ground, I observed the enemy descending from their position in three masses, preceded by numerous skirmishers. Our picquets were at this time retiring in some confusion. Sir J. Moore desired me to ride to Sir E. Paget and to tell him to advance on the enemy's left, as he had agreed with him, and to tell Fane to draw out his brigade on the St. Iago road. On my return I found several companies of the 50th and 42nd retiring, and that Sir J. Moore had been wounded There was a heavy fire from behind all the hedges and enclosures, but scarcely any considerable force could be discovered on either side. The French maintained a heavy fire from their field-pieces on the position, directing them chiefly on the mounted officers. The enemy appeared to me to be retiring at every point towards their own position.

17th. On the 17th the enemy did not appear till 7 o'clock, when a small corps of cavalry advanced cautiously. About three in the evening the enemy brought forward a few field-pieces to the high ground near the water and opened a fire on some of the transports near the citadel. At this moment I was about to embark.

I have copied an old journal which was written in great haste, and have related the substance of that which came under my own view. The whole of Noble's account is false. The absurd stuff about Betanzos being intended to be destroyed must be his own invention. It may be asserted safely that we never saw the enemy on the march in any force except at Lugo, and that all their fighting was with the stragglers.

The bridge of Castro Gonzalo was burnt. I believe you

know more about this than I do. Crauford superintended it. With respect to the Engineers' tools, I heard Pasley complaining of the want of them. There was at that time no staff corps or any establishment attached to that department, and all work of mining was performed by working parties, and tools were issued by the Quartermaster-General's Department or by the Commissariat. At Astorga, I believe, among the camp equipage destroyed, the entrenching tools shared the same fate.

The next bridge attempted to be destroyed was not far from Nogales, on the Rio Herrerias, but when the bridge was proposed to be destroyed Sir J. Moore himself rather objected to it, knowing the river could be forded a few hundred yards below.

The next bridge was between Lugo and Betanzos, I believe over the Miño. Jones has exaggerated the occurrences on this day's march.

We may affirm that all the straggling before the march from Lugo was of that kind which is common to all British columns, and that the stragglers up to that day were chiefly composed of drunkards. Two divisions which were quartered in the villages near the position in front of Lugo marched by a narrow lane instead of at once striking into the main road. Thus marching on this bad road on a dark night the rear of the column was not far from Lugo till two o'clock on the morning of the 9th. But even this was not of much importance; for the whole had passed the river and halted three leagues from Lugo before one o'clock p.m. I observed few stragglers that had not passed the river, and arrived at the bivouac near Venta Bahamondo or Venta de Guteniz before 2 p.m.

The French did not enter Lugo before 9 o'clock and were not seen during this march. There was a small rearguard of cavalry. The columns marched about 7 or 8 o'clock on the evening of the 9th. The weather was dreadful and it rained the whole night, and in the divisions that were suffered to halt during the night and put in motion before half the men were assembled there was a great deal of confusion, and during the whole of this day there were many that could not find their divisions. Two regiments (the 59th, I believe, was one) did not arrive at Betanzos with more than 150 men. Sir J. Moore passed these dispersed divisions early in the morning. From this imprudent halt alone arose all the horrors which Jones ascribes unjustly to hard marching. It is evident that the reserve marched in perfect order, although the different corps of that division had more work than the others. Thus, if the generals of division had been more expert, the divisions would have arrived at Corunna without ever once seeing the enemy except at Lugo.

The reserve halted in a good position in front of Betanzos. I rode out to Sir E. Paget and everything appeared in perfect order, but stragglers were passing in great numbers. Jones says that he could discover nothing like an organized army.

On the 10th we halted

At Betanzos a mine was sprung at the end of the town on the road leading to Corunna. This detained the French cavalry some time. The divisions marched in one column and everything appeared to go on very regularly. The cavalry retired to Corunna independently. There could have been nothing but a rearguard affair between Lugo and Corunna, and no kind of skirmish took place. The 76th were at Villa Franca, the 59th and 51st, I believe, did not march further than Lugo nor the 23rd; but I am not quite certain of this.

You are nearly right in your estimate of the army at Lugo. However, I think the cavalry fit for service must have been under 1,500. You are nearly right in your estimate of the combatants at Corunna, *viz.*, 14,600. Noble's plan of the battle appears correct, and, I think, better than ours.

Sir J. Moore, you must recollect, moved in the direction of Mayorga to ensure his junction with Baird, and from that place to Carrion by Sahagun, and by the direct road, there is not more than four or five miles difference. But as a good place to concentrate, and a short distance to march from and to communicate with Romana at Mavilla, Sahagun was preferable to Mayorga to march from with an intention of making an attack. Besides, Sir J. Moore had the choice of marching on Saldanha at the same time.

Sir John Moore would probably have pushed on Sir E. Paget further and supported him with Fane's Brigade had he . . . .

I think you should dwell much on his intention of going to Vigo to put everything right, and on the folly of Baird's allowing the signal to be hoisted for all the transports to steer for England before the officers had been trans-shipped to their own battalions, &c.

I am sorry I cannot give you a better account of the march; but in the papers which I gave you at Cobham and the preceding ones describing the march from Lisbon, I took great care that the dates were correct by comparing them with old records. I recollect having had some discussion about the date of the 6th and 7th January some years since. Jones has copied most of his narrative from James Moore, and assumed that as the data of his arguments. The order dated Lugo, the 9th, is certainly a mistake. I have written this in much haste to save the packet, so that I fear you will have as much trouble in reading it as I had in deciphering yours.

Do read Southey's second volume. He has completely ruined his character as an historian. His work ought to be reviewed immediately. I will transmit to you what I think should be published respecting his errors and bitterness against Sir John. That story about Bonaparte's having said that he would have shot Soult if he had issued his proclamation declaring himself King of Portugal I suspect to be one of his ridiculous anecdotes for which he has no authority. He states that Sir John Moore's movements had some effect, but not by any means in proportion to 'the sacrifice' he made, and that if he had fought in Gallicia the Spaniards would have attacked Madrid! Against this statement we have only to produce St. Infantado's letters. However, his book will save you much trouble. Do not be disheartened. The important documents will always make your work the best that has been circulated.

Yours sincerely,
J. Colborne

Extracts from an Unpublished Article (1827) on Southey's *History Of The Peninsular War*

Southey's Accounts of Sir John Moore and Mr. Frere

The depreciation of the services of Sir John Moore and the defence of Mr. Frere seems the grand object of Mr. Southey's work. It is this bias that has induced him to assert with dogmatical presumption that 'Sir John Moore wanted faith in the courage of British soldiers,' a general that had confided in it more than any other, and that had fought with them in the first rank from his youth, and directed the most glorious and arduous operations of the British army.

Mr. Frere conducted himself, we think, as a conscientious and well-intentioned Minister, but he participated in the delusion and blindness of the Spanish Government, and his official letters and documents seem to partake of the arrogance of his patron and poet. He certainly deserves many of the eulogiums passed upon him, but if Mr. Southey has attempted to wind him up at the expense of a man whose reputation was basely sacrificed to party spirit, who had devoted his whole life and energies to his country and profession, whose ability and decision did materially aid the Spanish people, he has for ever forfeited any claim he might have had to the character of a just and diligent historian, and far better would it have been for his fame had he never ventured beyond his strength beyond the Remains of Henry Kirke White and the precincts of biography.

Sir John Moore Right in Not Fighting an Action Earlier

A battle should not be fought except an important object is to be gained. Sir John Moore had taken the lead with an inferior force, and the movements of his adversary became subordinate to his. In uniting the British army and directing it with the aid of Romana's Division against an isolated corps, he effected a total change in the enemy's combinations. He was aware that no consideration but the actual crisis at which Spanish affairs had arrived should induce him to give up Portugal and his communications with Lisbon. On military principles he perceived his movement was faulty, yet a glorious cause and the representations of the Spanish authorities, the attention he was bound to pay to their reports of the exertions they were making on the Tagus, in La Mancha and Estremadura, demanded that a trial of the activity and perseverance of the provinces should be made. His friend, Mr. Stuart, informed him that a retrograde movement on Portugal would produce an effect not less serious than the most decisive victory of the enemy.

His offensive movement, then, was founded on the exaggerated statements from Aranjuez, Toledo and the southern provinces. He drew the principal mass of the hostile force on him, but he attracted it from Saragossa, from the capital, from the pursuit of the hunted divisions of Castanos, St. Juan and Galuzzo; he protected the straggling mob of Blake and gave Romana an opportunity of organizing it. He might defeat Soult and destroy his corps or some of the divisions of the 8th Corps on the march to Madrid.

The most important part of his project had been accomplished; to risk his army in carrying into effect a secondary operation from which a certain loss would have been sustained without an important result might have suited the tactics of Cuesta, Venegas, Carbaojal and Arezaga, but not those of an officer of experience.

In few cases can a commander be justified in bringing on an action to save what is termed the 'honour of the nation.' Why should Sir John Moore, who had gained his first object, and then found it necessary to conduct his army by a retrograde movement and steadily pursued his purpose, lose his army to increase his own reputation?

Straggling on Sir John Moore's Campaign

In no one movement during the whole campaign were we able to prevent straggling to an immense amount. Luckily we generally advanced when we recovered our stragglers. In every British army the great majority of the men are well-conducted, brave, the best soldiers; by practice they become intelligent and excellent in every respect. I suppose the army given up by the Duke of Wellington at Bordeaux was the most compact and movable army that had ever been assembled. But let us not suppose that to the very last we effected the elimination of straggling; the disease of straggling was incurable. The system of recruiting is so defective and so radically bad that in every regiment we must say there are from 50 to 100 bad characters that neither punishment nor any kind of discipline can restrain. In quarters they are kept in some measure restrained, but the moment the army is in movement they separate from their regiment. Their object is to march independently and ultimately to get into some hospital. So that for the most part these kind of characters are absent and unserviceable.

So that in this campaign, when we talk of disorder and disorganization, the disorganization was confined entirely to this species of straggling occasioned by drunkards, or a preference to march independently and overtake their divisions at their leisure. We appeal to every regiment on this retreat whether there was any disobedience or disorder but this. The divisions of Hope and Fraser being a head one and Sir D. Baird's being ahead of the corps which covered the retreat these divisions never having seen the enemy till their arrival at Lugo proves that the rapidity of the march was not the cause of the straggling, besides, the stragglers of the covering corps, which had to fight, were comparatively fewer; and the whole march was performed with great regularity. We must except one night, the night after the march to Lugo, but this was purely accidental.

Letter to Lady Napier on Sir John Moore's Choice of Corunna as His Port of Embarkation

109, Eaton Square
28th May, 1850

My Dear Lady Napier,

In reply to your queries, you must first be made acquainted that when Sir J. Moore was assured that Napoleon was in full march in search of him, he despatched Colonel Fletcher, Commanding Engineer, with instructions to visit Vigo, Betanzos, Corunna and Ferrol, and report on the facilities or advantages offered at each of those places as points of embarkation for troops pursued by an enemy. At Lugo, I believe, Fletcher returned with his report, and on the night of our arrival read it to the Military Secretary half asleep from fatigue. In the morning early it was laid before the Commander-in-Chief. Sir J. Moore had many years before been employed by the Duke of York at the desire of the Minister of the day in making an inspection of the coast in the vicinity of Ferrol, and from his own recollection imagined that vessels tacking out of the river would be exposed to the fire of an enemy.

Corunna, therefore, was decided on under the circumstances of the case, as the point from which troops could embark with less risk and with reference to the stand which might be safely made at Betanzos en route, and its short distance from Corunna, and the march which could easily and safely be accomplished by the columns retiring from that position. The needless march and countermarch of Fraser's Division, the slow progress of the several corps in retiring from the position taken up at Lugo, the forced night march and imprudent halt of Baird's Division and consequent dispersion of the troops in barns and sheltered fields, determined Sir J. Moore to continue his march with as little delay as possible from Betanzos in the expectation of seeing the transports in the Bay of Corunna prepared to receive artillery, baggage and troops. Yours very sincerely,

J. Colborne

Appendix 2
Colborne's Accounts of Waterloo

OBSERVATIONS ON COLONEL GAWLER'S
CRISIS OF THE ACTION AT WATERLOO

To establish the precise time when the battle was no longer doubtful and the movements which were the immediate cause of hastening the crisis is the object of the writer. And as he is persuaded that the movements of Sir H. Clinton's Division and of General Adam's Brigade, and of the 52nd Regiment in particular, tended greatly to hasten the crisis, it is necessary to describe the several positions of the division from half-past three o'clock to half-past seven, fixing from seven to half-past seven as the critical half hour, but time passes so quickly in an action, and everyone is so occupied in performing his own duty, that it will be difficult to find persons agree as to time. However that may be, it is clear that while the columns of Napoleon, which made the unsuccessful attack on the point which is usually called our right centre, advanced in full march towards the troops occupying our centre (the Brunswickers retiring and the British Guards closing in), no one who was looking steadfastly at the movements of the Imperial Guards at that time could say that the battle did not look critical, or but that the Imperial Guards had the appearance of success, and also that our centre was on the point of being penetrated. This, then, we must fix as the time when no change for the better on our side had taken place, and that we were in the greatest danger; but the moment the Imperial Guards halted and formed square in consequence of a menaced attack on their left flank, our prospects were immediately changed for the better. It was the 'crisis,' and half an hour afterwards, when they were thrown into confusion and they retreated towards La Belle Alliance, the battle was won. They had no reserve formed worth the name of a reserve. All attacks of cavalry or infantry after that moment were the necessary consequence of the flight and the endeavour to save such part of the crew of the wreck as could be brought off without incurring further risk.

Therefore, however splendid the conduct of any corps might have been, after the first flight of the French, in reaping the fruits of the victory and in completing the rout of the retiring columns, they took no part in the critical affair on the plateau of La Haye Sainte or plain below it which the left flank of Napoleon's columns overlooked.

Assuming that the three regiments, the 52nd, 71st and 95th passed the cross-road which runs a few hundred yards in rear of La Haye Sainte and forms an acute angle with the Nivelles road, at half-past three or four o'clock, the 52nd halted in the low ground three or four hundred yards in front of that road, and about 700 yards from the nearest angle of Hougomont. Remaining there an hour, the 52nd Regiment, being a strong regiment, formed two squares, the 71st formed square 200 yards to the right of the 52nd, and on the approach of the French cavalry towards the 71st, the 95th, apparently not more than two companies, formed close to the rear of the 52nd. Colonel Nicolay of the staff corps and several officers ran into the square of the 52nd. Two of the enemy's guns were on the high bank or ridge in front of the 52nd, apparently about 200 yards from the squares; but were only to be seen by the mounted officers. A mounted officer, Sir John Colborne, who had ascertained the exact position of these guns, called out from the commencement of the ascent to a captain of the

52nd to say whether he could see the guns from his part of the square. These guns and a howitzer fired constantly on the squares. The right and front faces of the right square of the 52nd opened a fire obliquely on the French Cuirassiers, who made a movement towards the rear of Hougomont, towards the 71st. The remainder of Clinton's Division were formed to the rear of the right of the 71st Regiment.

The Duke of Wellington sent a message to the 52nd by Colonel Hervey to retire up the hill, about half-past five; but Colonel Hervey was requested by Sir John Colborne to inform the Duke that the regiment was not in danger from the guns in front, if the order was given from the apparent vicinity of the guns. However, on the Nassau Regiment, or some of the allied troops, running rapidly out of the wood of Hougomont towards our line, the 52nd prepared to retire and form two lines the right sub-divisions forming one line and the left sub-divisions the other and retired rapidly up the hill towards the cross-road which they had crossed an hour before. While they were retiring, a field officer of the Cuirassiers galloped out of the enemy's columns and came at full speed down the hill towards the 52nd, hallooing lustily, *'Vive le Roi!'* as he approached. This officer pointed out the spot where Napoleon was and where the Imperial Guards were on the march to make a grand attack. The 52nd halted in two lines about 10 yards behind the cross-road where the ground sloped towards our position. The officer of the Cuirassiers pointed out to the officer commanding the 52nd, Sir John Colborne, the exact spot where Napoleon was with the Imperial Guards. The guns, under Lieut.-Colonel C. Gold, on the cross-road were all silent, there was scarcely any firing except in the rear of La Haye Sainte and on that part of our centre. The dense columns of the French were in full march on the plateau of La Haye Sainte, near the farm, and the flank of the columns at this time appeared to form a right angle with the 52nd, supposing the left of the line of the 52nd to be prolonged. A few minutes before this an officer, Sir John Colborne, had occasion to look at his watch and said, 'The wounded had better be left where they are, the action must be over in half an hour.' Therefore, at seven, we will say, the 52nd wheeled the left company nearly a quarter of a circle to the left and formed the remainder on the new line, with the intention of moving on the left-flank of the Imperial column and firing into the column to retard the movement. The 52nd thus, at seven o'clock, were formed into two lines, not four deep, but each left sub-division in rear of its right, the whole forming two complete lines, the rear line keeping the wheeling distance of a sub-division from the front line. At this time the 95th, apparently a small number, formed on the left of the 52nd. A strong company of the 52nd was sent to skirmish in front and to fire into the Imperial column. At this moment General Adam came to the 52nd from the 71st, seeing the 52nd moving on. The Duke, it appears, at the same time had sent Colonel Percy to the 52nd. The 52nd, however, were already in motion, its right flank totally unprotected, and moved off in two lines well formed, and covered by skirmishers commanded by Lieutenants Anderson and Campbell, who had directions to push on and look to the whole battalion as their support.

Whether the 95th moved off with the 52nd is not certain. They certainly did not continue on the left flank the whole time of the march towards the front. The 52nd moved steadily on. The instant the French columns felt the fire of Anderson's skirmishers they halted, appeared to be in some confusion, and opened a heavy fire on the 52nd. The two officers of the skirmishers were wounded and the greater part of the men; the right of the battalion also suffered severely. The 52nd still moved on, passing the entire front of Byng's[1] Brigade of Brit-

---

1. Most of Byng's own brigade was at Hougomont. Colborne means Maitland's Brigade, with whom Byng was, as he had succeeded to the command of the whole division through Cooke's being wounded.

ish Guards (who were stationary and not firing) at about 300 yards or so in front of them, and forming probably a right angle, or perhaps an obtuse angle, with the line of the Guards.

At the moment the 52nd commenced the movement Lord Hill was near the British Guards commanded by Maitland, and no movement on their part had then taken place. Therefore it is imagined that when the 52nd commenced the movement they were shortly followed by the 71st and the whole of Clinton's Division the Imperial troops saw that their flank and rear were menaced by a mass of troops they halted; but the moment this halt took place our centre also made a forward movement, which was resisted by the attacking corps of the French.[2] The 52nd in the meantime had proceeded to within a short distance of the rising ground on which the French were formed, when a body of British cavalry were perceived at full speed approaching the front of the left company of the 52nd. The officer of the company gave orders to fire, supposing they had come from the enemy's column. The three adjoining companies wheeled back to form square. The battalion at the time was under a heavy fire from the Imperial Guards, and the regiment was halted for a few minutes to enable the companies to rectify their line. At this moment while the three companies were forming up, the Duke was close in the rear and said, 'Well, never mind go on, go on!'

This halt brought the 71st, which corps had not been so much exposed to the fire as the 52nd, close on the right of the 52nd. The 52nd then advanced at full speed. The greater part of the French gave way in confusion, but some remained formed close to the deep road running direct from La Haye Sainte to La Belle Alliance. Captain Cross called out, 'They are coming over, don't fire!'

The French, however, opened a straggling fire, some run-

---

2. Colborne means that he imagines whatever movement was made by the Guards, took place at this time.

ning across the road and a few remaining till the 52nd were within six or seven yards of them. The whole of the 52nd charged briskly till they were impeded by the deep road, when they halted for a minute or two till they received the word to pass. They had some difficulty in getting over. When they had passed they formed line and wheeled to the right. Sir John Colborne's horse was here shot, and he mounted one of the gun horses. They found a gun on the plateau fully horsed and moved on in line, keeping their right on the road, and passed La Belle Alliance, and were joined by the skirmishers at the head of Bülow's Corps, which shortly after that came obliquely from the left.

In the meantime the 71st had proceeded towards Rossomme and did not pass the road where the 52nd did. The whole of Sir H. Clinton's Division, the moment the French were observed in retreat and in confusion, had struck to their right towards Rossomme. The 52nd passed about 80 pieces of cannon and tumbrels within a quarter of an hour after they had passed the Charleroi road from Waterloo. The skirmishing or attack that took place in the retreat from Rossomme or Planchenoit, the 52nd took no part in; they halted when the evening closed. Bülow's corps in column passed the 52nd after the regiment had halted.

The writer has never been on the ground since; but he is positive, as far as his memory can be relied on, that these facts are correctly stated, and is thus certain that no corps whatever passed between the 52nd and the French from the time the 52nd moved on the flank of the French, for the 52nd were under a heavy fire the whole time and were opposed to the moment they touched the Charleroi road. When they were formed to the left of the Charleroi road no corps was near them. The only corps of cavalry near the 52nd or the French column during the attack was the regiment of cavalry that moved in the direction of the left company of the 52nd. Thus it appears that the movement to which Sir H. Vivian alludes[3] must have been the attack made in retreat, and that all the troops that came in contact with the French must have moved across the track of the 52nd in their movement from the crossroad to the Charleroi road and while the 52nd were charging up to the plateau of La Haye Sainte.

(Dictated to Colonel W. Rowan, at Toronto, 1835)

> *Note by Sir William Rowan:* When the 52nd had halted and taken up its ground for the night I went to look for my brother.... At some distance in the rear I fell in with the Guards, also halted with piled arms. While talking to Captain Davies, formerly of the 52nd, Sir John Byng came up and said, 'We saw the 52nd behaving nobly, as it always has done.'

Correspondence With Captain Siborne

Kitley
Yealmpton
22nd February, 1843

I have been so fully occupied since the year 1815 that I have seldom had time or inclination to read any of the accounts of the battle of Waterloo. Indeed, it has always been a most unpleasant task to refer to our past military operations, which are connected with many painful recollections.

I have cautiously abstained from giving opinions on controverted points that would draw me into discussions. I think, however, that it almost becomes my duty to give you every assistance in my power to enable you to compare the facts in my statement with the information which you have received from various sources, and to correct the errors which appear in the account you have forwarded to me.

We were all so intent in performing our own parts that we are disposed to imagine that the brigade or corps with

---

3. In his controversy with Colonel Gawler in the *United Service Journal*, 1833.

which we were engaged played a most distinguished part, and attribute more importance to the movements under our own immediate observation than they deserved. I am persuaded that none but mounted officers can give a correct account of the battle, and very few of those had an opportunity of seeing much beyond the limited space which they traversed.

I have, in great haste, from the impressions which I strongly retain at this moment, written down the principal facts which occurred under my observation, a kind of log-book from 11 o'clock to the close of the action. . . .

I remain, &c.,
Seaton

Memoranda: 24th February, 1843

It was eleven o'clock when our batteries (of 20 guns, I believe) in position on the rising ground to our left of Hougomont opened their fire on a column advancing on Hougomont.

The French commandant of the Premier Legere mentioned to me a few days after the battle that he was in the front of that column, and that the first shot from our guns killed and wounded three of his regiment. At this time several shots reached the 52nd Regiment, then halted in column to the rear of the road leading to Merbe Braine and the point of intersection of that road and the Nivelles road.

Desirous of seeing the commencement of the action, I rode with Colonel Rowan to a commanding eminence. My attention was directed to the French Lancers, which showed themselves near the cross-road leading to Braine-la-Leud, and cheering. After this cheer a large space of our position to the left of Hougomont appeared covered with our dispersed cavalry, rapidly retiring. Two large masses of French cavalry followed them in good order. They passed the batteries of 20 guns to which I have referred, which appeared abandoned and had ceased to fire.

I returned to the 52nd Regiment, which was on the march in column and advancing towards the cross-road that connects the high road from Genappe to Waterloo and the road from Nivelles to Waterloo. The 52nd continued its march to the valley which separated the right central part of our position from the enemy and halted about 500 yards in front of the cross-road. I rode up the opposite ascent and observed two guns pointed and firing at our column. I returned and called out to Captain Shedden, the officer leading the column, and desired him to tell me whether he could see these guns. I formed two squares on the appearance of the masses of heavy cavalry to our right, but nearer to the 71st Regiment than to the 52nd.

Several shells fell near the left angle of our more advanced square and the left side of it was grazed by a sharp fire. Lieutenant-Colonel Charles Rowan was anxious to take the command of the left square, in which Colonel Chalmers was, but on my acquainting him that I should superintend both the squares, he remained, at my request, with me. The front and right faces of this square opened fire on the French Cuirassiers advancing towards us, and the French cavalry halted and retired and appeared in disorder.

Colonel Hervey, one of the Duke of Wellington's aides-de-camp, brought up an order from the Duke for the 52nd to retire up the hill. I mentioned to him that if the Duke had ordered us to retire with reference to our exposed position, that we were protected by the ground in front.

'Very well,' he replied, 'I will mention this.'

However, soon after I had received this order I heard a great noise and clamour in the direction of Hougomont, and observed the Nassau Regiment, I believe, running in disorder out of the wood; and supposing that Hougomont would be abandoned and our flank would be exposed, I formed columns from squares and wheeled into two lines, and this formation being completed we faced about and retired in two lines through the Belgian guns under the command of Colonel Gold,[4] and as we were ascending the hill a French colonel of the Cuirassiers galloped out of the French ranks, shouting out, *'Vive le Roi!'* repeatedly, and rode up to me, addressed me and said, *'Ce—Napoleon est là avec les Gardès. Voilà l'attaque qui sefait.'* This officer remained with me for some time.

On our arriving near the cross-road on the summit of the hill, near the Belgian guns, I halted the 52nd. Many of our wounded were lying a few paces in our front. My anxious attention had been attracted to the dense columns moving on the Genappe road towards the centre of our position, and observing their rapid advance I ordered our left-hand company to wheel to the left and formed the remaining companies on that company. Colonel Charles Rowan assisted in completing this formation, with whom I had had some conversation on the intended movement and on the necessity of menacing the flank of the French columns.

This movement placed us nearly parallel with the moving columns of the French Imperial Guards. I ordered a strong company to extend in our front, and at this moment Sir F. Adam rode up and asked me what I was going to do. I think I said, 'To make that column feel our fire.' Sir F. Adam then ordered me to move on and that the 71st should follow, and rode away towards the 71st.

I instantly ordered the extended company of the 52nd, about 100 men under the command of Lieutenant Anderson, to advance as quickly as possible without any support except from the battalion, and to fire into the French column at any distance. Thus the 52nd formed in two lines of half-companies, the rear line at 10 paces distance from the front, after giving three cheers, followed the extended company, passed along the front of the Brigade of Guards in line, commanded by Sir John Byng, and about 500 yards in

---

4. Colonel Gold's guns were British.

front of them. If our line had been produced it would have formed an obtuse angle with this Brigade of Guards.

I observed that as soon as the French columns were sharply attacked by our skirmishers, a considerable part of the column halted and formed a line facing towards the 52nd and opened a very sharp fire on the skirmishers and on the battalion. The only skirmishers, I think, that were out on that day from our brigade were those of the 52nd which I have mentioned, but I am certain that none fired but those of the 52nd. Three or four companies of the 95th were formed on our left, rather to the rear of our line; the remainder of the brigade, the 71st, must have been at least 600 yards to the rear[5] when the 52nd commenced its movement towards the Imperial Guards; but I think I observed the 71st moving on, as well as the whole of Sir H. Clinton's Division, when we had advanced a few hundred paces.

I have no doubt that the fire on the flank of the French column from the 52nd skirmishers and the appearance of a general attack on its flank from Sir F. Adam's Brigade and Sir H. Clinton's Division generally, was the cause of the first check received, or halt made, by the Imperial Guards. The 52nd suffered severely from the fire of the enemy; the loss of skirmishers was severe and the two officers of the company were wounded. The right wing of the 52nd lost nearly 150 men during the advance; the officer carrying the regimental colour was killed.[6]

At this moment two or three squadrons of the 23rd Dragoons appeared directly in front of the line of the 52nd, approaching rapidly towards the line. The two companies on the left halted and fired into them, supposing them to be the enemy's cavalry. My horse was wounded; I called out to the adjutant to stop the fire, and whilst we were rectifying this

---

5. Siborne says 'not more than 150 yards.'
6. According to Leeke, Ensign Nettles was killed while the 52nd was retiring just before the attack by the Imperial Guards.

mistake which had occurred, the only one that had occurred during the day, and which interrupted our march, the Duke of Wellington came to the rear of the left of our line near the two companies which had fired. I said to his Grace, 'It is our own cavalry which has caused this firing.'

His Grace replied, 'Never mind, go on, go on.'

We continued our advance, which soon brought us under the hill or ascent occupied by the Imperial Guards, and we found ourselves protected from their fire by the hill. Our line, from the badness of the ground and the interruption to which I have alluded, had thrown the two right-hand companies into some disorder, and I, suspecting the French cavalry were not far from our right, called out to the officers commanding Nos. 1 and 2 Companies to halt and bring up their companies in good line, and whilst I was restraining the disorderly impetuosity of these companies under great excitement, several officers in front, Colonel Churchill and Colonel Chalmers, were cheering and waving their hats and caps in front.

At this time the 71st formed on our right flank and I ordered the bugles to sound the advance and the whole line charged up the hill, and on our arriving at the edge of the deep road, the opposite side of which the Imperial Guards had occupied, the 52nd fired, at least, most of the companies. We observed the enemy in great confusion, some firing, others throwing away their packs and running to the rear.

Captain Cross called out that the French soldiers near us were going to surrender, but on their continuing to fire on us, I ordered the 52nd Regiment to 'pass the road,' and the whole passed through the guns and carriages, &c., and we formed columns of companies, our right resting on the road to Genappe. We moved on in column and passed, I think, 80 guns or carriages in about 10 minutes after this new formation. No cavalry whatever could be seen on our left or to the left of the Genappe road, and I am sure that no British cavalry were between us and the French for the last hour of the battle. I think, therefore, that the attacks of our cavalry at this time must have been made by the cavalry which had passed in rear of the 52nd and to the right of the Genappe road.

I observed smoke and firing towards Planchenoit and to the right and left of the Genappe road. The 71st did not cross the Genappe road but moved to the right as well as part of the other brigade of Sir H. Clinton's Division.

At the junction of the Genappe road and the road leading, I believe, from Wavre to Nivelles, the skirmishers of the 52nd and the advance of the Prussians under General Bülow mixed. When we passed this point it was nearly dark. We halted a few hundred yards from it and the whole of General Bülow's Corps passed our right on the road leading to Genappe.

The Duke of Wellington, on returning, I suppose, from Belle Alliance, passed the left of our column and inquired for me and left a message that we were to halt for the night.

Sir John Byng mentioned to me at Paris that he observed our movement in front of his brigade, and that at this time his brigade had no ammunition left. Lord Hill mentioned to me also that he was near the Brigade of Guards when he observed the 52nd moving across the plain, that some men of the British Guards were retiring, that he ordered them to advance, waving his hat to them.

I think, therefore, that this was the time when a portion of the Imperial Guards halted to fire on the 52nd, and that immediately after this halt the British Guards charged and made their forward movement. It appears to me evident, if this statement be correct, the movement of the 52nd took place some time before any forward movement was made by the Guards.

'Perhaps this information and the minute details which I have mentioned may enable you, with the different accounts which you have received from other officers, to correct the many errors into which you have fallen in your account of the close of the engagement. If Colonel Charles Rowan, Lord Strafford[7] and Sir F. Adam confirm these details, you may consider this account of the last two hours of the battle of Waterloo authentic, and a correct version.[8]

I have been particular in stating many unimportant occurrences, because I am persuaded several absurd blunders and stories have originated from the movements of the 52nd and General Adam's Brigade having been misrepresented.

Seaton

Corfu
22nd April, 1843

Dear Sir,

Private and Confidential

I was so much occupied previously to my departure from England that I had not time to reply to your letter of 27th February.

Although I think it incumbent on me again to offer some remarks on the battle of Waterloo, with reference to my observations on the errors which it appeared to me you had fallen into, I send you my explanations, persuaded that we of the 52nd, who have so freely given our notions of the results of the movements towards the close of the action, were little qualified to furnish correct information on the subject of the general operations of our army, in consequence of our whole attention having been absorbed by the movements which we were actively engaged in carrying into effect, and that you, who have had access to the evidence of officers posted in every part of the field, must be enabled to form a just conclusion as to the grand features of the battle.

I met in town with several officers of the 52nd who were

---

7. Previously, Sir J. Byng.
8. This paragraph from 'perhaps' is omitted in the published Waterloo Letters, its place being supplied by stars.

near me at the close of the action, and as they all differ materially in their accounts of it, I beg you will destroy the confidential statement which I forwarded to you, and which I drew up after being acquainted with your earnest desire to collect information on certain points, under the impression only that some of the details mentioned by me might tend to confirm other accounts in your possession.

Sir Frederick Adam and myself are persuaded that there was only one attack made by the Imperial Guards, and that that attack was in progress at the moment when the 52nd Regiment wheeled to its left and advanced, unsupported by any other corps excepting four companies of the 95th, and that the Imperial Guards halted and fell back precisely at that time and opened a fire from the left flank of their formation, and that their hesitation in moving to the front and change of position took place in consequence of the fire of the 52nd, its steady advance, and the appearance of the supporting line of the rest of Adam's Brigade and the whole of Sir H. Clinton's Division.

I was in a position which enabled me to observe the moment at which the columns of the Imperial Guards halted and closed to the rear and my attention was chiefly and anxiously directed, to the point where they halted.

I am, therefore, confident that the whole of the columns of the attack of the Imperial Guards that approached the line defended by the Brigade of British Guards were on march at the time the 52nd wheeled, and continued their march till the fire of the regiment was felt by them; and that the attack of the 52nd commenced after it had advanced 50 or 60 paces, and before any forward movement on the part of the British Guards.

I conclude, then, that the Imperial Guards assumed a defensive position at that time, and remained on the defensive till they were assailed and dispersed by General Adam's Brigade, and that when the 52nd commenced its first advance it was at least 300 yards in front of any other corps except the 95th and that no other regiment was near the 52nd on its reaching the point occupied by the Imperial Guards, behind the road encumbered by the French artillery, except the 71st, which regiment had moved to its right and did not cross the road in front.

The Duke of Wellington states, I believe, in his memorandum of the battle of Waterloo that he sent an order to Sir H. Clinton to advance and attack the Imperial Guards as they were approaching our line. This order was carried by Colonel Percy, who mentioned to me that he saw the 52nd advancing along the plain as he was conveying the Duke's message. The forward movement of the British Guards must therefore have taken place about the time he left the Duke.

All subsequent operations were defensive on the part of the French, and were occasioned probably by the simultaneous movements of the British Guards and the 52nd, the menaced advance of Sir H. Clinton, and the approach of the Prussians which had compelled Napoleon to throw back his right wing.

I remain, dear sir, yours faithfully,
Seaton

Answers to Questions Put by Captain W. C. Yonge

> At what period was Adam wounded, and if he did not continue with the brigade during the whole battle, at what time did he leave the field, and who succeeded to the command?

He was wounded either during or immediately after the wheeling up of the 52nd to the left for the purpose of taking in flank the French advancing column in their final attack, and then left the field. No one assumed the command of the brigade; the commanding officer of each regiment acted according to his discretion.

Did Sir John Colborne order the formation of four deep, and did he direct the advance and charge of the 52nd on his own responsibility or through direction of the Duke?

The Duke of Wellington had some time previously ordered the formation of four deep. Sir John Colborne, thinking such a formation in the ordinary manner (*i.e.*, with intervals between the files) inexpedient, did not comply with the order. But the 52nd were subsequently formed in two squares on the slope of the hill in advance of the position, from whence, after some time, they were withdrawn to the crest of the hill, and then Sir John Colborne, as the safest way of complying with the order, placed the left wing of the regiment in rear of the right wing, closed up.

He received no directions from anyone for the wheeling of the regiment and the attack on the flank of the French column. A few minutes previously a colonel of French Cuirassiers had galloped in, shouting, *'Vive le Roi,'* and coming to Sir John Colborne, informed him that Napoleon was forming a column of attack and pointed out where the formation was going on. As soon as this column advanced, Sir John Colborne, said to the adjutant, Winterbottom, 'We must bring the regiment up on their flank.'

Winterbottom said, 'We cannot do it; we cannot wheel the regiment.'

To which Sir John Colborne replied, 'Wheel the left company, and the others will conform to it.'

During the movement Adam came up and asked, 'What are you about?'

To which Sir John Colborne replied, 'Don't you see that advancing column?'

Almost immediately afterwards Adam's wound took place and he left the field.

> When the 52nd were formed four deep with their right shoulder forward, what was the exact position of the 71st?

The 71st, having been in line to the right of the 52nd, it will be obvious that when the wheel of the 52nd had taken place so as to bring their line at right angles to the position, the 71st were considerably in their rear. The forward movement of the 52nd was retarded by two circumstances. 1: The French column being, as usual, flanked by skirmishers, Sir John Colborne desired to throw out some to answer them, and requested the officer commanding two companies of the Rifle Corps (attached to the brigade) to deploy for this purpose. He refused, and then Sir John Colborne ordered out the right companies of the 52nd, checking for the time the advance of the regiment. The other cause was that some English Light Dragoons being charged by the enemy, were driven in with such haste that they galloped directly on the line of the 52nd, followed closely by the French, several of whom were shot close upon and even within our line, the men opening intervals to let them through and shooting them as they passed. These two causes of delay in the advance of the 52nd enabled the 71st, who had followed our movement, to come up, and they advanced on our right, I believe, at about the ordinary interval of battalions in line.

> Did the 71st co-operate instantly with the 52nd advance, and yield them efficient support, and how near was the left of the 71st to the right of the 52nd at any one moment during their movement, first to La Haye Sainte and continued up to La Belle Alliance?

The first part of this question is answered above. When the French column was driven back and the regiments, bringing up their left shoulders, followed them, the 71st gradually increased their distance, diverging to their right and going to the right of the road while the 52nd went to the left.

I think the 71st did not approach the 52nd again until both the regiments arrived at La Belle Alliance.

> What was the force of the Imperial Guards with which the 52nd came into immediate contact, and what was the total force brought up to sustain the attack?

The French column appeared to consist of six or seven thousand men. I cannot at all say what portion of them were of the Imperial Guard. After their repulse the 52nd followed them rapidly, at a run, so as to overtake and pass a considerable number who were entangled in a hollow cross-road, and then passed on to the attack of a body of apparently between 2,000 and 3,000 of the Guards, who had preserved their order and occupied a hill rather to the left of the direct line of advance towards La Belle Alliance. I think there were three battalions of them. They opened a heavy fire on us as we advanced in line till we came within 50 or 60 yards, when moving off in good order, our men being rather blown with their long run, by the time we got to the crest of the hill they had disappeared on the other side and we saw no more of them. A considerable space of ground was passed between the hollow cross-road which I have mentioned and the hill where these battalions were posted. In going over this ground the Duke was immediately in rear of the 52nd, and when, in consequence of seeing that parties of Cuirassiers who were retiring before us were continually trying to form, apparently with the intention of charging us, several of the officers were rather checking the pace of the men for fear of the ranks becoming disordered, he two or three times called out, 'Go on, go on,' and so it was that these Cuirassiers were fairly driven off without ever being able to make any head.

> Was the charge of Maitland's Brigade or a battalion thereof seen by the 52nd, and, if so, in what state did they retire after breaking, as it is said they did, the leading column of the French Guard?

This charge and the reported expression of the Duke of Wellington, 'Up, Guards, and at them,' are altogether apocryphal,[9] and to be classed with that fiction on the part of the French, *'La Garde meurt, mais ne se rend pas'* which they assert to have been uttered in answer to a summons to surrender by those very battalions of the Imperial Guards whom I have described as conveying themselves away so cleverly before we could get to the top of the hill on which they were posted.

To those who claim for the Guards the credit of repelling this column of attack, we might say as Prince Hal to Falstaff, 'Mark how plain a tale shall put you down.' The 52nd having, as before mentioned, changed front to the left so as to bring their line to a slightly obtuse angle with the line of the position, and the 71st having come up on their right, they advanced on the flank of the enemy's column, and the left of the 52nd outflanked the head of the column. On our approach the French halted and retired in confusion, receiving a severe fire from the two regiments which, bringing up their left shoulders, pursued them so that the 52nd passed over the ground on which the enemy's column had advanced. It is evident that had the Guards charged the head of the column, they must have been intermingled with the left of the 52nd, whereas, in fact, as to Byng's Brigade, they were stationary, doing nothing, like a regiment on parade, and this was accounted for shortly after by Sir John Byng, who told Colborne that they had no ammunition left, adding, 'I was very glad to see you coming in our front.'

As to Maitland's, they had been falling back a short distance, but on our movement taking place advanced again and halted in line with Byng. The Duke also on our advance gal-

---

9. To this hasty dictum we must not attach too much importance. In his communications to Colonel Rowan and Captain Siborne, Colborne had tried to reconcile his recollections with the accounts given by the Guards. See also his letter to Colonel Bentham below.

loped forward, as Major Percy, one of his aides-de-camp, said, with a very different expression of countenance from that which he had worn for some while before.

Not a word was heard of any charge made by the Guards until after our arrival at Paris, when the despatch had come out, and astonished everyone by the omission of all mention of the circumstances of the repulse of this last effort of the enemy, and when Lord Bathurst, in the House of Lords, had said, in giving an account of the action, that the English Guards had ... *(remainder missing)*.

LETTER TO CAPTAIN W. C. YONGE

7th February, 1852

From some questions put to me, I fear it may be the intention of Bentham, or some of our 52nd friends, to bring before the public the exploits of our old corps and its officers. Nothing can be more disagreeable or create more jealousy than thrusting continually before readers the claims, or supposed merits, of particular corps or officers long after the events, to be discussed or recorded, as a tribute to their exertions. It does no good to individuals or generals, and such notices are very properly considered as *puffs*, or as published for some interested motive. I heard the Duke of Wellington say at his own table at Paris in 1815, 'Let the battle of Waterloo stand where it does; we are satisfied.'

He knew that the first impressions given could not be removed easily, and that the merit of the English army being brought into an authorised controversy would become depreciated by the advocacy of some and the jealousy of others. Dr. Moore annoyed his son, Sir John, and exposed him to bitter sarcasms by his continual insertion in the papers of eulogiums on his gallant and successful service. Sir Sydney Smith, a man of extraordinary qualifications, destroyed his character by his talking and writing, so that he passed for a charlatan *par tout*.

Letter and Memorandum to Colonel Bentham

Deer Park
Honiton
15th October, 1853

My Dear Bentham,

. . . . It may be more satisfactory to you, instead of replying to your queries, to draw your attention to the principal movements which accelerated the termination of the battle of Waterloo, and to the facts which would be admitted as evidence in support of the claims of the 52nd to the merit of having first checked the advance of the Imperial Guards at the crisis of the battle and of having completed their *déroute* by marching directly on their dense columns, and, by a flank movement, charging them so vigorously that the whole gave way and retired in confusion. The statements of officers engaged at Waterloo I found were generally so difficult and conflicting that it was impossible to draw up any correct account from them.

Captain Siborne, I believe, consulted every officer in command with whom he was acquainted or to whom he was introduced, and endeavoured to make their versions correspond with the facts generally known relative to the movements of divisions, brigades and regiments. I have never read his account. If you bring the 52nd into a contest with the Guards by attempting to prove from rumour that the latter was retiring at the time they are said to have charged and defeated the French troops, you will raise up a host of opponents to your account, which would rather injure the cause of the 52nd.

I suppose that the Guards must have made some forward movement and that many officers must have seen it, but I contend that the French columns had been checked and thrown into disorder before the Guards moved. I saw the column of the Imperial Guards steadily advancing to a certain point and I observed them halt, which was precisely as the skirmishers of the 52nd opened fire on their flank. My attention was so completely drawn to our position and dangerous advance, a large mass of cavalry having been seen on our right, exposed as it was, that I could see no movement whatever on the part of the Guards; and, indeed, as we advanced, I believe we were too much under their position to have had them in sight. Sir J. Byng's Brigade remained in line without firing or making any movement while we passed along its front, our line forming a right angle with that brigade, and about 200 yards nearer to the French. Sir J. Byng told me afterwards at Paris that he had his whole attention drawn to our movement, and that his brigade had no ammunition left. He gave us at that time full credit for our advance. Till the Duke of Wellington's despatch was made known at Paris we had never heard of the charge of the Guards, and I am inclined to believe that the attack of the French had been checked by the advance of the 52nd and the movements afterwards of the whole of Sir H. Clinton's Division, before any forward movement had been made by the brigade commanded by Sir P. Maitland. This account corresponds with that given me by Lord Hill, who was close to the Guards and saw no moving across the plain.

When we followed the French to La Belle Alliance no troops from the part of the position occupied by the Guards were near us, and we passed 80 guns and carriages a short time after the French had retired, which they had left on the road from La Haye Sainte to La Belle Alliance.

I have written this as circumstances occurred to me to remind me of the part we performed, without method, but with these remarks and the facts mentioned in the enclosure you may be able to judge correctly of the claims of the 52nd.

Yours very faithfully,
Seaton

Enclosure

The 52nd crossed the road running in the direction of Hougomont, and halting in the low ground, formed two squares. A large mass of cavalry menaced several times the front and right faces of the square nearest Hougomont. and their guns opened fire, on which the cavalry retired, but not far. At the same time two guns opened on the same square, enfilading the left face of it. A shell burst at the angle, killing and wounding several men. At this moment Colonel C. Rowan said to Sir J. Colborne, 'Do you think we can stand this?'

He replied, 'But you see it is not a simultaneous attack.'

A few minutes afterwards Colonel Hervey, an aide-de-camp to the Duke of Wellington, rode into the square and delivered the message, 'The Duke wishes you to retire up the hill.'

Sir John Colborne replied, 'Acquaint the Duke, if he thinks we are too exposed, that we are not suffering from the fire of those guns.'

'Very well,' he said, 'I will mention that.'

There was, however, a sudden rush of several companies of the Nassau Regiment out of the wood of Hougomont, from which it was supposed that the wood was occupied by the enemy. Therefore the 52nd formed two lines from square and retired up the slope to the left (right?) of Sir John Byng's Brigade. A few minutes before the 52nd began to retire an officer galloped out from the French cavalry down the hill, shouting, *'Vive le Roi!'* and riding up to Sir J. Colborne and Colonel Rowan, stated that Napoleon was advancing 'there,' pointing to the road leading to La Haye Sainte, to attack with his columns.

Sir John Colborne retired with this officer in rear of the 52nd, passing through the batteries commanded by Colonel Gold, and after posting the 52nd in line, ordered the adjutant to take the wounded to the rear.

At about half-past six o'clock, after he had been anxiously looking at the dense columns moving towards La Haye Sainte and afterwards advancing rapidly on that road, he ordered the 52nd to wheel to the left on the left company. This brought the 52nd parallel with the flank of the French column of attack. A strong company, commanded by Lieutenant Anderson, was ordered to extend, skirmish in front, and feel the enemy, and the regiment immediately advanced. The French troops, on feeling the fire of the skirmishers, appeared checked, halted, and opened a heavy fire on the 52nd.

The Imperial troops had been in movement up to this time, and no forward movement on the part of the Guards had as yet taken place. Lord Hill said a few days afterwards, 'I saw the 52nd moving across the plain.' It is, therefore, believed that the flank movement of the 52nd and the advance of Sir H. Clintons Division afterwards compelled the French column to halt, and whatever movement on the part of the Guards took place must have been ordered after the 52nd had occasioned the halt of the French.

The 52nd, as they closed on the French, saw only in their front the troops opposed to them. The French cavalry on the right of the 52nd had retired, having probably been withdrawn when the Prussians first appeared marching on Planchenoit. The 52nd passed in front of the Brigade of Guards commanded by Sir J. Byng, advancing always on the Imperial Guards, who had wheeled from column and continued their fire till the 52nd arrived at the crest of the deep road which divided them. They then dispersed, and the 52nd, crossing the road, advanced in pursuit. At this time General Bülow's skirmishers appeared on the left of the 52nd and firing increased in the direction of Planchenoit. The 52nd must have been at least half an hour moving on the flank of the French from the time the regiment first wheeled till the charge took place.

The crisis may be called the period when the French columns, advancing with the intention of penetrating our centre, were checked and compelled to halt by the flank movement and fire of the 52nd. This was the very first appearance of a change in our favour. The attackers were attacked and checked in their assault and driven from the ground which they had gained before they could deploy.

The whole of the Imperial columns advanced at the same time and their flank was first attacked by the 52nd before any forward movement was made to check them in front. The Prussians could not have attracted the attention of the French so as to cause the throwing back of their right wing till after the Imperial Guards had commenced the attack on our centre. The 52nd marched in pursuit till 9 o'clock. Bülow's column passed at the crossroad near Belle Alliance.

Colonel Percy was ordered by the Duke to carry a message to Sir H. Clinton to advance with his division, and saw the 52nd advancing along the plain as he left the Duke and before any movement whatever had been made by the Guards.

The 52nd opened fire when some squadrons of our own cavalry appeared in front of the left company of the 52nd. This impeded their march for some minutes. No regiment except the 52nd fired on the flank of the Imperial Guards, while this attack of the 52nd was going on so close to the position of the Guards. The 52nd having been actually engaged closely with the divisions of the halted column for half an hour, there can be no difficulty, perhaps, in ascertaining the precise time the British Guards charged, as their forward movement must have taken place during that half hour, and the Imperial Guards were not finally dispersed till the 52nd charged up the hill close to the road, behind which the Imperial Guards had been half an hour, it may be said, in position.

Seaton
October, 1853

www.ingramcontent.com/pod-product-compliance
Lightning Source LLC
Chambersburg PA
CBHW031621160426
43196CB00006B/231